MEMORIES
OF
CHINESE
LIFE

Chen Yu

 China Intercontinental Press China Light Industry Press

图书在版编目（CIP）数据

中国百姓生活记忆：英文 / 陈煜编著；刘晓霜，李娜，刘燕译.
-- 北京：五洲传播出版社，2014.9

ISBN 978-7-5085-2894-6

Ⅰ.①中… Ⅱ.①陈… ②刘… ③李… ④刘…
Ⅲ.①社会生活 – 概况 – 中国 – 1949～2014 – 英文 Ⅳ.①D669

中国版本图书馆CIP数据核字(2014)第214678号

中国百姓生活记忆

出 版 人：荆孝敏
编　　著：陈　煜
译　　者：刘晓霜　李　娜　刘　燕
策　　划：刘忠波
责任编辑：苏　谦
装帧设计：北京正视文化艺术有限责任公司
出版发行：五洲传播出版社
　　　　　中国轻工业出版社
地　　址：北京市海淀区北三环中路31号生产力大楼B座7层
邮　　编：100088
电　　话：010-82005927，82007837
网　　址：www.cicc.org.cn
承 印 者：北京华联印刷有限公司
版　　次：2014年9月第1版第1次印刷
开　　本：720×965mm　1/16
印　　张：20
字　　数：200千字
定　　价：138.00元

Preface

In the 65 years after the founding of the People's Republic of China, Chinese people have experienced significant changes in life. The improvements in basic necessities of daily life and the enrichment of political, spiritual and cultural life reflect the social progress.

The book *Memories of Chinese Life* aims to reflect such progress in dribs and drabs. It selects minor matters in daily life that could touch the deep memories of people like the Lenin Coat, food coupons and water supply stations in the lanes of Shanghai in the 1950s, the "Little Red Book" in the 1960s, the Eight Model Operas, picture-story books, and bell-bottoms in the 1970s, red skirts, fake collars, disco, Teresa Teng, and "dageda"(cell phones) in the 1980s, the Shopping Basket Program, stock markets, supermarkets, League A, the Tang suit, home mortgage slavery in the 1990s...The description of such trivialities in daily life can help those who experienced these periods regain memories and the later generations to learn about daily life in the past.

The book is dedicated to the 65th anniversary of the founding of the People's Republic of China and the industrious and brave Chinese people, who love life.

Contents

Memories of Chinese Life

1960s

1970s

Memories of Chinese Life

1980s

Memories of Chinese Life

1990s

21st Century

Memories of ★ Chinese Life in 1949

Many things needed to be done

On October 1, 1949, 300,000 servicemen and civilians held the founding ceremony in Tiananmen Square, Beijing. Mao Zedong read the announcement of the Central Government and solemnly declared the founding the People's Republic of China to the world.

The China Economic Yearbook 1981 published some economic data for 1949, including:

In 1949, China had a population of 541.67 million, a birth rate 36‰, a death rate of 20‰, and life expectancy was 35 years.

Other figures included:

Gross output value of industry and agriculture: RMB46.6 billion;

National revenue: RMB35.8 billion;

Total retail sales of consumer goods: RMB14.05 billion;

Raw coal: 32 million tons;

Electric power generation: 4.3 billion kWh;

Crude oil: 120,000 tons;

Steel: 158,000 tons;

Cloth: 1.89 billion meters;

Sugar: 200,000 tons;

Grains: 113.20million tons;

Cotton: 445,000 tons;

Oil plant: 2.564 million tons;

Aquatic products: 450,000 tons.

Industrial products in 1949: sewing machine 2,000 sets;

Radio sets: 4,000 sets

Bicycles: 14,000

With this information, per capita data can be easily calculated, which makes it easy to see how backwards and poor Chinese society was in 1949.

In 1949, the per capita annual gross output value of industry and agriculture was only RMB86; per capita annual national revenue was RMB69.29; per capita annual total retail sales of consumer goods were RMB25.94; per capita annual raw coal added up to 59kg; per capita annual electric power generation was 7.9 kWh; per capita annual crude oil 0.2kg; per capita annual steel production 0.29kg; per capita annual cloth 3.49 meters; per capita annual sugar 0.37kg; per capita annual grains 209kg; per capita annual cotton 0.82kg; per capita annual oil plants 4.7kg; per capita annual aquatic products 0.83kg.

If calculating in details, we can reach the following conclusions:

The Chinese people in 1949 could only have 0.572kg grains, 0.013kg oil plants, 0.017kg meat and 0.0023kg of fish per day per person.

In the same year, the country suffered from drought, frost, plagues, storms, hail and floods. Floods were especially serious, resulting in about 100 million *mu* of arable land being drowned and 20 million victims.

The People's Republic of China, newly founded, started "post-war economic recovery" under conditions of extremely poor economic foundation. The country was very poor and backward with people living in harsh conditions. Many things needed to be done. That was the reality of New China of that time.

Against poverty and backwardness, industrious and brave Chinese people worked hard to develop the economy and rebuild their homes independently and wholeheartedly and created miracles one after another and the most beautiful picture.

On October 1, 1949, Mao Zedong declared the founding of the People's Republic of China at the Tiananmen Gate tower.

Provided by Beijing Municipal Archives

MEMORIES OF
CHINESE LIFE IN THE

1950s

In the 1950s, many things were waiting to be done.

The basic necessities of life of the common people were simple and could be summarized like the lyrics of a folk song: "Four-pocket Chinese tunic coat, tasty millet and sorghum, several households consisting of a village and visiting relatives on foot."

The revolutionary passion and ideal dominated the life of people in the 1950s. They neither complained about the miscellaneous works and impoverished life nor lost heart in the face of difficulties. Although they had broken their iron pans for smelting steel, or thought the per *mu* yield of grains to be thousands kilograms, their yearning for the happy life gave no cause for much criticism.

Some people still think of the 1950s to this day and remember how simple life was at that time.

Chinese tunic suit replaced the western-style clothes and chi-pao

When New China was founded, people's clothing was still in the style of the Republic of China. The male citizens in urban areas normally wore long gowns with buttons down on one side and women wore chi-paos. In rural areas, men often wore Chinese style short jackets with buttons down on the front and trousers and women wore short gown with buttons down the left side and trousers or a longuette. The clothes were mostly machine-made, or hopsacking or flax. In addition, western-style clothes and Chinese tunic suit were also popular.

Chairman Mao Zedong and Premier Zhou Enlai also wore Chinese tunic suits.

Provided by the National Costume Museum of Beijing Institute of Fashion Technology

⊙

Pure woolen gabardine Chinese tunic suit, the formal attire of men of China at that time.

Provided by the National Costume Museum of Beijing Institute of Fashion Technology

In the 1950s, people's clothes were often closely linked with the revolution. The western-style clothes and chi-paos were gradually regarded as bourgeois and died out for dozens of years. Men started to replace the long gown and mandarin jacket with Chinese tunic suits and women wore clothes with buttons down the front and did not bind their feet any longer. Chinese tunic suits became the most solemn and most popular clothes of Chinese people.

In the early days the Chinese tunic suit had many buttons and the four packets were neat and simple. However the style was too stiff and orthodox and lacked innovation.

It was enviable at the time to have a set of woolen Chinese tunic suit. Wearing one or two pens in the right pocket of the Chinese tunic coat was a symbol of the knowledgeable and literate.

Later, the Chinese tunic suit was worn by young students inspired by the revolution and by their respect for CPC cadres. Later, neater and more lively "people's suits", "youth suits" and "student suits" were designed based on the characteristics of the Chinese tunic suit.

There was a kind of slightly improved Chinese tunic suit that had a larger collar band and lapel and was very popular at that time. Mao Zedong, leader of the People's Republic of China, liked this style of Chinese tunic coat. At the founding ceremony, leaders of New China appeared on the Gate Tower of Tiananmen Square as a group for the first time. The image of Mao and the other leaders in Chinese tunic suits attracted world attention. Since then, this style of the Chinese tunic suit became known as "Mao suit" in the west.

Fashionable "Lenin Coat"

Nanjing had some children's folk rhymes in the early days after New China's founding: "The drawing room is bright, with a large beautiful bed, gals wearing colorful clothes and lads wearing Lenin Coat."

In the early days after New China's founding, Soviet Union clothes naturally became the symbol of the revolution and deeply influenced urban citizens. The Lenin Coat became the most popular item for a while.

The Lenin Coat was named after the fact that Lenin often wore that style of coat before and after the October Revolution. It had a western-style open collar, two rows of buttons, slanting pockets at the bottom of the front and a belt with three buttons on each side. It could be unlined or cotton-padded.

Standard Lenin Coat.

Provided by the National Costume Museum of Beijing Institute of Fashion Technology

The Lenin Coat was originally a man's jacket, but women's dress was developed on this basis and became a revolutionary "fashion" enjoying the same reputation as the Chinese tunic coat. Wearing a Lenin Coat - the widely recognized "Soviet Union style" of clothes – was fashionable and ideologically advanced and became a classical costume for women cadres of governmental organs. As a result, this style was also called "cadre suit".

The Lenin Coat had some decorative elements such as a double line of buttons and large lapels and a belt helpful to highlight the female body line.

This coat later became the favorite "fashionable dress" of numerous Chinese women. Wearing a Lenin Coat and short hair was the fashion of young women of the time. They looked simple, able and valiant. China's first woman tractor driver Liang Jun, and the first woman train driver Tian Guiying were both models of the Lenin Coat. The example of model workers led the fashion trend of the times.

Youth in Lenin Coat. Lenin Coat was the mainstream attire of the literate women and female cadres in the 1950s.

Provided by the National Costume Museum of Beijing Institute of Fashion Technology

Pitifully there were few choices of color for the Lenin Coat. The simple blue, grey and black reflected the mood of the times for plain living.

Girls keen on bib overall

Since 1949, the working classes in the production field enjoyed improving social status. Working hard was most glorious and simplicity was a fashion, wearing the bib overall became an honor. Young women were keen on wearing the men's strap overall and plaid shirts for a while.

The bib overall has a pair of suspenders with a pocket on the breast. It normally goes with a round hap with a front brim and a pair of rubber-soled cloth shoes, often hand made. In addition, rubber-soled shoes, with the front and rear parts coated with rubber were named "Liberation Shoes" because

⟨↑⟩

Men's bib overall (left).Women's bib overall (right). This baggy overall is convenient for work and was often worn with a white towel and a blue liberation hat. In the times when the working class led everything, this workers' attire was very fashionable.

Provided by the National Costume Museum of Beijing Institute of Fashion Technology

servicemen of the People's Liberation Army wore them. This pattern became widely used and popular among urban citizens.

The new shoes were often pinned with a heel before wearing and children's shoes were normally repaired with a tip binding on both the front and the heel. It was common for boys' shoes to be repaired with a patch along the big toe.

After the founding of New China, the silk and satins with the color of traditional Chinese culture seemed to have some strong feudal flavor. Therefore women workers and female students abandoned the silk fabrics and chose color cotton prints which had the peasant culture characteristics for clothes to show their vicinity to the working class and farmers.

When wearing the cotton-padded coats, people often wore a single-layer dustcoat in order to maintain the advanced image and prevent the coat from being soiled (to avoid frequent washing). In the 1950s, most women used Lenin Coats as their dustcoats.

Little swallow wearing color clothes: "platye"

On May 17, 1955, the *Youth Daily of Shanghai* published the article Supporting Girls Wear Bright-Colored Clothes, which was signed by Qixin. The article held that people could dress beautifully, but girls often wore "single-colored" clothes and some only wore blue clothes. The article called for people to dress the motherland into a large garden with all flowers blossoming, but also dress girls like a flower or a piece of gem. The article concluded with a call for girls to wear bright-colored clothes.

In 1956, with living standards improving, popular colors had diversified from blue and grey. A woman's button-up dress platye imported from the former Soviet Union became the most popular choice: featuring loose short sleeves, pleated hemlines, round-collars, dense flowers prints, tartans or stripped patterns and a cloth belt.

Platye was the informal clothing choice of Soviet women. In the 1950s, what Chinese people saw were mostly illustrated magazines, periodicals and films from the Soviet Union. The attire of heroines in Soviet literature and the especially fashion columns of such publications influenced the common

Girls trying on the platye.

Provided by the National Costume Museum of Beijing Institute of Fashion Technology

people indirectly. Soviet female experts working in China who wore platye become the direct object of imitation of the common people.

All Chinese women, from the well-known women and celebrities to the grassroots on the street or lane, or the construction site, had a platye; even little girls in kindergartens had their own platye. A group of young women, vibrant and passionate in revolution, wearing a big smile, a long pigtail or short hair with bangs cut hanging over the forehead dressed in colorful platye, sang pop songs, went to school or work, attended a meeting or an assembly, or visited a park, devoting themselves to the construction of New China.

Later when the relation between China and former Soviet Union worsened, the name "platye" was not longer used but *lianyiqun*– the paraphrase of "platye" – emerged.

Food coupon starts the coupon era

In the 1950s, the food supply was short in China. The Government Administration Council issued an order in October 1953 that China was to implement the planned food supply and that food was supplied through quota coupons. Consequently, food coupons appeared.

On November 1, 1953, Beijing issued flour purchase permits for the first time, which were marked with "No post-register for lost permits. Overdue permits are void."

In October 1955, the Ministry of Food issued the National Food Coupon after the food quota supply plan was implemented.

The widely accepted time of the beginning of coupon era in academic circles was 1955, marked by the issuance of the first set of National Food Coupons. Later, edible oil coupons and clothing coupons appeared. More than 2,000 cities and counties issued and used various coupons for the planned supply of goods. In addition, some large factories and mines and schools also issued various coupons.

The use of coupons is such variety, geographical involvement, duration and quantity as in China was rare in the world.

The coupon-based quota food supply started in 1955 in urban areas. The Interim Measures on the Urban Food Quota Supply issued by the State Council decided nine supply criteria according to division of labor, age and food consumption habits of citizens.

With regard to non-staple food, except for edible oils (including sesame paste) which had been included in the planned supply under the management of the food administration, eight kinds of non-staple foods, including pork, beef, mutton, fresh egg, white sugar and black sugar, bean vermicelli and cake, were supplied through coupons.

People of the Han nationality could have six *liang* of pork (300g) and five *liang* of beef and mutton (250g) per month per person. People of the Hui could have 700g beef and mutton per person per month and 200g of white sugar and black sugar respectively and two fresh eggs. In addition, fresh fish was supplied on May 1, and the traditional Chinese rice pudding on the Dragon Boats Festival. Such goods were supplied over three to seven days with the method of ensuring a wide coverage of households with a small quantity for each household.

Such food coupons and permits were part of a planned food supply and were priceless securities (document security). All citizens who had meals at the mess halls or relatives' and needed to purchase grains and the non-staple food had to provide food coupons of the location by presenting grain coupons to the designated grain store within the quota plan.

The appearance of the food coupon in the 1950s marked the beginning of the coupon-based goods supply system that lasted 40 years. The small food coupons accompanied all Chinese people.

⊕

On October 21, 1955, the People's Committee of Beijing forwarded a notice on several issues concerning the use of the food coupon.

Provided by Beijing Municipal Archives

⊕

The flour purchase permits issued by the Food Bureau of Beijing in 1954.

Provided by Beijing Municipal Archives

Residence booklet to control influxes into the urban area

In 1953 after the 1st Five-Year Plan was implemented, factories recruited millions of workers in an effort of industrialization. However, the Central Government found that many of them were actually farmers who sought non-agriculture employment. The government issued an order requiring state-owned factories not to recruit workers from rural areas. What's more, the government started to control the "blind influx" into urban areas. Since then, the term "blind influx" has referred to farmers with a job but no household registration in an urban area.

On June 22, 1955, the State Council officially issued the *Instruction on Establishing a Regular Household Registration System*, requiring anybody or any household to report to the county-level government and get a migration card when moving in or moving out.

On January 9, 1958, China's first household registration management regulation the *Household Registration Regulations of the People's Republic of China* was promulgated and enacted. Since then, Chinese people were divided by region. The household registration system limited the free flow of people like an intangible binder.

How did such a small residence booklet have such binding force? The function of the household registration was related to many of the functions given to it. It was linked to employment, housing, education, social welfare and other rights and interests of people.

The household registration system was seriously affected during the Great Leap Forward period. From 1957 to 1959, the urban population increased from 15 percent to 20 percent and the number of workers at state-owned factories increased from 15 million in 1957 to 39 million in 1960. People that took part in the "blind influx" could find a job in urban areas but without food, it was another story. After the Great Leap Forward, the economy was seriously undermined and severe famine swept China, especially remote rural areas. During the national economic adjustment from 1961 to 1962, more than 8 million workers and 500,000 cadres and their families were transferred to rural areas. In the following dozens of years, the rigid household registration system was kept unchanged.

The household registration system maintained urban-rural differences. However, it was the best of a bad bunch of options given the situation in China at the time.

Free public eateries

In 1958, "eating your fill and working hard" emerged as a famous slogan across the country.

After implementing the "eating your fill" policy, many public eateries aimed only to ensure a supply of staples and dishes without limit. What's more, they focused on providing a variety of dishes through a week or even a longer period.

Workers have meals in a public eatery.

Provided by Beijing Municipal Archives

In that period, many public eateries ran open-chair banquets to serve commune members as they arrived. Some areas even offered convenience for travelers and tried to persuade them to enjoy free meals.

With the implementation of the "free meal" and "eating your fill" measures, most public eateries went through their supplies in several months.

On October 25, 1958, the *People's Daily* published the editorial Running the Public Eateries. The editorial put forward specific requirements on public eateries, for example diversified food and dishes, well-matched coarse grains and wheat flour and rice and free supply of seasonings such as sauce, vinegar, shallot, garlic and hot pepper. The public eateries were required to improve their meals, provide meat dishes several times a month, hold dinner parties on festivals, pay attention to hygiene, develop their own vegetable bases, offer special care for senior commune members, children, patients and pregnant women or new mothers, and renovate old houses into eateries or build simple eateries.

Public eateries and the supply system were designed seemingly with not basis of the reality of China and exceeded the consciousness of people. And some practices were ridiculous.

Dusky and greasy "row houses"

After the founding of New China, Beijing first renovated the dirty Longxugou, dilapidated Hepingli and built residential houses in the eastern and western outskirts.

The "row houses" of Beijing were also named "barrack-style housing". It was said that this type of south-facing row houses were used for temporary living of servicemen of the Eight Banners and their families during the period of Emperor Kangxi of the Qing Dynasty. This type of house was material-effective, was easy to manage, was warm and was widely used at the time.

The space between rows of this type of houses was about three to four meters. The house, with an area of 14-16 square meters, had no separate kitchen, toilet and other living facilities. The middle room was sometimes divided into two parts for two neighboring families. The front half was south-facing while the

Beijing's first dilapidated housing renovation demonstration area, the Debao Housing Renovation Community.

Provided by Beijing Municipal Archives

rear half had only a north-facing window.

This type of house was shallow and everything in the room could be taken in at a glance. Most families built a small kitchen in front of the front window. As the kitchen blocked the sunlight, the room was dusky and greasy. Normally a row of houses or several rows shared a public water supply tap. The first building on the row of houses was normally a public toilet, featuring poor sanitary conditions. The neighbors often referred to "going home by following the smell".

In 1958, the "Great Leap Forward" and "People Commune Movement" started and the quadrangle courtyard began to move towards public ownership. At the time most quadrangle courtyards were privately owned. Beijing had about 1.2 million rooms with 920,000 under private ownership. The urban construction of Beijing forced a large batch of farmers to transfer to urban household registration and enjoy the same treatment as Beijingers. However, they had no houses and lived in the collective dormitories built by the units. The public ownership attempt of the quadrangle courtyards opened a door for many migrant workers who faced the pressure of marriage and having children.

Family members distributed the rooms of the quadrangle courtyards equally. Normally a family could get a room and some had two rooms. In this way, a quadrangle courtyard had several families and some even dozens of families.

Water supply station in Shanghai lanes

The public water supply station first appeared in 1928 in Shanghai. The station was also named the retailing water station. Stations were set up in shantytowns for poverty-stricken people. However, there were more than 1 million people in shantytowns with no access to running water before 1949.

After the founding of New China, water stations were set up in areas without running water. In 1950, Shanghai had 355 public water stations for nearly 200,000 people. Many areas had to use well water. In 1966, Shanghai had 3,903 water stations that covered about 1.6 million people. More than 400 people shared a water supply station on average. In 1979, the number of water stations reached 4,490, the highest in history. In the early days the stations were normally located in the center of a shantytown. A large water tank was filled with water for people's to use directly in peak times to save queuing time. More importantly, the water tank also worked as the water source for fire control. Lanes were normally narrow and fire engines could not enter them. In case of a fire, the water tank was the lifesaving water source.

Shanghai citizens could tell you many stories about the public water stations. In the early morning they had to get up to get water and waited in line when there were too many people. Later somebody put a bucket to hold a place in the line by the tank. Sometimes the queue was so long that it even extended to

A water station in Shanghai.

the lanes. Sometimes people in the queue would get into quarrels or fights. In the cold winter, the water pipe often froze and needed to be melted with hot water. Sometimes the hot water failed, people had to wait for the frozen pipe to thaw. Sometimes the water pipe burst, and no water was supplied. What's more, when water spilled and froze, the ground became slippery and some seniors could fall.

Without washing machines, people had to wash clothes by the water tank with a basin. When the washing machine appeared, people rushed to connect the washing machine with the water tap before dawn. In this way it was hard to avoid complaints from those who were waiting in the line to take water. For many Shanghai citizens, a day started with the water station. At dawn, people got up and came to the water station to wash their faces and brush their teeth, wash vegetables or clean buckets. Nearly everyone had to go to the water station at least once a day. It was even busy in the break days and festivals with people washing clothes and vegetables and gossiping around the water station. The water station was just a small epitome of society.

In June 1999, the last public water station was dismantled in No.713 Lane, Liyuan Road, Luwan District.

Walking-based transportation

"Transportation depends on walking, communications depends on shouting, heating depends on shaking and security depends on dogs". The first sentence of the humorous verse described the reality of transportation tools in most areas of China in the 1950s. In rural areas in the 1950s, the vast majority of people had no access to buses and only a very few of families which had workers in the family had a bicycle. The number of bicycles per 100 households was 13 in 1956 and 16 in 1957. People mainly depended on walking, animal-driven carts and animals in travel and single-wheel cart (wooden wheels), dray and flatbed carts (solid tyres) for transportation. There were basically no transportation options and people had to visit relatives on foot.

In urban areas, although the number of buses increased, people still could not rely on buses to travel. As a result, the bicycle became a main urban mode of transportation, in addition to the motor vehicle.

In 1958, Beijing had nine tram routes and each had a number plate of different color.

Before 1958, Shanghai had eight tram routes, 10 trolleybuses and 49 bus routes.

In 1955, bus tickets were rated at 4 cents, a dime, 15 cents and 2 dimes. The trolleybus was rated at 4 cents, 7 cents, a dime and 13 cents. The tram was rated at 3 cents, 6 cents, 9 cents and 12 cents.

In July 1958, the Shanghai Public Transportation Company (SPTC) was set up. The Tram Repair and Production Factory of SPTC trial-produced the Red Flag branded coach and the first articulated coach (trolley bus) in Beijing and Shanghai.

"Dangdang Bus" reminds pedestrians to keep away from cars with bells

In the 1950s, Beijing had the "dangdang bus". The dangdang bus was the name for trams in Beiping (old Beijing). In history Beijing's first tram was put into operation on December 17, 1924 from Qianmen. At the time, there were 10 trams running between Qianmen and Xizhimen. The connectors on top of the bus and the noise they made led to common people calling them "modian car" or "dangdang bus". The buses had a copper bell on the front. When the

Dangdang bus on Chang'an Street in Beijing.
Provided by Beijing Municipal Archives

driver stepped on the footplate, the bell would give out a sound that sounded like "dangdang" to remind pedestrians to keep away. It was the first generation of modern transportation. The tram in Qianmen first used French models and later Japanese and China-made models.

In 1958, the tram in Qianmen stopped operating.

In the beginning of 2008, the iron rail was set up on Qianmen Street after trams were renovated, allowing for the reappearance of the dangdang bus after 50 years.

In the 1950s, motorcycles were rare and seldom used in daily transportation.

There were taxies in the big cities such as Beijing and Shanghai, but beyond the access of the common people. In the early days after the founding of New China, Shanghai had 29 taxi companies with nearly 400 taxies in service. In Beijing, the government imported a batch of new Warszawa and Victory sedans from East Europe and the former Soviet Union to use as taxi. In addition, there was also pedicab in service but the price was not low. For example it cost 20 cents from Qianmen Station to Xidan Station.

Cartoon dance needs a "big brother"

The Youth Daily of Shanghai introduced a dance on January 30, 1951: The cartoon dance. It was an interesting collective dance without limits on quantity or shape, but it needed a leader. Whatever action the leader took, the others followed. And all actions were created by the leader who must have some dance foundations. The dance required changing actions, slow or fast, funny like the walking of clowns in the cartoons to increase the pleasure of the dance.

In today's term, the dance needed a "big brother".

There was also the hand-in-hand dance which had no limit on the number of dancers, but required an even number. Two dancers formed a team face-to-face to form two circles. The two dancers joined their left and rights *hands*.

There was also an orgiastic dance with all participants forming a circle without limit on the number of dancers. Some danced in the circle in freestyle moves and when certain beats appeared, the dancers in the circle must find a friend and salute with the right hand.

The People's Daily criticized the balls of Shanghai in 1956: "It was very popular to hold balls in factories and institutional organs in Shanghai. Some bad tendencies appeared such as extravagance and waste, corruption and affray."

The investigation showed that two of the three factories of the state-owned Shanghai Broadcasting Equipment Factory had enough space for dancing, but they rented famous ballrooms such as the Four Sisters Ballroom. To collect money for the rent they sold tickets for the ball and the tickets were rated at 10 cents, 20 cents or even 60 cents or 80 cents. Consequently corruption appeared.

A divorce is hereby granted as mediation failed

In May 1950, China's first Marriage Law was promulgated and enacted.

The first clause of the Marriage Law declared: "The feudal marriage system, which features forced marriage, male chauvinism and ignorance to children's interests, is abolished. A new democratic marriage system is exercised which features free marriage, monogamy, equality of rights between men and women and protection of the legitimate interests of women and children."

The Marriage Law also set provisions on the minimum age for marriage: "Only after reaching 20 years of age for men and 18 years for women can they get married."

It also provided: "A divorce is granted when both parities are willing to divorce. In case a party insists on divorce, a divorce is granted only after mediation of the local people's government and the judicial institution fails." With this provision, many women ended miserable marriages.

When the new Marriage Law was enacted, serious social problems were caused because of poor implementation in some areas. According to the *Youth Daily* on February 3, 1953, some women and young men were killed or committed suicide because of poor implementation of the law in areas of East China. Incomplete statistics show that 438 people were killed or committed

The wedding picture and wedding ceremony had rich
characteristics of the times in the 1960s.

suicide from January to July, 1952, in 57 counties of Zhejiang Province.
According to the statistics of 11 districts of Jimo and Jiaoxian counties of
Shandong Province, 37 of the 50 people who committed suicide in half of the
year were young. Of the 166 victims in Tengxian, 86 were young and most
were women.

Rural women have a bath in the bathhouse for the first time

In the 1950, it was common to see children waving a red banner on the street and singing: "Dear uncles and aunts, please listen to me. Do not spit on street, otherwise you will be fined a fine of 50 cents."

It was also a new phenomenon to mobilize people to develop good hygiene.

However, it was not easy to have a bath. *The Youth Daily of Shanghai* published an article on July 6, 1956, To Have a Bath in Laohuzao, reflecting difficulties in having a bath: "In the past, workers of Shanghai Capital Luggage Factory had difficulty in having a bath and 22 workers had to share a washbasin. In the evening all workers tried to get the washbasin for a bath before going to school or a meeting and sometimes even got into quarrels. The factory management could not solve the problem because of the financial hardships at the beginning. Later the management decided to buy water tickets and bathtub cubicles from laohuzao (Tiger Furnace, hot water supply stores). Then the bath difficulty was solved."

Laohuzao also ran the bathtub cubicles and low-end teahouses. In the past, the fuel port of the furnace of the hot water store was set up outside of the wall in the form of two small windows, like eyes of a tiger. The stokehole was opened on the right front, like the tiger's mouth; the furnace tail had a high chimney, like the tail of the tiger. So it was vividly named laohuzao(tiger furnace).

In 1958, Anhui's bathhouse became a highlight of the country: "Rural women have a bath in the bathhouse for the first time".

It was the news on both the transformation of the outmoded habit and custom and sanitation. At the beginning of the year, a commune stipulated that the commune members must have a bath every half a month and designated the bathing date for men and women respectively. But when the date for women was reached, no one would volunteer to go to the bathhouse. The commune leaders sent women activists to mobilize people and asked the female heads of the production teams and women cadres to take a lead. Eventually all women commune members were invited to the bathhouse. Since then, the bathhouse was nearly full of women everyday. This sounds like a sweeping approach.

However, no one could say paying attention to sanitation was wrong.

Transferring Shanghai haircutters to open Silian in Beijing

In the 1950s, heavy makeup was rare for women and their hairstyles changed remarkably. It was common for women to have straight short hair or a simple and neat ponytail.

Short hair was popular among the young and middle-aged women of Shanghai and some old women wore a round bun or a simple Taoist bun. In addition, a bun with geometry patterns was also popular. Pigtails were a common hairstyle of young women in Shanghai. They considered simplicity as beautiful. Girls also often bound their hair into two ponytails. After 1950, perms became popular among workwomen. The hairdressers of famous barbershops such as Nanjing, Xinxin, Hua'an, Baile, Hujiang and Ziluolan designed many new hairstyles.

In the late spring of 1956, more than 100 hairdressers, from Shanghai's most famous barbershops, namely Huaxin, Ziluolan, Yunshang and Xiangming, took a train from Shanghai to Beijing. They brought their tools such as boilers, chair, clips and whetstones for the hair clippers. After 36 hours, they arrived in Beijing.

The trip to Beijing was arranged under the instruction of Premier Zhou Enlai. With the field visit, these four barbershops decided to set up a large

China time-honored Brand Silian Hairdressing Shop.

barbershop named Silian (a joint-venture of these four barbershops).

Each of the four barbershops was outstanding, let alone the Silian Barbershop jointly set up by the four. At the time, it normally cost 40 cents to have hair cut in a famous barbershop in Beijing, but 80 cents in Silian. However, the high charge was reasonable. In the early days, the barbershops only offered services such as shaving for men. After the founding of New China, the technology of barbershops in Beijing was backward and only a few hairdressers could use the hair clippers. When Silian opened, the 10 barber chairs imported from the US became a hot topic as were the fashionable hairstyles. Even the handicraft of the hairdressers, who held a roll brush with one hand and a hairdryer in another was worth seeing. Shanghai hairdressers paid special attentions to hairstyle design and exquisite technique. After haircutting, customers looked energetic and neat. The perm and hair blowing techniques are still the specialty of Silian. (Lu Yingbo, Silian Hairdressing: Stable Staffing and Stable Hairdressing Handicraft, April 13, 2008, The Economic Observer).

National steelmaking movement

"In the evening, the train runs in the field, passing by rows of furnaces. The flame made a 'birr' noise, lighting the night sky."

"Millions of iron armies marched into the barren wasteland, waking numerous mountains. Blasters fired the detonators in the quiet valley and endless minerals and coal flowed to the steel-making furnaces."

"Hundreds of roads were built, leading to the mines and furnaces. Both trains and ships accelerated for steel production."

That was the report Seething Days and Nights published by the *People's Daily*, honestly recording the fanatical scene of the national steel-making movement. Everything made way for steel-making. Numerous furnaces were established across the country with multitudes of people devoted to the task.

Backyard blast furnaces were set up everywhere across the country. Factories, corps, communes, institutional organs, schools and even the Ministry of Foreign Affairs set up steel furnaces and iron factories. All Chinese people, men and women, young and old, professionals and outsiders, became iron workers. In areas where there was no coal supply, they chopped trees to make charcoal; in the urban areas where there were no trees, they burnt furniture and bed boards as fuel. Without a supply of iron mineral, they used iron pans and cooking vessels. Without bricks and stones, they dismantled ancestral temples, temples, walls and pagodas. The bricks on the footpaths of Wangfujing Street of Beijing disappeared overnight and were used to build backyard blast furnaces.

Quiet schools also became seething with students putting down books and becoming iron workers. Even senior housewives stood up to send iron pans and iron hoes to use as raw material for steelmaking.

With extraordinary measures, China had more than 100 million of people working on the frontline of the steel-making sector by 1958, more than one sixth of the total population of the country. After several months of reckless

Beijing citizens deliver their iron products to the furnaces for steel-making. It was everyone's responsibility to support national development.

Provided by Beijing Municipal Archives

action, the declared steel output reached 11.08 million tons, pig iron 13.69 million tons, with considerable exaggeration. Actually the qualified steel output was only 8 million tons and qualified iron output 9 million tons. The rest was waste.

The national steel-making movement seriously damaged and wasted the ecological environment and material resources, worsening the difficulties of the common people. The products and output volume of light industry were sharply reduced, directly leading to extreme shortage of life necessities.

Wronged sparrow

In the 1950s, several hundreds of million of Chinese people were suppressing sparrows.

The small bird would never dream that it would be listed as a harmful bird and suppressed by several hundreds of millions of people.

In 1955, some farmers reported to Mao Zedong that sparrows had damaged their grain. Soon there was a decision that starting from 1956, efforts should be made to eliminate sparrows, rats, flies and mosquitoes in five years, seven years or 12 years.

Then sparrow became the enemy of human beings and was suppressed everywhere.

According to the incomplete statistics, more than 210 million of sparrows were killed in 1958 and not many of the birds were left. Many people had experiences killing sparrows:

"I lived in the rural area when I was a child. In harvest time, sparrows often came to eat grain. Farmers set up scarecrows in the wheat fields to scare sparrows. How could one protect the kernels drying in the sun? My father set up a wooden plank dressed in the form of a man. My brother propped a shallow bamboo basket with a chopstick, tied a thread to the chopstick and hid with one side of the thread in his hand. Soon a sparrow flew into the trap. Before the bird ate grains of rice, my brother pulled the thread and the basket fell down and trapped the bird. Watching the whole process, I was very happy." (Chen Lizhen, *Catching Sparrow, Xinmin News,* April 19, 2009)

中国共产党中央委员会、国务院
关于除四害讲卫生的指示

1958年 2 月12日

一个以除四害为中心的爱国卫生运动的高潮已经在全国形成。在全国各省市、广大群众正在大规模地行动起来，消灭老鼠、麻雀、苍蝇、蚊子，提倡卫生，扑灭危害严重人民最严重的疾病，并且纷纷提出规划，准备在几年时间内提前实现条国农业发展纲要（修正草案）所提出的要求。截至目前为止，倡不足全国统计，提前实现〔四无〕的省份直辖市：已经有北京定为两年，河南定为三年，上海定为三五五年，江苏定为四年，山东、山西、浙江、福建、广东、云南、甘肃、辽宁、黑龙江定为五年，安徽定为五至八年，决定在今年内就实现〔四无〕的市和县，有江苏的南京、常熟、苏江、南通，山东的济南、阳信、垦县，河南的郑州、开封、洛阳、焦作、璧封，甘肃的临州，山西的长治，河北的蓟县、河间。干部和群众在这一运动中充满了勤和信心，证参和工都有新的进展，目前党和政府的迫切任务，就是要坚决地地领地领导这一运动，在今年春夏用半把这一运动发展到全国一切已经基本上实现了社会主义所有制改造的地方，其正达到争取四年、人人动手的程度。要在今年争好，使每一省、市、自治县、每一县区、每个乡、每个合作社、厂矿企业、机关、学校、部队、都订出自己除四害讲卫生的年度计划和其期划，而且务必在今年内打下实现长期计划的巩固基础。

Instruction of the Central Committee of the CPC and the State Council on eliminating the four pests on February 12, 1958.

Provided by Beijing Municipal Archives

In March 1960, Mao Zedong instructed: "Do not kill sparrows any more." The slogan was changed to "eliminating rats, bedbugs, flies and mosquitoes."

Chinese people spared no efforts in eliminating the four pests. Water tanks, oil, spring clips and many other methods were used to eliminate rats. At the time, the number of eliminated rats was determined by the number of rat tails. Children submitted rat tails which were treated with revet to the schools or the neighborhood committees. People who killed rats were rewarded. In some areas, killing a rat could be rewarded with a box of matches or several rats could be traded for a bookmark. Some pupils even cut a tail into two pieces to fake the tails of two rats.

Women were bashful when doing radio calisthenics

On November 24, 1951, the first edition of the radio calisthenics was officially promulgated. On December 1, China National Radio broadcasted the music of the radio calisthenics for the first time.

The radio calisthenics were well received after promoting it for it was interesting and with beautiful activity. Gradually people's passion for radio calisthenics faded because the exercise did not meet their requirements.

In June 1952, Mao Zedong issued a call for the development of sports to strengthen people's health.

In July 1954, the second edition of the radio calisthenics was officially publicized, which increased the amount of exercise and stretches of the lower limbs.

The second edition was designed with help of the Soviet experts and some of the exercises were alien to many. Many women were bashful when doing the exercises and even tried to escape the exercise with various excuses. Leaders

Poster of the third edition of the radio calisthenics in 1957.

Pupils doing radio calisthenics.

Provided by Beijing Municipal Archives

at that time were serious and "drove" them out of the houses to do exercise. It took a long time for them to line up for roll call.

In 1957, the third edition of the radio calisthenics was officially publicized. The *People's Daily* published the news: "The third edition of radio calisthenics publicized". The article was interesting: "More than 90 percent of students of the Senior Party School of the Central Committee of the CPC insist on doing the radio calisthenics and the frequency has changed from twice a day to three times a day. According to the survey of 220 students, 67 students had increased the weight from 1kg to 6 kg, 13 fat students reported weight reductions; 29 reported increased appetites and 41 improved sleeping." (Radio calisthenics: a half-century long body-shaping memory, *Beijing Daily*, July 15, 2008).

Merit students

New China attached great importance to literacy.

China took a method of letting those who could serve as teachers to eliminate illiteracy, allowing the husband, wife or children of the literate to teach those who were illiterate. Teachers taught several Chinese characters a day and asked students to go over what they learned.

The anti-illiteracy class of some areas even stipulated 10 don'ts: Don't leave early, don't be late, don't fool around, don't laugh or play, don't smoke, don't wear a hat, don't chat, don't sleep, don't knit and don't read the newspaper in class.

On June 30, 1953, Mao Zedong said: "I have some words for the youth. First, wish them good health. Second, wish them to study well. And third, wish them do good work." That was probably the source of the "three goods".

In February 1955, the Rules for Primary School Students promulgated by the Ministry of Education dealt with the first clause: "Try to be a good student, keep good health, do a good work in assignments and conduct and be ready to serve the motherland and the people."

In May of the same year, the Rules for Secondary School Students were promulgated and the first clause made similar provisions as the Rules for Primary School Students.

In February 1957, Mao Zedong put forward: "Our education guideline shall focus on allowing the students to develop morally, intellectually and physically to become literate laborers with socialist awareness."

From then on the "three goods" evolved into the moral, intellectual and physical education with profound influence.

The first national salary reform

In 1956, the first national salary reform was implemented, which affected the interests of hundreds of millions of people across the country. On June 16, the State Council adopted the Decisions on Salary Reform. It laid a foundation for the salary system for the next 30 years and had a profound impact on China's administration of officials. "Rank" became an important standard for the political and economic life of various social groups except for farmers.

In the early days after the founding of New China, the supply system and the salary system co-existed. The domestic economy continued to grow until 1955, and a new round of salary reform was promulgated in response to the needs of the times. The central government decided to abolish pay points of the state organs and their affiliated institutional units and change to the currency salary system. The national salary reform started.

With the salary system reform, distribution systems were set up for state organs, enterprises and institutional units. The stage organs of the CPC and the government exercised the post-rank salary system which divided the cadres into 30 administrative ranks. Enterprise workers were divided into eight (seven for some branches of work) technical ranks. Professionals such as engineers, teachers, medical workers and literary and arts workers also were given corresponding ranks. The rank system of different categories could be converted, for example the literary rank 1 was equivalent to administrative rank 8 or the senior education rank 8 was equivalent to the administrative rank 17.

Meanwhile, the whole country was divided into 11 classes of salary according to natural conditions, commodity prices, living costs, transportation conditions and salaries of different regions, with appropriate considerations to key development areas and areas with harsh living conditions. The region of class 1 was considered as the benchmark and the salary was to increase by

Mei Lanfang, famous Peking Opera artist.

From Record of Disciples of the Art Circle

3 percent for promotion of each class (e.g., Zhejiang belonged to the Class 2 region; Anhui to the Class 3 region, Beijing to Class 6, Shanghai Class 8, Guangdong Class 10 and Qinghai Class 11). The higher the class, the higher the salary standards would be.

The classification standards were designed with a post divided into several classes and assessed according to title, virtues, talent and qualifications. Roughly the ministerial level was equal to Class 3 to Class 5. For example, Maodun was then Minister of Culture and his salary was rated as Class 4. The deputy-ministerial level was equal to Class 5 to Class 8. Zhou Yang was the then Deputy Minister of Culture and his salary was Class 6. The bureau level was equal to Class 8 to Class 10 and deputy bureau level Class 9 to Class 12, an so on.

The proportion between the highest salary and the lowest salary was about 21:1. With the reform, the salaries of all people were significantly improved. People of the academic circle and the cultural circle were willing to accept the classification and assessment. For example, Mei Lanfang's salary was RMB1,100 before the salary reform. He was content to be rated as Literary Class 1 and accepted RMB336 of salary. Guan Suchuang volunteered to be rated as Literary Class 2 and her salary was reduced from RMB800 to about RMB280. After implementation of the salary system, writers could choose between the literary class and administrative class. The salary of the literary class was higher than the administrative class under the same conditions, but many chose to be rated according to the administrative classes.

In addition to the self-discipline atmosphere of that time, there was another

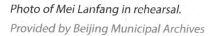

Photo of Mei Lanfang in rehearsal.
Provided by Beijing Municipal Archives

reason for them to choose the administrative class: The administrative class was linked with access to documents and reports or even subscriptions to the *Reference News* and senior cadre medical treatment and other benefits. For example, Zhao Shuli was rated to Administrative Class 10 and RMB209.9. Meanwhile, he could also be rated to be Literary Class 2 and RMB280. But Zhao chose the administrative class.

A batch of writers such as Bingxin, Zhang Tianyi, Zhou Libo and Qiqing were rated to be Literary Class 1. Before this salary system reform, professors had their own ranks, but they also attached importance to this rating. Chen Yinke, Liang Sicheng, Feng Youlan, Ji Xianlin and Zhong Jingwen were rated as Class 1. At that time, some 56 professors were rated to be Class 1. The rating was very strict and some provinces had only one Class 1 professor and some even had none. For example, Wu Mi, Chen Zizhan and Huang Kun and some other leading scholars of various disciplines were only rated to be Class 2.

Ji Xianlin was rated as a Class 1 professor and his salary was RMB345 in addition to a subsidy from the Chinese Academy of Sciences of RMB100, totaling RMB445. To have a dinner in Moscow Restaurant, it cost RMB1.5-2 with a service of soup, dishes, butter and bread and a cup of beer.

1949 1950S 1960S 1970S 1980S 1990S 21st Century

MEMORIES OF
CHINESE LIFE IN THE

1960s

The 1960s saw the birth of numerous heroes and their words and deeds were instilled into the daily life of common people. But in the 1960s, Chinese people experienced starvation and extreme shortages of life necessities. The harsh situation was caused by "30 percent natural disasters and 70 percent man-made disasters". When the "left-learning" errors prevailed and daily life became political life, the Cultural Revolution broke out and the whole nation paid the price.

The food substitute movement: Man-made meat essence and appeasing hunger with chlorella

In the late 1950s, the "general line", the "Great Leap Forward" and the "people communes movement" (collectively called Three Red Flags at the time) swept the country. With natural and man-made disasters, the Chinese people reached the so-called "Three Years of Natural Disasters" or the "Three Years of Hardship".

Rice expert Yuan Longping said: "Tens of millions of people died of starvation during those three years. During the Great Leap Forward, trees were cut to smelt iron and steel and the ecological environment was damaged. A drought in 1959 basically destroyed the harvest. I saw five starved corpses by the field, a bridge or road. I witnessed with my own eyes. It was miserable. In the spring of 1960, the shortages of food worsened. To cook more food with less grain, a national 'food increase cooking method' advanced experience exchange was held in Xi'an in January 1960. Heishan County, Liaoning Province, was the birthplace of the 'food increase method'. In May 1959, the Santaizi side-product production team of the Dahusha Weixing People's Commune created the method. Before promoting it, some cadres and common people expressed their suspicion, 'a wall cannot be built without soil; added water cannot work as food'. Some even made a joke: 'The food increase method is to swell the rice by soaking it. It cannot appease our hunger, but makes our bladder work harder.' However, the 'corn increase method' of Heishan County was promoted to the whole country. Meanwhile, due to the low grain rations and serious shortage of non-staple food, people could not take sufficient calories and many suffered from edema and hepatitis and other diseases."

At that time, some areas provided that only with the hospital "prescription" could a patient get a "pink rehabilitation ticket". With the ticket one could buy "rehabilitation powder" (a mixture of wheat bran, bean powder and granulated sugar) from the designated site and take the powder mixed with boiled water several times a day. One senior recalled that "the curative effect was acceptable."

Considering the tension caused by the famine in the rural area, the Central Committee of the CPC issued an order on August 10, 1960, requiring all regions lower the grain ration, "meanwhile, efforts shall be made to plant vegetable and develop side-products, food substitutes and the other substitutes". The Central Committee officially put forward requirements of "low standards and developing vegetable and melon food substitutes". On November 14, the Central Committee of the CPC issued an urgent instruction requiring an immediate large-scale mass movement for collection and production of food substitutes to get past the difficulties.

The so-called food substitutes referred to plants, animals, microorganism and synthetics that people used to appease their hunger but would not be considered food in normal days.

The food substitutes during those three years were mainly classified into four categories. The first category referred to the crop food substitutes, including straw, roots and leaves of crops that were not eaten during other years such as leaves, stalks and root from the rice paddies, wheat, barley, corn and sorghum and corn bran, corn core and rice hull and leaves, stems and roots of potatoes.

The second category referred to wild food substitutes such as straw, roots, leaves, peels and fruits of wild plants like elm leaves, bark and acorns.

The third category referred to chlorella, azolla and other phytoplankton. The cholorella is a kind of spherical algae, with a diameter of only a few microns and cup-shaped or plate-shaped green chloroplasts. It has great variety and grows in freshwater. It was originally used as pig feed. On July 6, 1960, the

Samples of vegetable coupon (valid for 10 days) in May 1962 in Beijing.

Provided by Beijing Municipal Archives

Samples of the food subsidy coupon for children two years old and below issued by the Beijing Municipal Non-staple Food Commercial Bureau in April 1963.

Provided by Beijing Municipal Archives

People's Daily made it clear that chlorella was not only good for feed but had high edible value.

The fourth category was synthesized food substitutes such as man-made meat essence, man-made meat and leaf protein. Compared with the first three categories, this category had certain technical content and was also called a fine food substitute.(Xiong Xinwen: Food Substitute Movements in the History of the People's Republic of China, *News Midday*, July 3, 2006)

Given the extreme food shortages, the masses could survive by collecting and producing various food substitutes. However, many food substitutes had virtually no nutrition and could not check edema and abnormal death.

Lying-in women provided with a lump sum subsidy of 1kg of eggs

On October 31, 1959, the Beijing Non-staple Food Commercial Bureau and the Beijing Municipal Public Sanitation Bureau jointly issued the Notice on Modifying the Supply Standards of Meat, Egg and Vegetable for Patients and stipulated lump subsidies to lying-in women of 1kg of eggs, 1kg of meat and 1kg black sugar.

From June 1, 1960, blood donors would be provided with subsidies of 500g meat for a 200cc of blood donation and 1000g of meat for a 400 cc blood donation. The children would be provided subsidies of 500g sugar, 125g of eggs, 750g cakes and biscuits and 1kg of dairy products. From January 1961, edema patients would be provided 1kg fresh fish. The supply of non-staple foods was tighter in 1960, e.g. the total stock of pork, beef and mutton was 1.805 million kg in Beijing on April 15, only enough for the quota supply for a month (200g per person per month). In light of the situation, the scope of goods supplied through coupons was significantly enlarged, in addition to the coupon-based quota supply of main non-staple foods.

A total of 21 kinds of commodities were supplied with coupons, including canned meat, cooked meat and dry goods (supplied with the meat coupon by converting them into an equivalent volume of meat), candy, cake, biscuit, dairy products, liqueur, dry vegetable, fresh vegetable, fish, seafood, dry and fresh fruit, soy sauce, seasoning, salt, bean products, starch, vermicelli and more in addition to meat, egg and sugar. In that year, sales of goods supplied with coupons accounted for 29.3 percent of the total retailing of non-staple food.

In 1961, the stock of meat, poultry and egg dropped sharply and the supply was extremely tight. For example, the meat could only meet the special procurement and the coupon issued to citizens could not be honored. From April, meat was supplied through an equivalent amount of fresh meat, cooked meat, fish and canned products. Given the lack of supply, from June 1961 to February 1962 no meat coupons were issued to citizens. Except in cases of special needs, patients, lying-in women and kindergartens, the daily supply of eggs basically stopped for citizens.

Gao Zhiyong, a cadre of the Second Commercial Bureau of Beijing, recalled the non-staple food supply during that difficult period:

The food supply was changed from the certificate-based supply to coupon-based supply. Citizens with official registered permanent residence in Beijing were supplied with food monthly. The food coupon was divided into coarse food grains coupons, flour coupons, rice coupons... The food quota was designed according to the age of the receiver and varied from 1,500g for infants, to between 3kg and 4kg for children and 10.5kg for adult... The flour supply accounted for 20 percent of the total supply, and rice accounted for 10

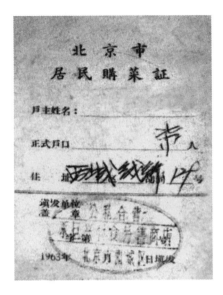

Vegetable purchase certificate of Beijing citizens in 1963.

Provided by Beijing Municipal Archives

percent. The others were coarse food grains such as corn meal, dried sweet potato chips or sorghum flour and fresh sweet potato.

Infants were supplied with two bottles of milk every day with a milk certificate and each bottle weighed a half pound. Those who were one year old were supplied with a bottle of milk and milk powder substitute. The children were supplied with a milk powder substitute coupon and an infant sugar coupon a month. With the coupon, one could buy 500g milk powder substitute (mixture of the soybean powder, rice powder and a small volume of milk powder) from the designated shop and 100g of brown sugar (imported from Cuba).

The food coupon was certainly hot. In 1961, a Beijing food coupon of 500g was sold at RMB3 in the black market. More than 80 percent of the frontline production workers earned between RMB30 and RMB40. At the same time, a national food coupon of 500g sold for RMB4 in the black market and a Beijing flour coupon of 500g sold for RMB5.

In 1960, the supply of pork dropped sharply. In July no fresh pork was available and canned meat was supplied. With several coupons one could acquire a can of meat.

Since 1961, the quota of meat coupons was reduced from 150g to 100g. In April that year, canned chicken, duck and fish were used as substitutes for fresh meat. From June to the end of the year, no pork was supplied to citizens.

According to official statistics, in 1961 per capita meat consumption was 425g for the whole year, the lowest in history, but much higher than other provinces and municipalities. (Beijing Non-staple Food Business Annals, 2002)

Quota supply of vegetable, shallot, ginger and garlic

In 1960, vegetable was officially classified as a National Grade II Good. The vegetable was supplied by quota and those who had official registered permanent residence in Beijing had access to 100g of fresh vegetable a day, selecting from any of radish, potato or cabbage, but mostly potato. In addition, a small number of "shallot coupons" were also issued. With the coupon, one could buy a handful of shallot, ginger, garlic, etc., mainly under the arrangement of the neighborhood committee with emphasis on the families of revolutionary martyrs and servicemen. Sometimes no vegetable was available even with coupons. However, with the coupon one could buy pickles or salted vegetable (pickles were supplied with coupon). Many goods were supplied with Beijing Non-staple Food Purchase Permit. For example, several kilograms of cabbage for the winter; 100 g sugar per person per month; 500g salt per household per month; 50g sesame paste and 50g tea per household for the Spring Festival, National Day and May 1. From 1959, tea was classified as a National Grade II Good and was rarely seen in the market. For festivals, 150g of vermicelli of various specifications, 25g of pepper, 25g of aniseed, 25g of agaric, 25g of citron day-lily and 25g of sodium carbonate were supplied per household.

Peanut and sunflower seeds were supplied once a year. For the Spring Festival, each household could buy 250g peanut and 100g fried sunflower seeds. Only until 1965 the supply was changed from 250g peanut and 100g of sunflower seeds per household to per person.

Edible oil was supplied to those with official registered permanent residence in Beijing and each person could get an oil coupon per month. With the coupon, one could buy 150g of edible oil, mainly soybean oil or cotton seed oil. The

Vegetable coupon in 1962, cake and biscuit coupon in 1963, subsidy oil coupon and barley coupon in 1964.

Provided by Beijing Municipal Archives

peanut oil was only supplied in small volumes during the Spring Festival and other festivals.

In addition, an additional festival subsidy oil coupon would be issued for each household for the Spring Festival. With the coupon, one could buy 50g sesame oil.

The sauce (low-end) and vinegar (bulk) was supplied without limit, but no more than 750g at a time. Fortunately there was no limit on purchase times.

Each month a household would get a coupon for cake and biscuit respectively. With the coupon and additionally a Beijing food coupon (national food coupons were not acceptable) of 200g, one could buy 250g of cake and 100g of biscuit. (From Memorial Citation on Goods Supply of Beijing in the Hard Time, Yan-Huang Historical Review, Issue 8, 2007).

From 1959, Shanghai also faced shortages of non-staple foods and adopted a quota supply or coupon-based supply for cabbage, radish, shallot, garlic and seasoning, cake and sugar according to population. Since then, the varieties of goods supplied by quota or coupon increased every year.

In the three years, the Shanghai commercial authority issued up to 53 kinds of goods supply coupons, totaling 141 specifications, to ensure the supply of basic necessities. The coupons and certificates issued to people or households were handed out by the grain stores on behalf of the competent authority.

Umbrella and alarm clocks were also supplied with coupon

In order to distribute a limited supply of goods, Beijing also issued coupons for soap, matches, chimneys, iron stoves, iron pans, aluminum kettles and even brushwood and coal. There were also coupons for wardrobes, wooden trunks, wooden beds, round tables, alarm clocks, watches, electric bulbs, sewing machines, bicycles and more. Such coupons were one-off and marked with allowed purchase quantity of the designated goods. According to incomplete statistics, as many as 61 different goods were supplied through coupons in 1961, excluding those supplied with permits.

At the end of 1961, Beijing started issuing industrial coupons. Since then all goods, except for those supplied through coupons or permits, were supplied by industrial coupons.

Industrial coupons were issued according to the salary of employees at a rate of one coupon for every RMB20 per salary. The purchase scope was wide for the industrial coupon: towels, blankets, wool, handkerchief, battery, spool cotton, iron pans, aluminum basins, aluminum lunch boxes, enamel basin, enamel cup, enamel bedpans, cotton gloves, iron-casing thermos, bamboo-casing thermos, sports shoes, umbrellas, cotton rubber shoes , needles, sewing thread, slicker, laminated raincoat, rayon products, nylon underwear, leather shoes, alarm clocks, radios, belt, knives, scissors, import blades, all kinds of bags and cases, chocolate, cigarettes, tea and wine out of the quota.

The supply of goods in the urban area was short, but it was even harder in the rural area. With the "people's commune movement", commune members were forced to eat meals at collective eateries.

Simple farmers responded to the call of the CPC and donated their iron pans and spoons for steel smelting. In 1961, the public eateries failed and the farmers had to cook for themselves. Unfortunately, they had nothing to cook in and had to travel to urban areas to purchase such articles. However, nearly all goods were supplied with permits or coupons and farmers could not buy anything.

There were too many kinds of coupons and permits and the farmers could hardly remember with which coupon to buy what.

It was complicated because sometimes temporary arrangements were made on which coupon was to be used for what goods. The shortage of goods and too many kinds of coupons and permits led to one of the most visible features of the Chinese market – queuing. When people saw queuing in the street they would join in before knowing what was being sold.

Consumers buying thermos in the market.

Provided by Beijing Municipal Archives

Clothes coupon from Beijing in 1961 (left).Rubber overshoes coupon from Beijing in 1960 (middle).Meat Coupon for the Spring Festival in 1964 (right).

Provided by Beijing Municipal Archives

It was common for people to queue for goods that were sold out. They had to go home disappointed and wait for the next time. They worried failing again and wasting a coupon.

"Three years in new, three years in old and three years in patched"

Material life in the 1960s was extremely harsh and was mainly reflected by the clothes people worn and the saying "three years in new, three years in old and three years in patched."

Families with many children could not afford new clothes for all and had to "make new clothes for the eldest, the old for the second eldest and the patched for the third". It was common to see people wearing ragged clothes and even worn clothes were used for patching and making soles.

Chinese people had their own ways to deal with difficulties, for example, turning over faded khaki clothes and cotton-wadded jacket, exchanging a new collar and repairing worn wristbands, shortening ragged trousers into pants and wearing long-sleeved blouses as short-sleeved or adding trouser legs or remaking worn trousers into skirts or T-shirt or dual-purpose shirts.

In 1960, the Central Committee of the CPC decided to reduce the supply of civilian cotton cloth. The cloth coupon was granted per capita. Those who had an official registered permanent residence in Beijing could have coupons for 4.5 chi (1.5m) of cloth a year, which was only enough for patching old clothing.

At that time, the washing and repairing sector was very busy. No matter how ragged the clothes they could be repaired back to perfection. For a patch, a cloth coupon was also needed according to the size of the patch in addition to the service fee.

After 1964, the situation improved and more cloth coupons were granted. In addition to the cloth coupons, coupons for cotton, sweatshirts, undershirts, vests, pants, rubber overshoes, cotton-wadded shoes and more were issued. For a period, cloth coupons were also charged for buying sewing thread and a coupon for a cun of cloth for a small ball of thread.

The blue uniform model originates from the Chinese tunic suit and was the most common male dress in the 1960s.

Provided by the National Costume Museum of Beijing Institute of Fashion Technology

Women workers dressed in frocks in the 1960s.

Provided by the National Costume Museum of
Beijing Institute of Fashion Technology

In the 1950s and 1960s, dressing materials were normally pingyang cloth, denim, twill, khaki, corduroy and poplin. Only in Spring Festival could one dress in new clothes.

Hand-made or store-bought new clothes were normally hung on the wooden stand before bed on the eve of the Spring Festival. Children often lied in the warm bed and stared at the new clothes with endless daydreams and sometimes they sat up to look at the clothes closely, forgetting it was chilly outside with the snow and ice. What they wanted was to dress in the new clothes to visit friends and relatives the next day. With such dreams, they could hardly fall sleep and just wished it for the dawn to arrive as quickly as possible. The following day, they did not hate getting up, but dressed in the new clothes and went out with their friends after eating breakfast. One of their first topics of conversation was to compare whose clothes were better.

No white buttons for white suit in Beijing

In the spring of 1960, Premier Zhou Enlai and Marshal Chen Yi planned to visit Cambodia after concluding a visit to Burma, India and Nepal. At that time Prince Norodom Sihanouk's father King Suramarit had passed away. After sending a letter of condolences, Zhou and Chen decided to visit Cambodia as planned, not only to pay a friendly visit but also to mourn the late King.

Zhou sent an urgent instruction to Beijing asking for a white suit for each member of the delegation to Kunming for them to exchange into clothes of condolence for Cambodia.

Although the clothes were made quickly, there was a big problem. At that time, everyone in the country dressed in blue and grey and workers could not find white buttons for the white suit anywhere in Beijing. They thought of all kinds of measures, but none worked and it would have been strange to match a white suit with blue, grey or black buttons.

A clerk at the Wangfujing Department Store showed quick wits in the emergency after noticing the ivory soap boxes that were made of plastic. With the ivory plastic soap case in hand, the clerk said: "I have an idea. How about making white buttons?"

They had no other choice and tried it. They cut the soap boxes into round buttons and sewed them on the white suits. The buttons and the suits matched perfectly. Then the workers bought dozens of soap boxes and cut them into buttons. Finally they prepared the suits in time and sent them to Kunming. (Quan Yanchi, *Secret Emissary of the People's Republic of China*, Guangming Daily Press, November 1990)

Countrified usher uniform

In the 1960s, children normally dressed in the cotton-wadded coats and trousers. Fat or thin, all were cumbersomely dressed. Later a new uniform-like coat appeared that combined the cotton-wadded coat and a blouse. However, the outfits still looked cumbersome and were difficult to clean and wash. Some young men refused to wear the coats to "play cool".

A kind of cloth shoes called "lazybones shoes" (loafers) were very popular. The shoes were cheap and convenient to wear. The most popular was the white-rim loafers with a black vamp, white rim and white plastic shoe sole. Tianjin Loafers produced in Tianjin were the best. The children in high school who liked to show off were big fans of this brand and paid no attention to other brands after getting a pair of them.

The five-hole cotton-waded shoes with corduroy vamp worn in winter were nicknamed "Beijing Cotton". Like the loafers, the shoes with white plastic sole

Dresses for young and middle-aged women. A reversible jacket and dark blue trousers were the common female dress in the 1960s.

Provided by the National Costume Museum of Beijing Institute of Fashion Technology

The "Red Guard" green military uniform was the special dresses of the youth during the Cultural Revolution. At that time, men or women were proud of dressing in the military uniform. Wearing a waistbelt, a red sleeve emblem on the left arm, a badge of Mao Zedong on the chest, matched with an army cap, liberation shoes and a military bag.

Provided by the National Costume Museum of Beijing Institute of Fashion Technology

were the most popular. In snow days, children liked to skate and such shoes were especially slippery.

Breathing masks were an important ornament in those years. The mask was not worn, but tucked into the jacket between the second and the third buttons with the string left outside. It was a vogue mark that could not be neglectable, functioning like a tie or jewelry. Normally careless, children often found they forgot to take the mask with them on the way to school and had to go back to get it. Otherwise no matter how fashionable the clothes were, they would think themselves out of fashion. That the breathing mask string was the most stylish gadget reflected the simplicity and tedium of children's dresses.

In the mid-1960s, people started wearing a cloth blouse with a boat collar, a collar of western-style clothes and five buttons. The design was once called "usher uniform" probably because it could be dressed when receiving foreign guests and on other important occasions. This design was different in the collar and pocket from men's Chinese tunic. The so-called "usher uniform" could be used as outer wear in the spring and autumn and was very popular in the decade from the mid-1960s to the mid-1970s. Then it went out of fashion, but was still popular among the middle-aged and old women (especially some female teachers and cadres) until the late 1990s.

Military uniforms were popular across the whole country. In the 1960s, the military uniform led fashion trends. In the popular doggerel, one could be "arrogant or not, depending on whether you have a set of beige military uniform or not".

The outfit with an army cap, a "national defense green" jacket or a set of "national defense green" uniform, a pair of loafers, a military bag, a 26-model bicycle and a wire lock in hand, could be called "cool" or in "vogue", "arrogant" or "stylish".

The practice of everybody dressing in military uniforms faded with the fall of the "Gang of Four" and the reform and opening-up.

Red Guard hairstyle

On May 2, 1964, *Tianjin Evening News* published a letter from reader Dong Chunyan "Why My New Hairstyle was Criticized?":

"I am a woman worker and like dressing up. I'd like to have a new hairstyle or new fashionable clothes. But there were somebody making sarcastic comments about me. I believe diversity of hairstyles is a specific symbol of improvement of people's livelihoods. I think everyone has a dream of beauty, especially for us young people. It is not good for every woman to have a ponytail or short hair."

On the same day, *Tianjin Evening News* published another letter titled "What Kind of Beauty do We Want" from Ma Jin'an, a cadre at the CYL of Tianjin Steel Factory. He said:

"Some young people in our factory wear an oily 'coattail style' slicked-back hair, or have a beard, dress weird... Although they are only a small part of us, they require our attention."

When the Cultural Revolution started, those with fashionable hairstyles were seen as practicing the rotten lifestyle of feudalism, capitalism or revisionism and forced to have get hair cut if they were found in the street. Showing any reluctance, they would be forced to shave half their heads and punished by parading through the streets. For the male members of the Red Guards, most

Red Guard Propaganda Team. The girls have the "iron girl" hairstyles like a pigtail or short hair and the boys a flattop.

Provided by the National Costume Museum of Beijing Institute of Fashion Technology

of them had a buzz cut and looked brave. Most girls had a short cut or pigtail and looked heroic. The Red Guard Hairstyle of woman red guards was a braid cut to the length of the neck, a neat fringe, and center-parted hair hooped into two brush-like braids.

State Council cuts sales of lipstick in China

Li Shuqin, a clerk at the cosmetic division of the Xidan Department Store of Beijing, was familiar with cosmetics and helped customers. She introduced vermilion rouge for those who planned to buy for their children and purple for girls of ethnic groups with sun-burnt complexions. For male customers who wanted to buy "snowflakes" in summer, she introduced "Almond Honey" as the cream that did not make the wearer look pale or smell sharply fragrant.

In the 1960s, lipstick and make-up gradually became unacceptable by the "revolution".

On September 23, 1966, the Central Committee of the CPC approved and forwarded the Report on Policies on Finance, Trade and Handicraft Industry of the Office of Finance and Trade of the State Council and the National Economic Committee, which stipulated that woolen cloth, silk, cigarettes, liquor and cosmetics used on stage and films would be continuously produced. The varieties of goods should not be cancelled without consideration. Cosmetics such as lipsticks could not be sold domestically.

Renovating Fangua Lane

In the 1960s, many farmers started to build new houses. Generally speaking, no large changes were made, and most built thatched cottages. Some with better economic conditions built simple tile-roofed houses. The groundsill of the tile-roofed houses was built with bricks or stone cubes, with walls built with soil or the walls with bricks and inner side soil. The best walls were completely built with bricks. The house rack was normally built in the style in the 1950s with girders, purlins and bundles. The tile-roofed houses of the rich generally did not use bundles, but a kind of thin square bricks especially made.

In the early days, when New China was founded, houses in the outskirts or rural areas were normally simple tile-roofed ones. The building materials of the houses were mainly soil with the outer sides built with bricks. Some were shabby with only the front walls built with bricks and the other three walls with soil.

On October 15, 1960, the Ministry of Construction Engineering submitted a report to the Central Government on urban area housing. It said that the sharp increase in the urban population, meant the total living area was far short of actual needs and many could not get married or live separately after getting married or several families had to share a house because of shortage in housing. It suggested mobilizing forces of the Central Government, local governments, industrial and mining factories and the general public to build residential houses and tried to solve the short supply of residential housing in three to five years.

The central area of Shanghai had many legacy shabby houses and shanty houses. In the 1960s, the old housing renovation plan was rolled out. Fangua

When Fangua Lane of Shanghai was renovated, people moved to the new residences happily.

Provided by Beijing Municipal Archives

Lane was renovated in 1962, Mingyuan Village in 1972, and the neighborhood west to Caoxi Road, opposite to Wantiguan in 1975. The renovation of Fangua Lane was successful.

The total area of Fangua Lane was 4.45 hectares and the renovation program removed 26,900 square meters of shanty houses and 340 square meters of public buildings, involving 1,964 households and totaling 8,771 people. With the plan, the per capita construction area was increased from 3.06 square meters to 7.27 square meters and the environment with concentrated shabby houses and low pool zones was changed to beautiful residential neighborhood with green belts and neatly arranged residential houses.

Nine-storey Anhua Building nicknamed "high-ranking official building"

Beijing used to have three "peoples' communes" buildings, namely Fusuijing Building in Xicheng District, Beiguanting Building in Dongcheng District and Anhua Building in Chongwen District.

Anhua Building was named as it was built on the site of dismantled Anhua Temple. It was completed in May 1960 and used to be the most popular building of Beijing, or China's earliest "serviced apartment" with Beijing's first community chamber.

The main building of the Anhua Building was nine-storeys high while the wing building was an eight-storey complex. The total construction area was nearly 20,000 square meters, quite huge at that time. The buildings made a great flutter when it was completed and few people did not know that building at that time.

Each floor of the building was equipped with five large glass droplights and four glass doors, dividing the long corridor systematically. The corridor was 3 meters wide, leaving a large space at the corner for stacking sundries and airing washed clothes. It had direct ventilation and lighting.

The structure of the Anhua Building fully reflected the principle of a commune by providing no living facilities such as kitchens. All the service facilities were provided on the first floor where the public eatery and boiled water room were located. In work days, residents ate at their units and children were sent to kindergarten, therefore few ate at the public eatery.

The workers of the public eatery would ask residents one by one on the evening of one day about their dinner and whether they wanted to order meals for the next day. They wrote down what was ordered, sent the meals door-to-door and took the empty thermos back and sent the filled ones back.

Living in Anhua Building required not only high status, but also high income. Most residents living in this building in 1962 had a salary about RMB200 and the rent of the two-bedroom suite was more than RMB10, equaling the monthly salary of a common worker of Beijing. Therefore this building was also nicknamed "high-ranking official building".

In the history of Beijing, Anhua Building was the first equipped with elevators. In the center of the building, two elevators were installed, the single-door model. On the east side of the building, space was preserved for another two elevators. For the purpose of cost saving, those two were not installed.

At that time, children in the neighborhood liked to come to Anhua Building to take the elevator. The internal area of the elevator was less than 3 square meters and could accommodate five to six persons at the most, in addition to the operator and her table and chair and the electric heating. Children and adults, near and far, came to see the elevator. Children even considered the elevator a toy and took it up and down repeatedly. At that time, Anhua Building was regarded as good as a hotel.

Although the design of Anhua Building had no kitchen, it had a spacious toilet and a bathtub. The bathtub was not installed because of the high cost, but the space was preserved.

In 1964, the long abandoned eatery on each floor was equipped with a supply of coal gas and became the public kitchen. Residents cooked in the kitchen. Against the wall was a row of cooking stoves in the kitchen. It must have been very busy and interesting when every household was cooking at the same time. (Fang Lu, The Last Commune Building of Beijing, Caixin Century, July 1, 2005)

From honeycomb briquette to gas tank

In the 1960s, rural areas used straw and firewood as the fuel while urban areas used honeycomb briquettes. In winter there was no heating and stove were used for heating. Before winter, residents needed to buy an iron stovepipe and install the stove themselves. In the 1960s, LPG was available for common people. (Across Beijing, Volume I)

It was not easy to ignite a stove. First, one needed to put a piece of scrunched paper into the hearth with a piece of turf for igniting, on which honeycomb briquette was put. Then one needed to ignite the paper which lighted the turf and the coal in order. Step by step, the stove was ignited. In the process, smoke was strong and filled the whole room.

It was not that hard to learn how to ignite the stove. What was difficult was to keep the flame and reach the purpose of heating.

Many had a similar experience. Every day they started with opening the stove, cleaning coal ash, feeding coal to the stove and then sealing the stove after 15-20 minutes; when they returned from work, they first opened the stove, cleaned coal ash and fed fuel to the stove. It was nearly 8 o'clock in night when the flame was roaring. After enjoying heating for about two hours, it would be time to sleep. Therefore the highest room temperature in night was about 10 to 13 degrees Celsius.

However, it was common for the stove to be extinguished.

The highest worry of using the honeycomb briquette was carbon monoxide poisoning, or "gas poisoning".

When the coalmen delivered briquettes to door, he was always well received with tea and a cigarette to get more dry briquettes. The newly made briquettes were wet and could hardly be ignited. What's more, wet briquettes could easily produce carbon monoxide. Therefore everybody was nice to coalmen. Of course, neighbors were considerate to coalmen. A cart of briquettes weighed several hundred kilograms and the coalman needed to push the cart and carry the briquettes himself. It was laborious and the coalman could sweat even in the late autumn after delivering a cart of briquettes. Everybody earned money the hard way, so they sent what they could to the coalman.

Normally the briquettes would be aired in the yard for several days until they were dry. Then the whole family moved the briquettes to their own coal tank or under the windowsill. The stacked briquettes would be covered with a layer of plastic cloth. The whole family depended on the briquettes for the winter and nobody wanted rain to fall on them.

In November 1965, the first LPG service station for civil use was established in the outskirts of Beijing and consumers in residential areas surfaced. At that time, a cylinder of gas was RMB2.7 and the negotiated price RMB3.2.

Forever, Phoenix and Flying Pigeon

The bicycle industry started in the 1950s in China.

The lamp was a rare spare part on today's bicycle but used to be a permit at night in the 1950s. At that time, many areas had no street lamps. For safety, bicycling without a lamp was not allowed at night. The key spare part of the bicycle lamp was the dynamo-powered device that turned friction into electric power for lighting. The dynamo-powered device was expensive and many could not afford it. Therefore a specially designed flashlight appeared. It was square and powered by two batteries and was installed on the bicycle basket for lighting. Poor people could only use the papered lantern.

Not everybody could afford a famous brand bicycle.

In the 1960s, Forever, Phoenix and Flying Pigeon became famous brands and ranked at the top three in national competition.

At that time, the bicycle was not only a basic transportation tool, but also an important asset of common families. For example, Beijing had 940,000 bicycles in 1965, 1.44 million in 1970 and 2.23 million in 1975.

Not many people could afford a bicycle of any of these three brands at the time. It was an enviable asset like today's Mercedes Benz and BMW. From the 1960s to the 1970s, a bicycle was one of four must-have betrothal presents.

First Beijing subway built secretly

On July 1, 1965, at 9:00am, the launch ceremony for the Phase I project of the subway construction in Beijing was held under two ginkgo trees at the west side of Yuquan Road in western Beijing. Peng Zhen, then mayor of Beijing, presided over the ceremony. Zhu De, Deng Xiaoping, Luo Ruiqing and many other state leaders attended the ceremony. Zhu De broke ground for the project with a shovel with a red silk ribbon.

However, considering it was a project for preparedness against war and needed to be kept secret, only a few media organizations, including Xinhua News Agency and the *People's Daily*, were invited to attend the ceremony on the condition that they would not disclose any information about the ceremony and only keep the information for internal reference and recording.

Then, the Phase I project of the subway of Beijing was secretly launched.

At the time, there was smaller traffic flow so the project didn't have impact on traffic.

On October 1, 1969, the first subway train drove out of the Gucheng Station. The Phase I project took four years and three months, more than one year after the original deadline. However, it was completed before the 20th anniversary of the New China.

In 1971, the first subway tickets were sold, at a price of RMB0.1. (The First Beijing Subway, by Huang Jiajia, *Beijing Daily*, September 25, 2007)

Since it was a project to prepare for war and China lacked experience in

Beijing's first subway train drives into the Bajiaocun Station (currently the Bajiao Amusement Park Station of Subway Line 1 in Beijing).

Provided by Beijing Municipal Archives

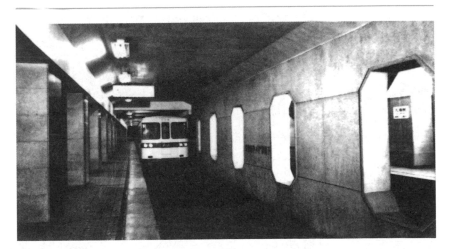

In October 1969, the first subway line of Beijing was built, with a total length of 23.6 kilometers and designed daily transportation volume of 1.5 million people.

commissioning equipment and management, the subway was only opened for a few of visitors after it started operating in October 1969. People who wanted to experience or visit the subway had to get a coupon from their work units first. The subway became part of the scenery of Beijing. Many people from units outside Beijing visited it. There were even guide staff in service.

We don't accept tips

In the 1960s, people lived a hard life. So, few people had the chance to travel abroad. Therefore, generally, tourism only meant inbound tourism at the time.

Since 1956, the number of overseas Chinese and compatriots from Hong Kong and Macao visiting the Chinese mainland grew. Under such circumstances, many cities established travel agencies to provide services for overseas Chinese travelling in the Chinese mainland. With increasing diplomatic activities in 1956 and 1957 China International Travel Service established business connections with travel agencies in the Soviet Union, Eastern Europe, the People's Republic of Mongolia and 23 western countries and began to provide services for foreign travelers.

In 1957, travelers from the Soviet Union and Eastern Europe accounted for 95% of the total number of travelers. However, in the middle of the 1960s, the number of travelers from western countries began to account for a dominant proportion. For example, in 1965, western travelers accounted for more than 80%. However, each year, there were only about 4,000 to 5,000 foreign travelers who traveled to the Chinese mainland.

On November 2, 1964, the China Tourism Administration held the first working conference on tourism. A goal was set to accept 8,000 travelers in 1965 and 45,000 by 1969 and generate income of USD43 million from tourism within five years.

There is a story.

In the 1960s, two old ladies from Singapore checked in at the Shanghai Overseas Chinese Hotel. Liu Lirong, a staff member of the hotel, provided services for them. Before leaving, the two ladies gave more than RMB2 to Liu as a tip. However, Liu told them that they didn't accept tips.

The ladies were very confused and said: "We always have to pay tips in Singapore and Hong Kong for the hotel and restaurant services. We even have to pay tips for using the washroom."

One of them said: "I remember that tips were accepted in the past."

Liu answered: "That only happened before the liberation."

"Yes, it was," said the old lady. "How kind you are to provide such good services without accepting tips. The country has been greatly changed."

As mentioned by the old lady, tips had a history in China. They used to be called gratuities. However, in the New China, especially in the 1960s, when campaigns to combat and prevent revisionism and foster proletarian ideology and eliminate bourgeois ideology were being carried out, who would accept tips?

Hundred Thousand Whys

At the beginning of the 1960s, *Hundred Thousand Whys*, a series of books on popular science, were published. Later, the books were revised and republished several times. A total of more than 100 million volumes were printed. They were widely known as encyclopedic books for popular science reading.

The knowledge of science and technology contained in these books was deeply impressed on the memory of little readers. Many people got lifelong benefits from them.

The readers then knew that they needed to observe and think deeply about the things that they didn't known and learn general knowledge from the daily life. For example: Why we should eat fruits? Why dogs barked at strangers? Or, why gingival bleeding happened when people brushed their teeth?

The readers learnt that the largest flower in the world is Rafflesia, which has a stink that helps attract mosquitoes and flies for pollination. The smallest bird in the world is the hummingbird. The whale is not fish. Stars in the sky have different ranges of brightness. The vast universe has many planets that are similar to the earth. Jupiter is very large but has low density.

The *Hundred Thousand Whys* books taught many people that science is power and knowledge is wealth. The books are like knowledgeable teachers. Many people began to be highly interested in science and technology and chose science and engineering courses at universities and colleges.

Han Han, a well-known Chinese writer born in 1980s, said on many occasions: "You will be accustomed to asking why after reading the *Hundred Thousand Whys* books. Many people don't like to ask ask why, because they believe things should be the way that they look like. However, I always ask why."

Learn from Daqing Oilfield for industrial production and learn from Dazhai for agricultural production

In 1964, Mao Zedong gave an instruction: Learn from Daqing Oilfield for industrial production, learn from Dazhai for agricultural production and learn from the People's Liberation Army.

The instruction was etched into the memory of people of that generation.

At the end of 1963, the Daqing Oilfield of China was put into operation, marking the end of the dependence of the Chinese people on imported oil. Meanwhile, a well-organized and hardworking team was created in the petroleum industry.

The campaign to learn from Daqing Oilfield for industrial production began in early 1964. It called for carrying forward the "spirit of Daqing" to work hard for industrial development without consideration of individual honor and benefits and to realize self-dependence.

One of the most famous examples during the campaign was Wang Jinxi, who once said: "When there are conditions, go ahead; when there are no such conditions, create them and go ahead."

Dazhai refers to a production brigade (equal to a village) of the Dazhai Commune at Xiyang County, Shanxi. It was located in the Taihang Mountain area with extremely hard environmental and climate conditions. However, under the leadership of Chen Yonggui and Guo Fenglian, the production brigade overcame the difficulties and reclaimed terraced fields in the mountainous areas and built up an impounding reservoir on the top of mountain. In this way, they changed the situation to live in natural conditions.

Floating red flags at Daqing Oilfield.

Learn from Daqing Oilfield for industrial production. Wang Jinxi was honored as the "iron man".

The advocacy to "learn from Dazhai for agricultural production" led numerous cadres and the masses to launch the campaign to make long-term and great efforts to reclaim farmland in mountainous areas, carry out water conservancy projects and improve quality of soil to fully enhance agricultural infrastructure construction, improve conditions for agricultural production and strive for a good harvest.

However, impacted by the ultra-left ideological trend, abuse of resources from people and unscientific practices during the campaign resulted in adverse consequences.

Follow the good example of Lei Feng

In the history of the New China, there has never been any figure as great and warm as Lei Feng.

On March 5, 1963, the *People's Daily* published the inscriptions by Chairman Mao Zedong: "Follow the good example of Lei Feng." Since then, activities to learn from Lei Feng were launched nationwide.

Lei Feng was a squad leader at the engineering corps of the Shenyang Army of the People's Liberation Army. He was born in a poor rural family at Wangcheng County (currently Changsha County) of Hunan in December 1939. Later, he became an orphan. In 1957, Lei Feng joined the Communist Youth League. In 1960, he joined the army and later became a member of the CPC. He was then elected squad leader. On August 15, 1962, Lei Feng died while on duty.

Lei Feng set a good example in the following aspects:

First, even though he was born in a poor family and had a bitter childhood under the oppression of the landowner, he was optimistic.

On March 5, 1963, Beijing Daily published the inscriptions by Chairman Mao Zedong: "Follow the good example of Lei Feng".

Provided by Beijing Municipal Archives

A still of the movie Lei Feng.

In the 1960s, a great number of activities to learn from Lei Feng were launched in Beijing. The picture shows students of No.6 Girls' Middle School (currently No.156 Middle School) reading reports on Lei Feng.

Provided by Beijing Municipal Archives

Second, he lived a plain and hardworking life. His clothes were full of patches.

Third, he was ready to help others. He often sent money he saved to the people who really needed it.

Fourth, he carried forward the "spirit of screw". He compared himself to a screw that had been ready to serve wherever and whenever was needed. This showed the determination of Lei Feng to obey orders as a member of the People's Liberation Army.

Fifth, his diary encouraged many people to form the habit of keeping a diary and even had deep influence on the literature and rhetoric of people at the time.

He said in his diary that: "One's life is finite, whereas one's passion for serving the people is infinite. I will devote my limited life to serving the people." This encouraged many people.

Discussion about Lei Feng has never stopped.

More than 30 years later, the movie named *The Days Without Lei Feng* first revealed the cause of his death. The hero died in an accident but not a hero's death as many people supposed.

Along with that revelation, it is also known that Lei Feng was not a stoic, because a luxury watch and a well-preserved leather jacket were found among the things he left. It indicates that Lei Feng also pursued fashion. What's more, in accordance with later disclosures, Lei Feng also had romance.

Many people knew the song named *Follow the Good Example of Lei Feng*:

Follow the good example of Lei Feng, be loyal to the revolution and the Party, have a clearcut stand on what to love and what to hate and never forget the past suffering, and take the firm stand to fight with great enthusiasm.

RMB4 as cash gift and 1 kilogram of candies as betrothal present

An album of wedding photos of Shanghai people records the change of the wedding dresses of the Shanghai people. In the 1950s and the 1960s, the bride and groom just wore clothes they usually wore at the wedding. At that time, a couple might get married only with the following properties: a double bed, a thermos, a washbasin and a spittoon.

A woman who got married in 1965 said: "My boyfriend came to my home to propose a marriage with RMB4 as the cash gift and 1 kilogram of candies as betrothal present. On the wedding day, he brought me and my dowries (clothes, washbasin and bucket) to our home by bike. We invited our relatives and friends to have lunch at our home. It was simple. We obtained the marriage certificate and got married."

In the 1960s, both love and marriage were low-key.

In December 19, 1964, the *Youth Daily* gave a report on two young brides, who worked at the Shanghai Children's Hospital. One bride wore a dirndl dress at her wedding and lipstick. The other bride wore long earrings, a necklace with lock-shaped pendant, white-yarn gloves with hollowed design

Certificate for a new couple to purchase a cabinet.

Provided by Beijing Municipal Archives

and a bracelet. The daring dresses and decorations of these two brides caused hot discussions among the young people.

Newly-married couples bowed to the portrait of Chairman Mao Zedong

In the 1960s, love and marriage were integrated with the revolution.

On September 19, 1964, the *Youth Daily of Shanghai* made a report on the wedding of Ye Peijun, a younger worker at Shanghai Optical Instruments Factory. The wedding was held in the Dormitory Club. In the middle of the room, there was a portrait of Chairman Mao Zedong. On the wall of the room, there were couplets presented by colleagues of the newly-married couple, with the Chinese characters meaning "getting married and starting the career at the age of 30..."

As many other couples, the groom and the bride wore the clothes they usually wore in daily life and a big red flower on the chest. At the beginning of the wedding, the new couple bowed to the portrait of Chairman Mao Zedong in an attitude of respect. Then, the secretary of the CPC committee of the factory and the other colleagues congratulated the new couple. They sang for them, and some people performed cross-talk. At last, the wedding ended in the song titled *Socialism is Good* sung by the groom and the bride.

Usually, weddings were held in the evening, because people had to work in the daytime. Basically, a wedding included the following steps: The groom and the bride sang a song together, such as *The East Is Red* or *Sailing on the Sea with the Helmsman*. The newly-married couple bowed to the portrait of Chairman Mao Zedong three times; bowed to their parents three times; extended a salute to the guests and gave them wedding candies (hard candy was priced at RMB0.96/500g). Generally, there was no dinner. Most of the time, the newly married couple would provide noodles for people who had provided assistance for the wedding and, in each bowl of noodles, there were two poached eggs.

Weddings in rural areas were different.

The parts of singing the songs, reciting *Quotations from Chairman Mao Zedong* and bowing to the portrait of Chairman Mao Zedong were the same but a dinner would be provided after the wedding with simple dishes, including stewed cabbage with pork head meat and offals and stewed Chinese cabbage and radish with fat meat and pork skin. In addition, each table would be provided with one liter of white wine.

In rural areas, it was also popular to pitch together for a wedding. Each family contributed at least RMB0.2 and at most RMB2. A family might enjoy the dinner mentioned above if they contributed at least RMB0.5.

Some people gave presents to the newly-married couple, mainly washbasins, thermos, towels and quilt covers. In many places, especially the urban area, people gave a badge with the profile of Chairman Mao and the plaster statue of Chairman Mao as presents to the newly-married couple.

Even the love tokens of the affianced couple were related to the revolution: Badges with the profile of Chairman Mao and *Quotations from Chairman Mao Zedong* (the Little Red Book).

In addition, some girls would buy some woolen yarn and make a sweater for their boyfriends. The boyfriends might give their girlfriends plain-color handkerchiefs and notebooks. On the title page of a notebook, there might be sentences such as "sail through the wind and waves" and "seek for mutual improvement".

During the Cultural Revolution, love between the couples was completely overwhelmed by class struggle. A husband and his wife might fall out with each other due to differences in class, opinions and guidelines. Family members might blow the whistle on each other or set up clear boundaries with each other. However, many people still got married, though family background became the first determinant for marriage. The best spouses were CPC members, followed by workers and poor and lower-middle farmers. It was hard for the sons or daughters of landowners, rich peasants, counterrevolutionaries, evildoers and rightists to have a well-matched marriage, even though they might be of good appearance. That was the trend of the time, even though it was unreasonable.

Each family has the Little Red Book

In the 1960s, especially during the Great Cultural Revolution, people liked to quote some words of Chairman Mao before doing something.

There was a dialogue between an elder women and a vegetable seller in the market.

The seller said: "'Serve the people.' May I help you?"

The elder women answered: "'Faith will move mountains.' I want some radishes."

Then, she tried to pick the best radishes from the basket, which made the seller impatient. "'Challenge selfishness and criticize revisionism'," said the seller.

The elder women replied without raising her head: "'There must be absolutely no carelessness or negligence!'"

At that time, reciting the *Quotations from Chairman Mao Zedong* in the Little

In the 1960s, people liked to take pictures with the Little Red Book in hand to show their respect to Chairman Mao Zedong.

Red Book was not just a fashion trend but also a living need. The quotations were widely applied in daily life. When people went for a haircut or to buy vegetables and got involved in debates and quarrels, they always recited the quotations. The more quotations they recited, the more convincing they would be.

The *Quotations from Chairman Mao Zedong* was a collection of selected quotations from Chairman Mao Zedong's writings. Since it usually had a red cover and its content was about the important opinions of the leader of the Red Revolution, it was called the Little Red Book. Everybody had a Little Red Book and they took it everywhere.

During the "Great Cultural Revolution", more than 500 versions of Little Red Book in more than 50 languages (more than 5 billion volumes) were published. Then, the world had a total of a more than 3 billion people. Therefore, on average, there were about 1.5 volumes of Little Red Book for each person. The book was universally accepted as the "most popular book in the world in the 20th century" and the "book with the most readers in the world". Even today, much of the content of the Little Red Book is still applicable such as "no investigation, no right to speak", "modesty makes progress and pride makes one fall behind" and "lay down the burden and start the machine".

The content has had deep influence on the growth and ideological development of generations of Chinese people.

However, only a few of the books have been handed down.

Today, the Little Red Book has become a kind of cultural relic highly appreciated by many collectors. The price of such book at the market of cultural relics has been rising. In the early 21st century, a *Quotations from Chairman Mao Zedong* published in 1964 was auctioned by Sotheby's for more than RMB120,000.

There was a story. A man named Wang Zengfu took the Little Red Book instead of other family property out of a fire that suddenly broke out at his house one night. He was highly praised for protecting the Little Red Book. He said: "The book of Chairman Mao is the lifeblood of the poor and lower-middle farmers. I can lose the house, but I cannot lose the book."

Badge bearing Chairman Mao's profile worn on the chest

At that time, a badge bearing Chairman Mao's profile was a symbol to show loyalty to Chairman Mao more than an ornament. Everybody wore it.

Bookstores and shops would release "great news" when they had such badges in stock. Then the people would rush about telling each other the news. They did not call it "buying the badge" but "respectfully inviting it".

When someone needed to give another person a gift to ask for help, the best gift was the badge. In order to show loyalty, some people wore several such badges at the same time and some people even wore more than ten badges. There was a case that someone wore more than 300 badges on his chest, shoulder and the other parts of the upper body.

The earliest badge about the size of a fingernail. Then, larger badges were made. There was a kind of badge with a diameter of 80 millimeters, with the head portrait of Chairman Mao above and the pattern of a sailing steamer under a red sun below. It was almost as big as piece of cake.

There was another kind of badge with a diameter of 200 millimeters. It had to be worn on the neck with a red silk belt.

Meanwhile, every family had some kind of portrait or ceramic or plaster statue of Chairman Mao for worship.

The badge with Chairman Mao's profile was a symbol to show loyalty to Chairman Mao more than an ornament.

Loyalty dance

In the 1960s, the "loyalty dance" was the only type of dance of China.

The "loyalty dance" was a kind of group dance created during the "Great Cultural Revolution" to show the people's loyalty to Chairman Mao Zedong. It was very popular from 1966 to 1968. People danced to songs named *Sailing on the Sea with the Helmsman, Dear Chairman Mao, The Golden Mountain (Holy Mountain) of Beijing, Full of Enthusiasm to Welcome the 9th National Congress of the CPC* and the songs of quotations from Chairman Mao Zedong.

The "loyalty dance" featured simple and exaggerated movements and expression by glyphs and graphs. Major movements included hands held highly to show respect to the red sun; inclined bow step to show the determination to follow Chairman Mao, the great mentor; pointing at somebody (something) with anger to show the determination to completely smash the bourgeoisie; tightly clenched hands to show the determination to carry the revolution through to the end. The dancers always held the *Quotations from Chairman Mao Zedong* (Little Red Book) or red satin towel in hand as stage properties.

The movements of the "loyalty dance" were similar to radio calisthenics, but

All the songs broadcast in radio were about the revolution. The songs like Sailing on the Sea with the Helmsman and Dear Chairman Mao were very popular throughout the country.

The Mao Zedong Thought Publicity Team at the Ancheng Coal Mine to put on a special performance as an expression of gratitude.

were simple, rigid and short of aesthetic sense. The dancers, men and women, old and young, danced at the workshops, sports ground, wharfs, streets and field day and night. Every morning, "loyalty dances" were seen everywhere.

The "loyalty dance" thus became one of the symbols of the time.

For parades, the "loyalty dance" group might including hundreds or thousands of people, who danced to the music and moved ahead. Sometimes, the dance lasted for hours and the people moved for several kilometers. They danced and then walked, and then danced again. The grand spectacle was unprecedented.

The Red Guards take public transportation for free across the country to exchange revolutionary ideas

On August 18, 1966, Chairman Mao Zedong first gave an interview to a group of Red Guards. Responding to the call of Chairman Mao, the Red Guards and the students participated in the movement to take public transportation for free across the country to exchange revolutionary ideas. It was an unprecedented movement in terms of the number of participants or its coverage.

On September 5, 1966, the Central Government issued a formal notification to allow the Red Guards to take public transportation for free to participate in the movement, and the government would provide living subsidies for them. That's to say, free transportation, food and accommodation were provided for the participants of the movement. Therefore, all college, middle school and even some primary school students stopped their study to join in the movement to "experience the hardship in life and broaden their horizons".

At the same time, reception stations for the Red Guards were established nationwide to provide accommodation and transportation services for the Red Guards. The result was that great turbulence was caused and heavy burdens were imposed on local governments at different levels.

Later, it was advocated that the Red Guards walk to fulfill their tasks. There was an example: Twenty young people walked thousands of miles for 46 days from Shanghai to Beijing to visit Chairman Mao. Actually, only a few people attended the movement by walking.

Since August 20, 1966, the Red Guards began to visit Shanghai. In September, large crowds of Red Guards visited Shanghai. Related statistics indicate that about 380,000 people arrived at Shanghai during the first 50 days. There was a record of about 14,000 Red Guards entering Shanghai in one day. Shanghai Jiaotong University, which had more than 4,000 students, received more than 7,000 participants.

In later October, some Red Guards who admired the northern scenery went to Harbin by train. However, they did not leave the train station due to the extreme cold in Harbin, even though they wore military coats borrowed in Beijing. They got back on the train and travelled back south.

To sum up, the Red Guards participated in the movement mainly for the following purposes: Naively for revolution, for ideological education, for stirring up trouble or for travel.

Take the people that participated in the movement for the purpose of ideological education. They followed the steps of their predecessors engaged in the Chinese revolution to walk along the Long March route to visit Shaoshan, Ruijin, Jinggangshan and Yan'an.

Most of the people participated in the movement for free travel. Many of them travelled more than half of the country and then got back home when the weather was cold, like vagrants.

In February 1967, related departments issued a notification to stop the walking tours.

The movement had left a funny and bitter page in history.

Open-door schooling: Learning industrial production, agricultural production and military affairs

The term "open-door schooling" appeared during the "Great Cultural Revolution" when students were encouraged to attend industrial production, agricultural production and military affairs outside school as a way of learning.

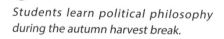

Students learn political philosophy during the autumn harvest break.

Young people in a rural area.

Provided by the Ethnic Costumes Museum at the Beijing Institute of Fashion Technology

Every school had a school-run factory and farm as the basis for open-door schooling, which was carried out once every semester and usually lasted for two to four weeks. Such practice destroyed the regular curriculum system and education order of the schools.

Of course, students who did not like attending classes were very excited to attend the open-door schooling, because they did not have to attend classes

Students dispatched to the machine tool plant.

Chairman Mao Zedong and Premier Zhou Enlai met with the militia members of Beijing.

Chairman Mao Zedong and farmers.

Provided by the Ethnic Costumes Museum at the Beijing Institute of Fashion Technology in school and obey classroom discipline and they had no homework and examination when "adventuring" in the society.

Some students were dispatched to the electrical machinery plants to learn how to operate the punching machine and related accessories and wrap wire. Some were dispatched to machine tool plants to learn lathing, clamping, milling, planing and grinding skills.

To learn agricultural production skills and provide support for farm work, some students went to work for production teams where they transplanted rice seedlings and did farm work together with the farmers. Some students went to the gardening farms to learn grafting and cultivation of saplings. Some students learnt to drive hand tractors and use plough and harrow to do farm work. Some students went to school-run farms to reclaim farmland and grow vegetables. Some students went to school-run livestock farms to learn to raise pigs.

Later, some people believed that open-door schooling had positive influence on students by encouraging them to participate in social activities to accumulate social experience and learn work skills so that they could be accustomed to cooperating with others to overcome difficulties, taking care of and supporting themselves, being confident and continuously pursuing self-improvement. However, some people still believed that open-door schooling was formalist and caused students to abandon their studies.

Educated youth go and work in the countryside and mountainous areas

In December 1968, Chairman Mao Zedong gave an instruction: "It's necessary for the educated youth to go and work in rural areas to receive reeducation among the poor and lower-middle farmers."

A campaign for educated youth to go to countryside and mountainous areas was launched. In 1968, all students of junior and senior high schools (who enrolled in school in 1966, 1967 and 1968) went to rural areas.

It was common to see educated youth wearing green army clothes without a collar, badges and army caps without insignias standing on the train to say goodbye to their parents and friends, with a bright red flower on their chest.

In April 1969, a group of educated youth bid farewell to their hometown before going to the countryside and mountainous areas.

The red flower was usually connected with a ribbon printed with "Guang Rong" (honor in English).

The educated youth prepared the army caps and haversacks by themselves. The haversacks usually had embroidered red Chinese characters, meaning "serve the people". Army clothes were very popular at the time. People paid great attention to figuring out whether army clothes worn by a person were real. If someone's cap was stolen it was usually because it was real.

During the "Great Cultural Revolution", more than 16 million educated youth went to the countryside and mountainous areas, meaning that one tenth of the urban population went to the rural area. It was a great population migration rare in modern history. Nearly all urban families were related to the campaign in some way.

The youth went to different areas, including Yunnan, Guizhou, Hunan, Inner Mongolia, Heilongjiang and other places. The government designated the places for the educated youth to live in, usually remote counties with the worst economic development and living conditions. The practice was soon made into a policy.

At that time, some of the youth were engaged in the campaign with great

"To dedicate to the revolution together with Chairman Mao for the whole life" was a dream for youth.

Provided by the Ethnic Costumes Museum at the Beijing Institute of Fashion Technology

enthusiasm. They were determined to follow Chairman Mao and enhance their loyalty working in the countryside and mountainous areas. Some people even wrote letters of commitment in their own blood to show their determination to settle in the countryside and mountainous areas. Some made a vow at Tian'anmen Square and in front of the monuments to revolutionary martyrs. Some secretly went through related procedures despite of the objection of their parents.

However, most youth were forced to leave home and went to the countryside and mountainous areas. They felt it was harder to live in these areas.

Many of the youth became members of production teams. Some lived in quite a different way, namely a paramilitary life, as members of production and construction corps.

In poverty-stricken areas, educated youth could not continue studying. The only thing they could do was farm work and contribute to the construction of rural and border areas. Many of them even paid for it with their lives.

Entering the 1970s, some policies were made to enable these educated youth to return to the urban areas as recruits of urban enterprises, attending examinations, or to give medical treatment, fill certain jobs, take care of their parents or become worker-peasant-soldier students.

In October 1978, the National Working Conference on Educated Youth to Go and Work at Countryside and Mountainous Areas decided to stop the campaign and help the youth to return from the rural areas and find jobs. After 1979, most of the educated youth returned to the urban area. However, some stayed and got married in the rural areas.

Some of the people who had attended the campaign became writers, including Shi Tisheng, Ye Xin, Liang Xiaosheng, Zhang Chengzhi and Zhang Kangkang. They created many works on the educated youth based on their own experiences. However, many of the youth also lost the chance for an education during the campaign.

"Barefoot doctor" helps the local people

In September 1968, the *Red Banner*, then most influential magazine, published an article titled The Direction of the Reform of Medical Education Indicated by the Development of Barefoot Doctors, which was published by the *People's Daily* on September 14, 1968.

Since then, the "barefoot doctor" became known nationwide.

The "barefoot doctor" was a result of the rural cooperative medical care system. It was a nickname of farmers who received minimal basic medical and paramedical training and worked in rural villages.

There were mainly three kinds of people who worked as "barefoot doctors": Members of families of doctors; people with high school diplomas and some

A still of the movie Spring's Seedling, which was about a female "barefoot doctor" providing medical services for rural residents.

knowledge of medicine and pathology; young people who went and worked in the countryside and mountainous areas.

The "barefoot doctors" made great contributions to solve problems caused by a lack of doctors and medicine in rural areas of China. The movies *Red Rain* directed by Cui Wei and *Spring's Seedling* directed by Xie Jin in 1975 were both about the "barefoot doctors".

By the end of 1977, 85% of the production brigades of the whole country adopted the cooperative medical care system. The number of "barefoot doctors" totalled more than 1.5 million.

On January 25, 1985, *People's Daily* published the article titled Stop the Services of Barefoot Doctors and Build Rural Doctors' Teams. Later, the number of "barefoot doctors" was decreasing. On January 1, 2004, the Regulations on the Administration of the Practice of Rural Doctors went into force. It stipulated that rural doctors should provide medical services after related registration and with related qualifications acquired through training. That's the end of the history of the "barefoot doctors".

Compared with today's medical services, the medical services provided by the "barefoot doctors" were very limited. So why do people have such deep memories of the "barefoot doctors"?

"Barefoot doctors" practiced medicine in order to help people in poverty. The core of their service was sincerity. The "barefoot doctors" didn't wear white uniforms. Their shoes were dirty because of their long walks and they usually wore coarse clothes. However, they served the people with heart and soul. In addition, the simple and effective medical mode they used met the requirements of most people.

Eggs as "cash"

In the latter 1960s, the Great Cultural Revolution caused great damage to the national economy of China. Chinese people lived in poverty.

In the rural area, in average, every family got a quota of 360 jin (180 kg) of grains throughout the year, no matter how hard they worked and how many adults and children each family had. Grain had to be bought with work points. Surplus work points would be converted into money and given to the owner of work points.

Generally, each farmer had to spend more than RMB30 to buy grain. Many people couldn't afford it with their yearly income. So, when there was some surplus, they would save money and put it to the best use.

In some places, due to large investments in water conservancy projects or other projects, which needed to be made up by the output value of crops, the farmers suffered losses. The higher their work points were, the more debt they would share. This was called "reverse dividend".

At that time, people rarely had cash. Most of them bought articles of daily use with eggs. Sometimes, they sold eggs for cash. When the children needed pencils and exercise books, the parents might give several eggs to their children so that they would change for things that they needed.

In the rural area, it was very common to use eggs as cash.

MEMORIES OF
CHINESE LIFE In The

1970s

Great changes happened in the 1970s, when the "Great Cultural Revolution" came to an end and the Reform and Opening-up began after the Third Plenary Session of the 11th Central Committee of the Communist Party of China. The turbulences in the state and in people's life ended and a new life began.

"With Dacron inside"

Dacron first emerged in China in the 1970s, when coarse cloth was the most common material for making clothes. It soon became a symbol of fashion and futurism. It was still popular in the 1980s. During this period, many people believed that wearing a Dacron shirt was fashionable.

Dacron is a polyester fabric (polyethylene terephthalate or PET) that was usually made into short-sleeve shirts. It is not environmentally friendly or comfortable. It is not very pretty and has low breathability and sweat absorbency. In addition, it may cause accidental exposure when it is wet. However, it does not crease and wears well. What's more important, it has

In the 1970s, only fashionable girls wore Dacron clothes.

colorful printings, which made the eyes of Chinese people used to wearing clothes of gloomy colors light up.

At that time, it was quite popular for a man to buy a Dacron skirt for his girlfriend, just as men of today men like to buy Cartier bracelets for their girlfriends. Girls or women liked to show off their Dacron clothes to their neighbors to show how much their boyfriends or husbands loved them. In addition to the pursuit of fashion, there was another reason for the popularity of the material: It was the easiest way to satisfy the demand for beauty among ordinary people.

In The History of 30 Years of Trifles: 30 Years of Everyone (published by *New Weekly* on November 26, 2008), Hu Fei wrote:

"There is a story to tell about how popular Dacron was in China. It happened in Sichuan, where Dacron was in short supply. One day, a young man walking on the street saw many people queuing to buy Dacron cloth. He joined them and waited to buy some cloth to make a shirt. However, when it was his turn, there was only one chi (1/3 meter) of cloth left. He felt disappointed, considering whether to buy it or not. The salesclerk asked, 'Do you want to buy it? If you don't, the people behind you may want to buy it.' The young man decided to buy it. The cloth was made into a pair of underpants. Then, the young man thought, 'how can I make the others know that I am wearing Dacron?' He finally got an idea. He made a sign on his trousers and wrote on the sign: 'With Dacron inside'. One day, he went to a public toilet, took off the sign and hung it on the door. However, he was surprised when he walked out of the public toilet. There was a long queue of people waiting outside. All the people asked, 'Where is the Dacron? When will you begin to sell it?'"

Dacron enabled most people to stop bothering with cloth coupons, because it was so durable. In addition, some stores offered 50 percent discount for buying Dacron cloth. Therefore, Dacron not only satisfied the need of the people for cloth but also met the requirements for "sentiment" to the largest extent.

Su Tong, a writer, noted:

In the 1970s, women usually wore blue, grey or army-green blouses or tops with small flower patterns. In the summer, some women might wear skirts.

However, only girls of school age might wear skirts with flower patterns. The adults could only wear blue, grey or black skirts with man-made creases. The most fashionable girls might wear white Dacron skirts. Due to the material, sometimes the color of the panty may be indistinctly exposed. Elderly women and females might look at the girls wearing such white skirt with disfavor, thinking that they were bad girls.

Romantic love and secret love happened at that time. A girl sitting on the back of her boyfriend's bicycle might be seen feeling shy when they passed through a street with neighbors on both sides.

Police officers chase young people wearing bell-bottoms

Pantshoes and bell-bottoms were the most popular dressing style in the 1970s as well as a symbol of the time.

Bell-bottoms are also called bell-mouth trousers. They are a kind of trouser with a short crotch, low waistline and trouser legs going wider and wider from top to bottom. The upper part above the knees usually wraps the hip and thighs tightly, while the lower part is wider and in the shape of a trumpet. The trouser leg usually reaches the heels so that they always touch the ground.

Bell-bottoms highlight the curves of the hip and the thighs, enabling women to directly show their charms. The pantshoes make women look more slender and elegant, feeling like that they are within sight but beyond reach.

Bell-bottoms broke up the uniformity and monotony that had been embraced by the great Eastern country for decades.

Bell-bottoms were first part of the sailor suit. The trouser legs were widened to cover the mouths of rubber boots to prevent seawater and water used to wash decks entering inside the boots. Since 1960, it became popular among hipsters in the United States. From the end of the 1960s to the ends of the 1970s, they became popular all over the world. When the Reform and Opening-up began, bell-bottoms were losing their popularity in the US. However, young Chinese accepted bell-bottoms nearly overnight, and the A-shaped dressing style soon became popular throughout the country.

Bell-bottoms became an invincible fashion. Walking on the street in bell-bottoms was equal to streaking. Young men who had long hair and wore bell-bottoms and sunglasses were deemed to be wicked and rascally.

So many people boycotted bell-bottoms. However, the young always lead fashion trends. They got their inspiration from the movies. The widened trouser legs reflected their rebellion after the Great Cultural Revolution.

Although bell-bottoms looked "strange", they broke up the uniform concept of design of Chinese clothes. That's why young people who liked to show their real selves to others favored them.

Bell-bottoms were banned soon after they became popular. It's said that bell-bottoms represented illusions, decline and decadence even though many people believed that they had nothing to do with ideology.

There was a scene in the TV play Bloom of Youth, where police officers chase a group of young people wearing bell-bottoms and order them to cut their pants with scissors.

Ai Jing, a Chinese female singer, wrote in her Story of Yanfen Street:

"One day, a boy who was older than me was captured by an elderly woman to parade through the streets after he walked on Yanfen Street wearing bell-bottoms. His bell-bottoms were torn. He lost his dignity with an expression that was hard to interpret on his face."

As bell-bottoms went popular, pantshoes became popular too. There was a very exaggerated story about a girl who was forced into a dead end by police and suddenly stopped and shouted loudly: "If you move closer, I will jump off the pantshoes."

Pierre Cardin and 12 models debuts at Beijing Cultural Palace of Nationalities

In 1978, Versace became the first international top-tier fashion brand to enter the Chinese market.

In the spring of 1979, the first fashion show was held at the T-stage temporarily set up at the Beijing Cultural Palace of Nationalities. Without experience in similar activities, the Chinese party was very prudent about the show and only people in the foreign trade and fashion circles were allowed to watch the show given by the great French designer Pierre Cardin and 12 models. The show challenged the aesthetic concepts of Chinese people.

Pierre Cardin had known China before because of a tapestry named The Great Wall, which was exhibited at the Expo of Chinese Light Industrial Products in Paris in 1976. The tapestry made Pierre Cardin curious about China. He bought the tapestry for a large sum of money and then started making plans to enter the Chinese market.

At that time, the Opening-up of China had not begun. Pierre Cardin was discouraged by his friends, who told him: "There is no fashion in China. The Chinese will not give you any money."

Obviously, this was not the case. Thanks to the Reform and Opening-up of China, the Pierre Cardin branch developed well in China. In November 1981,

In 1981, Pierre Cardin visited China.

the Pierre Cardin brand formally entered the Chinese market. In September 1983, the restaurant named Maxim's de Paris, with investment from Pierre Cardin, started operating in Beijing.

Following the steps of Pierre Cardin, a number of Japanese and American fashion shows were held in China. Many Chinese began to walk like models and dress themselves up. Chinese-style "fashion show" started.

A hubbub of voices in the tube-shaped apartments

In the 1970s, some enterprises and public institutions began to allocate houses for their staff. Most of the houses were tube-shaped apartments, which had been used as offices or dormitories of single staff.

At that time, the state government built houses for urban residents. The houses would then be allocated to staff based on a comprehensive evaluation of their working age, title and whether their spouses were working for the same units. Priority was given to seniority. Everyone was eager for this type of accommodation. Therefore, people competed in different ways to qualify, including bribery, abuse of authority and even threats with knives. House management divisions received ceaseless visits every day.

Numerous people were married and raised their children in the tube-shaped apartments. Their work colleagues were their neighbors. There was always a hubbub of voices when neighbors cooked in the corridor. Such scenes and lifestyle became memories for a generation.

The relationship as both colleagues and neighbors allowed people to treat each other as family. They cooked together in the corridor, tasted each other's food and shared materials. The children might have lunch at the neighbor's place if their parents were not at home. If someone forgot to turn off the gas tank, the others would do it for them.

At the later stage of the Great Cultural Revolution, residents of these tube-shaped apartments began to pay less attention to the revolution, looking to simply live. They wanted to buy food ingredients with coupons and cooked for themselves rather than go to the mess halls of their units. Someone would take the lead in using a coal stove in the corridor. Later, they found that the coal stove was not very good at retaining heat. So, they employed professional stove builders to build stoves that could be put aside at night. Therefore, in front of each apartment, there was a stove, a pile of coal dust balls and a shabby table. This was when the era of the tube-shaped apartments really started.

Some children would light the stove and cook a meal as soon as they got back from school. Sometimes, they might be too busy playing so that the meal may get burnt and everyone on the same floor would smell it. People usually got up before dawn to queue to buy pork and bean curd. Friends might save a place for each other. Children might grasp some dried bamboo shoots and soybean on the table of their neighbor before going to school, or take out an underdone sweet potato from the pot of others.

Later, the units finally got the idea of adding a kitchen in each floor. However, the water supply became a problem due to the installation of pipelines, especially in summer, when the water supply was frequently disrupted. As a solution, every family placed a large water vat in the kitchen to store water. Since water was usually supplied during the night, many people got up very early to collect water.

Many people who had grown up at the tube-shaped apartments went to work in the countryside and mountainous areas or joined the army or took part-time jobs. Whenever they thought of the days that they spent with their parents in the tube-shaped apartments and the kitchen in the corridor, they think of it as going back to heaven.

Later, many units built new apartments and many of the first residents of the tube-shaped apartments moved into new apartments and tube-shaped apartments were left to other staff.

Earthquake shelter-tents set up by making use of every single space

On July 28, 1976, an earthquake suddenly hit Tangshan. Beijing, hundreds of kilometers far away from Tangshan, also felt strong quake. Soon after, simple earthquake shelter-tents were set up on every street in Beijing. Nearly every place was used up.

In the early winter of 1976, earthquake shelter-tents were reinforced and thickened, with walls made of reed matting, yellow mud and bricks, roofs made of straws and asphalt felt as well as simple wood doors and windows. During winter, the sharp northwest wind penetrated the reed matting and was forever remembered by people in Beijing. It was not until 1977 that the aftermath of the earthquake gradually faded away.

In fact, many earthquake shelter-tents were built up in rural areas.

Through the 1970s, there was not great change in the houses in rural areas.

Wang Anyi, a female writer from Shanghai, wrote an article titled *The Houses* and recalled that she once lived in one in the 1970s. At the time, she worked with a production team in Daliu Village, in Wuhe, Huaibei, Anhui. Other people outside of the village believed it was a rich village, because it had many houses made of black bricks. Living there for some time, Wang Anyi discovered that the houses were divided into different classes. The best houses are totally made of black bricks, then there were houses made of bricks and adobe. The worst houses were made of adobe. Not a single house had a tile roof.

Wang Anyi lived in the best house of Daliu Village. She and four children of the "director" of the village and an educated girl from the urban area lived in the front three-room unit. Later, he learned that the length of the room was based

 Beijing courtyard.
Provided by Beijing Municipal Archives

on the girders of the house and was not actually a separate room. The house was separated by sorghum stalks: one for Wang Anyi and her roommates, and one used as living room and one used as the steel making room.

Some cities began to build houses. The high-rise residences at the Three Front Gates (the Front Gate, the Xuanwu Gate and the Chongwen Gate) areas, which were planned in May 1976, were the first high-rise residential buildings constructed by the government of Beijing. The government of Beijing was very proud of these projects, aiming to gradually give every household a bathroom. (At that time, most of the people had to go to public bath to take a bath).

In 1979, the completed housing construction projects for staff covered a total area of 62.56 million square meters. More than 4 million people moved into new houses.

The "Stone Gate" residence, not a "new horizon"

Shanghai had the tightest housing supply in the country. Three generations of people often lived in a 12-square-meter room. Most Shanghai people lived in 'Stone Gate' residences with small lanes. Some residences had new-style lanes and apartments, while some were just small simple houses, the residents of which were called slum-dwellers.

Typical traditional "Stone Gate" residences in lanes feature the following structure:

The bottom floor: The front door and back door. Inside the front door, there was a small dooryard, covering an area of four to six square meters. In front of the dooryard, was the living room, covering 20 to 28 square meters. Generally, this part was sunless and humid. Deep inside, via the stairway and the small bathroom, was a kitchen, covering six to eight square meters. The kitchen had a back door.

Up the stairs, there was a garret, covering 6 to 10 square meters, usually facing the north, gloomy and cold. Up more stairs, there was a room on the second floor, covering an area equal to the living room.

Continuing up, there was a flat roof, the roof of the garret. Continuing up, there was a "third-floor attic", with a triangular pitched roof and dormer. The area for people to stand up straight was about 12 square meters.

Originally, the house was designed for one family. The living room was used to receive visitors, while the room on the second floor was used as a bedroom. The garret and attic were used as storage rooms. The structure of the house was similar to that of a townhouse.

Compared with the slums, it was paradise here. If a girl's boyfriend lived in the slums, the girl's parents might not allow the girl to date him. Girls from the slums would not let others know that they lived in the slums. They might pretend to be fashionable and elegant and lied that they lived in the apartments at Huaihai Road.

In the kitchen of a "Stone Gate" residence there were always several sets of gas cookers, with independent lamps. The cookers might be locked in the daytime. The residents here might scramble for water to wash vegetables and rice. Sometimes, conflicts might happen. Some people even fought each other and broke things. (Reference: Records of Ten Years of Trifles: Commodity Supply in Shanghai during the "Great Cultural Revolution" by Ji Cong)

The Bund, the dimly-lit paradise for couples

In the 1970s, there were only a few of entertainment venues. Most of the time, young couples would like to go to the cinema for a date. They usually met at the gate of a park and then walked to the cinema one behind the other. They would enter the cinema after the movie started. They usually bought the tickets for the seats at the back of the cinema to avoid being noticed. They would leave just before the end of the movie. The whole process was like what spies did when connecting with each other.

Then, the boy would send the girl back home. In the dark, they walked hand in hand and kissed each other.

For many young couples, the most economical way to date was going for a walk along the road.

The parks were romantic places for dating. However, the date might be disrupted by management staff who usually walked around the parks with red armbands and flashlights. Sometimes, the young couple might be called "hooligans" and caught by members of the inspection team. The inspection team would call the managers of the units in which the couple worked.

Another place for dating was the Bund. The flood control wall at the Bund was called the "wall of lovers". There were many couples. The dimly-lit Bund was a paradise of couples.

Photo taken at the Bund. In the 1970s, the Bund was the paradise of the young people with great dreams.

There was a well-known "lovers' corner" at the Bund, with seats for the couples. There was an unwritten rule that two couples sat on the same chair. It's said that, sometimes, the boy of one couple might fall in love with the girl of the other couple.

When a couple decided to get married, the unit in which they were working for would allocate a house for them. Generally, the unit would consider the size and condition of the houses the couple were living in before they got married. If there was enough room for them to live after they got married, the unit would not allocate them a new housing unit. Rather, it would issue a certificate and coordinate with the house management division to build partitions. A couple that met related requirements for house allocation might get a garret covering an area of about eight square meters as their home, which might be full of new fittings, luggage, sewing machines and stools. The couple would feel proud if there were 10 to 20 quilts of different colors on the bed of their bridal chamber, though, in that case, they had to make great efforts to move the quilts onto the ground or sofa before going to sleep.

At that time, there were many advertisements to exchange houses. Some people might want to exchange a well-located house for a bigger one for their children who would get married. Some might want to exchange one house for two smaller ones. Different people had different demands. If the owner of a house knew someone working in the house management department, he or she might get a better house through the exchange.

In February 1979, the Shanghai Housing and Land Administration issued instructions to solve the problem caused by the shortage of houses for married couples above a certain age. Statistics showed 7,017 families in which the wife was aged 30 and above that had no home.

First 3,000 boxes of bottled Coca-Cola delivered to Beijing

Coca-Cola finally entered the Chinese market in 1979 after some setbacks due to the conventional view that suggested such beverage were a part of the Western capitalist lifestyle.

In 1978, before the Third Plenary Session of the 11th Central Committee of the CPC, Zhang Jianhua, then General Manager of China National Cereals Oils and Foodstuffs Import and Export Corporation (COFCO Corporation), proposed introducing Coca-Cola to the Chinese mainland. Li Qiang, then Minister of Foreign Trade and Economic Cooperation, approved the proposal.

Later, under an arrangement with the COFCO Corporation and the assistance of the Wufenghang Company (Hong Kong), the first 3,000 boxes of bottled Coca Cola were delivered to Beijing.

At that time, Coca Cola was only sold to foreigners who were working or traveling in China. It was mainly sold at the Friendship Store. Today, the Friendship Store, which is located near Jianguomen, is no longer mysterious to ordinary Chinese people. It still sells Coca-Cola. The manager of the Food Department of the store said a bottle of Coca Cola costed RMB0.4 in 1979.

During the period of the Planned Economy, the Friendship Store was a symbol of luxury. When reviewing the history of the development of Coca Cola in China, many media believed that it was a constraint for the CPC to only Coca-Cola to be sold only at the Friendship Store and some hotels at tourist destinations for foreigners.

However, some Chinese got the chance to taste the beverage before others. A newspaper report said that, Mr. Zhou Yueming, who resided at the Xicheng District of Beijing, bought Coca Cola and imported candies from the Friendship Store with the foreign exchange certificate provided by his second son, a diplomatic officer. These "new things" made the guest surprised and envious.

Eight model operas entertain 800 million people in eight years

In the early 1970s, the life of Chinese people, especially the cultural life, surrounded eight model operas. Later generations said that the eight model operas were seen by 800 million people over eight years.

The eight model operas include:

Beijing opera: *Shajiabang, The Red Lantern, Taking Tiger Mountain by Strategy,*

The Harbor and *Raid the White-Tiger Regiment*

Dance drama: *The Red Detachment of Women* and *The White-Haired Girl*

Symphony: *Shajiabang*

All the eight model operas were very popular among the masses. The leading

Stage photo of Shajiabang.

Stage photo of The Red Lantern.

Stage photo of Taking Tiger
Mountain by Strategy

roles of these operas were usually single men or women, who were staunch with moral integrity. They always sang with tightly clenched fist and a strong sense of righteousness. Every gesture showed their determination for revolution. The performers usually wore the same clothes and had the same face expressions.

It was hard for later art works to achieve the same popularity as the eight model operas. Of course, this was closely linked to the specific political environment at the time. People of the time may remember some of the lines in these model operas forever. For example, "the children of poor families share the household burden early" and "I have many uncles who will not visit us unless something important happens", sourced from *The Red Lantern*.

The most popular part of *Shajiabang* were the battle of wits between Aqingsao, Hu Chuankui and Diao Deyi. This battle of wits fully highlighted the elegant demeanor of Aqingsao, a woman who was the owner of a teahouse and was actually a clever spy of the CPC. She was capable of dealing with all the difficulties and achieving success one way or another.

Build the seven-star kitchen and boil the water.

Lay out the square table to receive the guests from all directions.

Everyone comes here is our guest.

Let's enjoy the happy hour together, and forget the troubles.

No sooner has the person gone away than the tea cools down.

The popular song of *Shajiabang* was widely known.

Later, there were ceaseless controversies on the model operas, with positive or negative attitudes. Some people liked model operas, because they had been accustomed to them. Some people disliked them, like Bajin, who said he had a nightmare about the Great Cultural Revolution after watching the replayed sample model opera.

Chinese movies are like news summaries

"People in Romanian movies frequently hug each other. People in Korean movies cry and smile. Albanian movies are unintelligible. Vietnamese movies always show wars. Chinese movies are like news summaries. "

This is an interesting summary of the movies in the 1970s.

In urban areas, people got together to watch movies. Some young people would watch the same movies again and again to date or kill time.

In rural areas, a lot of people walked long distances and tramped over hills to watch a movies. When the sun set in the west, the audience would sit on wooden benches or stools near the projector, waiting the projectionist to set up the screen, adjust the focus or change the filmstrip. Some people would put up their hands in the air and wave them toward the projection lamp so that shadows would appear on the screen. Then, they would feel very proud. Sometimes, the people would stay late at night to wait eagerly for the projectionist who had gone to another place to show movies.

There were usually large audiences, who almost surrounded the screen from all sides. Some people even climbed up roofs, trees and telegraph poles to watch the movies. Some people were injured during the process. Many people watched movies from the back of the screen, because there was not enough space in front. Some young people even fought each other.

The Girl Who Sells Flowers, a North Korean movie, was played again and again. Many audiences cried when watching it. It was said that men should bring two handkerchiefs while women should bring four to watch the movie.

Training rural projectionists.

Usually, news documentaries were played before the start of the movie. The documentaries were usually about Prince Norodom Sihanouk and Queen Monique. After that, the movie would start.

Chinese writer Ye Zhaoyan recalled that:

At that time, only a few foreign movies were on public shows, including *Lenin in October*, *Lenin in 1918* and several Albanian movies. There was an Albanian movie called *Mihai Viteazul*, which showed children swimming in a river while a girl wearing a bra and panties quickly passed by. It aroused great tumult among the audience. *Lenin in 1918* included a part of *Swan Lake*, a ballet. Many people bought tickets again and again to watch the movie. However, they just watched the dance, which lasted about half a minute and would leave after the dance.

Sandakan 8, *Proof of the Man* and *Kimi Yo Funme No Kawa O Watare*

In 1978, *Sandakan 8* was put on in China. The Japanese movie about the life of a Japanese girl who was sold to a brothel in Nanyang (an old name for Southeast Asia) reverberated more in China than in Japan.

Some people were extremely angry about what the movie. They even posted large banners on the streets, asking the government to ban and criticize the "blue movie". Finally, related departments cut off some scenes before putting it on again.

On the other hand, some people bought tickets just to watch a "blue movie". However, they were finally deeply moved by the story of Osaki, the leading role.

There was another Japanese movie named *Proof of the Man*, which also attracted great attention among Chinese people. Some people bought tickets again and again just to watch the short scene in which a character got naked to pee. However, most people were shocked by the behavior of the mother that killed her son to protect her fame and prestige. The theme song named *Straw Hat Song* was very popular. It was sung by Johnny, a black young man and son of Kyōko Yasugi, to show the love of a son for his mother and sadness of losing the mother's love:

Ma Ma, do you remember, the old straw hat that you gave to me? I lost that hat long ago.

Kimi Yo Funme No Kawa O Watare was another Japanese movie introduced to China in the 1970s. The tough guy played by Takakura Ken won great favor among Chinese audiences.

Many girls wanted to marry a man like Takakura Ken. Meanwhile, Mayumi, the girl with long hair and in leather boots, who seemed pure and was full of passion, became the dream lover of many Chinese men.

There is a classic clip in the movie:

"Jump, Jump, following Asakura, following Tangta."

In May 1979, soon after *Popular Cinema* magazine resumed publishing,

Poster of Sandakan 8 in 1978. The movie was based on the book Sandakan Brothel
No.8: An Episode in the History of the Lower-Class by Yamazaki Tomoko. Many
people watched the movie two or three times. The story in the movie led people to
think about human nature and aroused intense collisions of opinions and views.

A copy of Popular Cinema (No.2 Issue, 1980). On the cover was Li Rentang, who played the part of Zhu Keshi in the movie Tears. To some extent, the magazine witnessed the vigorous development of Chinese movies and the pursuit of art among Chinese filmmakers.

issue No.5 published a still from the British movie *The Slipper and the Rose* on its back cover. In the photo, the prince is kissing Cinderella in a splendid European palace.

The movie caused great upheaval.

A reader wrote to the magazine: "I cannot believe that. How could it happen in the socialist country established under the leadership of Chairman Mao Zedong and after the 'Great Cultural Revolution'. How can you be as degraded as the bourgeois magazines!"

Popular but not vulgar picture-story books

In the 1970s, picture-story books became very popular but not vulgar. They

In the time with extremely unsatisfied demand for both material and spiritual life,
picture-story books enriched the childhood of many people.

were good learning tools. For example, there were books adapted from the four
major classical novels and books about history and the four forms of poetry.

Picture-story books, also called "small comic books", were one of the most
important part of childhood for people born in the 1970s. *The Romance of
the Three Kingdoms*, *The Outlaws of the Marsh*, *The Legend of Yue Fei* and *The
Generals of the Yang Family* became the best options for children to spend
the weekend.

At that time, the authors of these picture-story books were very skillful. The
pictures were very beautiful and interesting. Usually, there were two kinds
of books: Those with drawn pictures and those with photos. The latter were
miraculous. They were made of photos of movies, with text captions. However,
limited by printing conditions and investment, only the covers of these books
had color, and the content inside was in black and white.

The most popular picture-story books were about fairy tales, such as the

Journey to the West and the *Investiture of the Gods*. In addition, those adapted from classics such as *The Romance of the Three Kingdoms* and *The Outlaws of the Marsh* were published in series. They were very popular, too.

A picture-story book usually cost several cents or tens of cents, which was expensive at the time. Therefore, children usually read the books in turn by borrowing from each other. Many people had experience collecting such books. They might put the books they bought and borrowed in paper boxes. Many of them had more than 20 books. Sometimes, they liked the books that they borrowed from others so much that they did not want to give them back.

Whenever a child got a new book, he would not like to finish reading it immediately. Instead, he would find a quiet place and sat down to read it. Soon, he would be absorbed in the story of the book. Most of the time, after he finished reading, he would find the time to read it again.

36 "legs" and "three betrothal presents with wheels and one with sound"

In the 1970s, three things were necessary for a men to propose, namely a bicycle, a wrist watch and a sewing machine, which were prepared for the daily use of a newly married couples and also to show the living standard

Titoni (a Shanghai brand) watch. (left)
SHANGHAI watch. (right)
Provided by Beijing Municipal Archives

Transistor radios in the 1970s.

Provided by Beijing Municipal
Archives

"Shanghai" sewing machine.

Provided by Beijing Municipal
Archives

of families. The families would feel proud if these things were shown at the wedding.

Later, the three things were seen as the "three betrothal presents with wheels". Some girls required their boyfriends to add a radio to the betrothal presents, which became known as the "betrothal present with sound". Therefore, the "three betrothal presents with wheels and one with sound" became widely accepted necessities for a proposal. Some families might not be able to afford a sewing machine so they had to borrow one for the wedding.

At the end of the 1970s, the conditions changed into 36 "legs" and "three betrothal presents with wheels and one with sound".

Of course, the 36 legs did not refer to the legs of people. It referred to the legs of furniture. It meant that the new home should have enough furniture. The composition of the furniture was different in different areas. In some areas, it even included a tripod that was usually placed in a corner.

Considering the living standard of the time, the newly married couple would be quite happy if the three betrothal presents with wheels were available before the wedding. Some richer families might buy a "Diamond" watch, a "Phoenix" bicycle and a "Five-Ram" sewing machine, all well-known brands. A Phoenix bicycle was equal to a private car now and would be admired by others.

From January to April 1979, sales of transistor radios increased 34.9 percent year-on-year. The long-term overstock turned to active demand.

Shanghai products sell well

In the 1970s, many Shanghai brands won great popularity nationwide due to their quality and design.

Given the shortage of supplies, Shanghai had the best-developed light industry throughout the country, with a number of durable and well-designed daily articles, including watches, sewing machine, bicycles and other products. Shanghai was proud of a variety of products, including Diamond and

 Shanghai products sell well. New "Shanghai" car

Baoshihua watches, Forever and Phoenix bicycles as well as Shanghai, Bee, Standard and Butterfly radios. At that time, the Shanghai products represented Chinese products and were popular all over the country.

People living outside Shanghai would buy items during their own business trips to Shanghai, or would ask others who would visit Shanghai to buy something for them.

A person who had visited Shanghai would bring back a lot of things for friends, because Shanghai products were very popular. No one would get back from Shanghai without buying something. As soon as they got back, they would immediately give the products to their friends.

Children liked the creamy candies produced in Shanghai. Girls likes the Dacron and corduroy material and clothes, which were high-grade products that they had been dreaming about. In the middle of the 1980s, the textile products of Shanghai had a diversified development, with a variety of new products: bulked yarn, grass-green Dacron poplin, thin stretch socks, imitated-decoration-firing overcoating and silk and satin brocade quilt covers and more.

The planned economy was based on planned supply. It was impossible to buy any Shanghai products without approval documents signed by leaders of the working units. The soaps, towels and malted milk powder were all hot consumer goods, though they may be unnoticeable today.

Shanghai products, boasting high quality, fashion design and reasonable price, were very popular nationwide. In addition, there were almost no counterfeits. In addition to the fashion design and durability, the memory of that time is another factor for the passion that Shanghai products generated.

The first TV commercial for ginseng tonic wine broadcasted at the first day of the Lunar Year

In the 1970s, there were almost no commercial advertisements. Newspapers and periodicals might reserve some space for advertisements for model operas. For example, on the fourth page of the *People's Daily* on February 5, 1970, there was an advertisement: The Great Victory of the Guideline for Art and Literature Development under Chairman Mao's Revolution model opera will be put on during the Spring Festival of 1970.

On January 14, 1979, *Wenhui Daily* published an article by Ding Yunpeng for the Shanghai Advertisement Company. The article titled Rectify the Opinions on Advertising said that the phenomenon of using advertising gimmicks, boasting and capitalist business models should be rectified.

Following that, a TV commercial appeared. On March 9, Shanghai Television rebroadcasted an international women's basketball game. To the surprise of the audience, a commercial advertisement was broadcasted at half time: Zhang Dawei, a famous Chinese basketball player, was drinking a kind of beverage called "Lucky Cola" with his teammate after a basketball game. At that time, advertisements were a new thing. The audience became confused and curious about the TV commercial. Some people even thought that the TV station made a mistake.

However, the advertisement was not the first TV commercial of China. The first one was advertisement for the ginseng tonic wine called "Shen Gui Bu Jiu", which was made with 16-millimeter photographic film at 15:05 on January 28, 1979 (the first day of the Lunar Year), 38 years after the world's first advertisement made in the US in 1941. It lasted 90 seconds.

Resumption of university entrance examination with an application fee of RMB0.5

In August 1977, Deng Xiaoping presided over the symposium on science and technology development and education and approved the resumption of university entrance examination system.

On September 19, Deng Xiaoping had a discussion with leaders of the Ministry of Education and proposed two standards to recruit students: Good individual performance and priority given to the best examinees.

On October 12, the State Council approved the Opinions of the Ministry of Education on Recruiting Students for Institutions of Higher Learning in 1979. It said that all workers, farmers, youth working in the countryside and mountainous areas, educated youth returned to the urban areas, ex-

Applicants attend the examination in Shanghai in 1977, when the university entrance examination system resumed. The examination changed the fate of generations of Chinese people and laid a solid foundation for science and technology development and the economic boom in China.

servicemen and current year graduates with high school or similar diploma were eligible to attend the examination. The applicants should apply for the examination on their own and then attend the unified examination.

The news spread throughout the country quickly. People rushed about telling each other the news, believing that the time for them to change their destiny through equal competition was coming.

The examinees hoped that the application fee could be set at RMB1. After collective discussion, the Political Bureau of the CPC Central Committee finally decided to set it at RMB0.5 to reduce the burden on applicants.

The university entrance examination of 1977 was held at the end of the year, with examination papers prepared by related departments of the provinces, municipalities and autonomous regions. Both applicants for courses of arts and science took the examinations for politics, Chinese and mathematics. Applicants for courses of arts also took the examination for history, while applicants for science courses took exams for physics and chemistry. New students enrolled in universities in the spring of 1978.

This was the largest-scale examination in the history of education around the world. However, ironically, there were not enough examination papers for all the applicants.

A report was made to Deng Xiaoping, who made a prompt decision to suspend the printing of the Fifth Volume of the Selected Works of Mao Zedong to give priority to the printing of examination papers.

In the winter of 1977, under instructions and directions of Deng Xiaoping, the university entrance examination was held for the first time in 10 years. It was the only university entrance examination held in winter since the resumption of the university entrance examination system. A total 5.7 million applicants got into the examination room. In the summer of 1978, a summer examination was held. A total of 11.6 million applicants attended the two examinations. So far, those remain the largest exams in history in terms of the number of applicants.

The applicants were of different many different ages. Some were more than 30 years old. They were married and even had children. Some were much younger. The applicants who passed the examination graduated in 1982. Some of them said, when recalling their school life, that one of the most popular jokes among the students was that the elder students always said to younger ones that they could be as old as their parents.

However, there were still many applicants who failed the examination. It was the times and not necessarily themselves that laid obstacles on their way. Through the examinations in winter and summer, the universities recruited more than 401,000 students, only 1 out of every 29 examination applicants.

Overseas Chinese students make a stir in the United States

On December 26, 1978, during Christmas holiday, 52 Chinese students arrived in the United States.

They were the first group of students to study in the United State after the founding of the New China and following the break of the deadlock between China and the United States that lasted for about 30 years.

The Chinese students made a stir among the Americans.

Liu Baicheng, a 74-year-old professor of the Department of Mechanical Engineering of Tsinghua University, was the leader the group of the students. He recalled that it was in September 1978 when the Central Committee of the CPC decided to send some students to study abroad. He had actually given up hope of being a member, because he had 45 years old at the time.

"My father had been a capitalist in Shanghai before the liberation of China. Such background was adverse to my application for studying abroad. Actually, I had applied for twice to study in the Soviet Union, but failed due to the background," he said.

However, this time and to his surprise, he received the notification from the department that he was working for informing him to attend the examination.

Many years later, he got to know that the chance for him to study abroad was due to a speech by Deng Xiaoping.

In June 1978, Deng Xiaoping, who had just resumed the leadership, listened to the report of the Ministry of Education on the work of Tsinghua University. Then, he said: "On the one hand, we should work hard to promote the development of our own universities. On the other hand, we should send people to study abroad and make comparisons so that we will know what we should do to run our universities. We should send thousands of students to study abroad, no matter how much it costs. The Ministry of Education may research on that. We may send 3,000 students out this year, and 10,000 the next year."

Then, Deng Xiaoping said: "The first task is to send the students out. Don't afraid that they will not come back. Even if 10 percent or 20 percent of them will not come back, there will still be 80 percent."

A report of the Ministry of Education was approved in September 1978 and the selection of people to be sent abroad began. Liu Baicheng said the candidates had to pass three examinations, including a preliminary examination organized by the department, written examination of schools that the candidates were working for and the unified examination organized by the Ministry of Education. (Reference: We Set Out before the Formal Establishment of Sino-US Diplomatic Relations by Cai Rupeng, No.3 Issue, 2009, *China Newsweek*)

In 1978, delegations of the Chinese government and many non-governmental institutions visited the United States, Japan, Canada and other countries. Meanwhile, many delegations of foreign countries visited China. During these visits, discussions about student exchanges were made and a number of cooperation agreements were signed and specific plans were made. Through government organizations, non-government organization, academic institutions and friendly individuals, diversified channels were opened for Chinese students to study abroad. The same year, a total of 3,000 students, including college students, non-degree advanced students and graduate students, were sent abroad.

With continuously expanded channels for Chinese students to study abroad and enhanced bilateral communication since 1981, overseas study supported by work units and self-funded overseas study have emerged as two other channels for Chinese to study abroad. The number of students sent abroad through these channels soon surpassed the number of the overseas students supported by the government.

By the end of 2012, China had 2.64 million students studying abroad.

Villagers of Xiaogang Village fingerprint for all-around contract

The Reform of China began in rural areas, while the reform in rural areas began with the promotion of the production responsibility system.

On December 1978, the Central Economic and Working Conference and the Third Plenary Session of the 11th Central Committee of the CPC were held. At the same time, in an evening, 18 farmers of Xiaogang Production Team of Fengyang County of Anhui got together at the thatched-roof cottage and affixed their fingerprints and seals on a written pledge on behalf of 20 households of the production unit. The written pledge said:

"We will distribute land to every family. The families should sign the written pledge. Every family should promise to fulfill the task for the annual agricultural tax to be paid in grain. Then, we will be able to support ourselves without laying any burden on the state government. If this mechanism fails, our cadres will shoulder the responsibility, even if we may be sentenced to death. In that case, please raise our children until they grow up to 18."

The written pledge marked with red fingerprints is now shown at the National Museum of China as a first-class cultural relic (No.GB54563).

In September 1980, at the central conference of representatives of the provinces, municipalities and autonomous regions, Chi Biqing, then first secretary of the CPC Guizhou Committee, made an aggressive proposal to fix farm output quotas on the household basis in accordance with the topographic features and economic development level of Guizhou. His proposal was immediately opposed by Yang Yichen, then first secretary of the CPC Heilongjiang Committee, who said: "You cannot do this." Chi responded: "Then, you go your way, and I will go mine."

Later, the dialogue between the two secretaries of the CPC provincial committees was published in a newspaper. "You go your way and I will go mine" became the most vivid representation of the discussion about whether the mechanism to fix farm output quotas on a household basis should be adopted or not.

The adoption and extension of the system of contracted responsibilities on a household basis with remuneration linked to output led to revolutionary changes in rural areas, becoming a milestone of China's Reform and Opening-up.

Watching CCTV News becomes a habit

On January 1, 1978, CCTV (China Central Television) News was first broadcast, with Li Juan and Zhao Zhongxiang as the news anchors.

As *Southern Weekend* said: "CCTV News has become the best-known TV program with the most audience all over the world over the past 30 years. Under suspicion and great pressure, it still has an audience of tens of millions who wait at seven o'clock every night to watch it, because it has become a habit for them. It is an ideological sign with profound symbolic meaning in the national publicity system. The news anchors who are always serious in speech and manner are called national faces. Government leaders at different levels are always shown in the programs for a limited time, which is exact to the second; the color and tone of the clothes of the news anchors always indicates the nature of the events to be broadcast; the change of the program or new anchors may be an omen for adjustment of the political pattern; whenever it's said "the news today may last about 59 minutes", some important events may have occurred. "

Since 1978, CCTV News became a window for Chinese people to know what happened in the country and the world. Chinese people firmly believe that CCTV News plays the role of a vane for Chinese politics and economy.

In the 1990s, Zhang Hongmin appeared in CCTV News in a Chinese tunic suit. This aroused great commentary in the embassies of many countries in China. They believed the choice showed a change in the political atmosphere. However, Zhang Hongmin wore the Chinese tunic suit because he had no other formal clothes when he was asked to cover for another news anchor that day.

The discussion showed that any change in CCTV News caught national and international attention.

All Chinese people listen to the Legend of Yue Fei told by Liu Lanfang

In 1979, Chinese people became hooked on The Legend of Yue Fei told by Liu Lanfang, a well-known Chinese Pingshu (storytelling) artist. In many cities, the streets were empty when people went home to listen to the story. At that time, few families had televisions. So, most people listened to the story through transistor radios. It was an unprecedented phenomenon in the history of the Chinese storytelling.

In the early stage of the Reform and Opening-up of China, Liu Lanfang and her husband Wang Yinquan edited and created The Legend of Yue Fei. The storytelling was broadcast by more than 100 radio stations while 1.1 million books were published, a record that still holds. Following that, other storytelling works were broadcast, including the Generals of the Yang Family and the Romance of Zhao Kuangyin. These works exposed the art of storytelling to audiences at home and abroad.

The performance of Liu Lanfang was easy to understand and vivid, making audiences feel as if they were on the scenes. The story was interesting and exciting. It was great!

The Legend of Yue Fei accompanied a generation of children. The first thing many children did after school was sit down on a stool near the radio and listen to stories about four brave generals under the leadership of Yue Fei. Liu Lanfang was not just telling stories about ancient people. What she wanted to do was to move and encourage audiences by the sagas of the heroes. If people born in the 1980s and 1990s ask their parents whether they listened to the storytelling of Liu Lanfang, most parents will say "yes". Many people are her fans.

"If you want to know what happened afterwards, listen to the next chapter." The conclusion of the storytelling always brought the audiences back.

Fragrance of puffed rice on the street

In the 1970s, people would become quite excited when some old man walked down the street with a black tin, which was actually a machine to make puffed rice. They would soon come to get some of the "puffed rice".

Following a series of sounds made by rolling the machine and then a "bang" the street was filled by the fragrance of the puffed rice.

At the time, puffed rice was a popular snack food. For children of the time it was similar to Mcdonald's, KFC or Haagen-Dazs today. It was especially exciting to have puffed rice. However, the chance only came during Spring Festival. So, children eagerly expected for the coming of Spring Festival.

The rice could only be bought using coupons. If someone came with 500g of rice, he or she must come from a rich family. Sometimes, a student might bring some puffed rice to school. Even on the way to the school, he or she might feel very happy. During breaks, he or she might take out and eat the puffed rice. The other children would look on with admiration, hoping that he or she might share some.

A sure sign that Spring Festival was near was when every family went to buy puffed rice.

People always queued for a long time to wait for the man to make puffed rice for them. On the first day of the lunar year, children would say blessing words, and the adults would give them some puffed rice.

To many people, the heavy black machine was part of the most cherished memory. It meant many people got together and enjoyed a merry festivity with delicious snack food. Sometimes, children would follow the old man who made puffed rice with the black machine from one street to another. They remembered the whole process: lighting a fire, adding firewood, pulling the bellow and jiggling the bar. They would like to listen to the sound of the "bang", which was always followed by black smoke and the fragrance of puffed rice. They would be very excited and shout. This was the happiest moment in the wait for the puffed rice.

The old man would usually open a small coal stove and add some coal into it. Then, he would put two mugs of rice into the calabash-shaped machine and tighten the cover before putting the machine on the fire. He would then pull the bellow with his left hand and jiggle the bar with his right hand which was followed by the "cling-clang, cling-clang" made by the machine.

MEMORIES OF
CHINESE LIFE IN THE

1980s

In 1980, China's per capita grain consumption stood at 428 *jin* (a *jin* equates half a kilogram).

In 1980, China's per capita expenditure on clothes was RMB42. Even though the cotton consumption of urban and rural people had not yet reached the level of 1957, the quality of clothes was much improved. In 1980, retail sales of leather shoes reached to RMB169 million, nine times larger than that in 1957.

In 1980, China's per capita expenditure on household goods was RMB42.4. The proportion of expenditure on bicycles, watches, sewing machines and televisions had increased from 0.5% of 1952 to 24.5% of 1980.

At the end of 1980, the per capita living space of urban residents was 3.9 square meters, 0.6 square meters smaller than the 4.5 square meters of 1952. According to statistics, in 1980, the per capita living space of rural residents was 11.6 square meters.

In 1980s, China remained a country with weak economic foundations. However the implementation of reform and opening up gave people confidence for the future.

Red dresses are in fashion

In the early 1980s, Chinese came to realize that bold dress did not necessarily have negative impact on a sound ideology.

According to *Beijing Evening News* on April 21, 1981, Beijing Youyi (Friendship) fashion factory designed a new type of dress that was pretty, unique and elegant. As soon as it was put on the market, it gained great popularity among many women.

Red Dress are in Fashion shot in 1984 reflected a conflict between a female model worker in a textile mill and a pretty dress. The "red dress" was a symbol to show that women in China began to liberate themselves from the single and rigid clothing and pursue a kind of clothes whose color and style were in line with their own character.

One day in the early 1980s, A Xiang, a country girl who worked in the Shanghai Dafeng Cotton Mill heard that Shanghai girls usually took part in a competition called "clothes killing" or "dress killing", in which all would wear beautiful clothes. A Xiang was fed up with being called a bumpkin, so she turned to Suzuki for help and bought a red silk dress from her clothes shop. Model worker Tao Xing'er liked the red dress very much and couldn't help trying it on. She looked very beautiful in this red dress. When A Xiang saw it, she invited her to the garden to compete. However, knowing that the shift foreman could not stand the red dress with bare shoulders, Xing'er quietly attached a white collar to it, which was ultimately torn off by her friends.

Encouraged by her friends, Tao Xing'er finally went to the garden with a crowd of female workers. She mustered up courage and boldly competed with other girls who were also dressed in beautiful clothes with various color and forms. However, it turned out that no one could match her. Tao Xing'er really enjoyed herself during the competition and at the same time, began to notice how old perceptions constrained her.

In the meantime, another film called *The Girl in Red* immediately became fashionable. The red clothes at the time were all the rage along with a classic line: "Don't be too attached, don't be prudish."

On July 12, 1986, *China Textile News* published an article about Beijing's early clothing market in the 4th edition, Vol. 28. The name of the article was *Yellow Dresses are Popular in Beijing*. The red dress fever was soon weakened. Women clothes ushered in a bright era with red and yellow coexisted.

Chinese models get attention

The first fashion magazine of China called *Fashion* was founded in Beijing in 1980.

That summer, semi-high-heeled sandals with rubber sole designed by Beijing Rubber Plant were launched and well received. The first fashion model team in mainland China was established in 1981. The organizer recruited students only in the name of "Clothes and Advertising Performing Arts Class", but to their surprise, the number of applicants was four times larger than what they had expected. Three years later, when the performance team visited Europe, it caused a great sensation. Westerners exclaimed: "Mao Zedong's children wore fashionable!" The fashion wind flowing from China displayed a new and open image to the world.

In October 1984, 10 arts academies including the Central Academy of Fine Arts and People's Liberation Army Academy of Arts issued an announcement on *Beijing Evening News* to openly recruit models for arts department. It was the first time since the foundation of the nation.

The announcement attracted 171 applicants, most unemployed youth. Twenty female models and ten male models aged between 17 and 30 were selected for a fixed salary of RMB40 per month and allowances for every hour of performance, altogether over RMB100 per month. The term of the employment contract was half a year.

At the beginning, models were introduced by teachers and students. Since the economic policy gave permission to the development of self-employed business, models became harder to find so open recruitment started, which was later consented by the Ministry of Culture.

Under the constraint of feudal tradition, being a model was considered shameful. Some applicants dared not tell their parents and asked schools not to have their names known.

In 1985, a nineteen-year-old rural girl named Chen Suhua got an opportunity from a friend to be a figure model in Nanjing University of the Arts.

Being naked to model for painters was regarded as an evil thing in the eyes of the local people. When her parents realized what their daughter did, they were enraged and forbade her to go out to make a spectacle of herself. Every day, there were villagers gossiping about her. Wherever she went, she was humiliated. Finally, she went insane, took off all her clothes and left the room.

Liu Haisu, a ninety-three-year-old artist, sent 1,000 Hong Kong dollars to Chen Suhua's family when he heard the story. (Tiantian: Abnormal Family of a Suffering Female Figure Model, published in *Family*, vol.10 in 1988) .

Compared with Chen Suhua, other models were much luckier. According to French newspaper *Le Figaro* on July 27, 1985, eight Chinese models made their debut on the runway of Paris for the show of Pierre Cardin. It was also the first time Chinese models were allowed to go abroad. In May, the show performed by the girls along with 25 male and female models won thunderous

Photo of contestants of Beauty of Youth contest in Guangzhou in 1985

applause in the Worker's Stadium. It was the fourth fashion show Pierre Cardin held in China. The latest clothing samples of the year in 1985 to 1986 designed by an outstanding fashion designer drew 15,000 enthusiastic people. However, too much exposure to bosom and shoulders and the high leg cut design for skin-tight skirts all surprised people and arose their antipathy.

Bikini tells us the best thing in life is freedom

In November 1986, the fourth national "Hercules Cup" was held in Shenzhen. In this annual top-level bodybuilding contest, Chinese female contestants were first encouraged to compete in bikinis (including a bra and a triangle pants, commonly known as Three-Point).

On the midnight of November 25, Huang Xuzuo, press director of the organizing committee was interviewed by reporters. He said: "The scheme of the competition is put forward by Shenzhen fitness club in light of the latest international rules and then approved by the organizing committee. According to the requirement of international contest, female athletes should compete in sports bikini. It is inappropriate to call it Three-Point for it may mislead people. As an official uniform required by the International Federation of Bodybuilding, bikini is the same as fencing clothes or wrestling clothes, which are involved in competition as well as its rules, so we don't have to make a big deal out of it." (Guo Dianqing: Male and Female Bodybuilding Invitation Tournament Recently Unveiled in Shenzhen published in *Life Weekly* on November 30, 1986.)

In China, for most women, the bikini is a kind of clothes just to be appreciated. On the beach, they all tend to wear relatively conservative swimsuits.

The bikini wave later blew from south to north, striking this ancient and conservative land. The bikini fever soon swept through the whole nation, which tested an old saying in western countries: "Bikini tells us the best thing in life is freedom."

In 1986, during a dance party of Hangzhou, a group of female actors from Shanghai ballet theatre performed aerobic dance in skimpy red bikini. When came on the stage, they didn't arose intense reaction. But later some said it was inappropriate to perform on stage with such revealing clothes.

City Beauties Pageant, the beginning of beauty contest

In early 1985, the Guangzhou Youth League committee started a beauty contest called "the First Yangcheng (nickname for Guangzhou) Beauty of Youth Contest", which was the first beauty contest held in city since the establishment of People's Republic of China.

The first round of contest began on February 3 at 7 pm. The contest was open to both men and women, who were not only judged on physical appearance but also on the cultural knowledge through written examinations. The contest attracted 550 handsome boys and beautiful girls, among which more than 130 passed to the second round at the Guangzhou Children's Palace on February 14. This time, some people were even asked to perform, sing or dance on the spot.

After the second round, the contest met much criticism and cases derived from which went all the way to the court in Beijing. Old scholars argued that to hold a beauty contest was to practice bourgeois liberalization for it only reinforced the idea of dressing, thus weakening the spirit of hard struggling.

It was at that time that Chang Yuping, the public relations manager of China Hotel, the first deluxe 5-star hotel run with Chinese and foreign capital, contacted me and claimed that China Hotel would be the exclusive venue sponsor for the contest after negotiations with the organizer. She invited beauticians and hair stylists from Hong Kong to dress up the 20 finalists (evenly split by gender). Now, in retrospect, it was the first time public relations girls, beauticians and hair stylists from this emerging industry appeared in China. In 1989, the TV series *Public Relations Girl* based on the story of Chang Yuping was aired on Guangdong TV Station and soon became enormously popular.

On March 6, the final contest was held in China Hotel of Guangzhou, during which five men and five women were selected as "Yangcheng Star". The female winner was Xie Ruoqi, the chief receptionist of the White Swan Hotel. In the final, she won the hearts of judges as well as thousands of audience by her graceful dance, sweet voice and impressive eloquence shown in her answer to the host. In the meantime, the male winner was also selected and his name was Wang Zijian.

However, due to some intervention, pictures of the beauty contest were not allowed published in domestic newspapers. (An Ge: *National History*)

In 1988, Guangzhou TV launched the first City Beauties Pageant to seek talent for TV commercials. The campaign was the first disguised form of beauty contest in China. In the same year, New Silk Road Model Look China started, marking the historical origin of Chinese model industry.

Although the content and purpose of the City Beauties Pageant completely met the criterion of beauty contest, it merely took on the name of "model contest" not beauty contest.

According to Ning Xiaozhou, director of the Arts Guidance Committee of City Beauties Pageant, the outcome of this pioneer activity was both expected and worrisome. However, to their surprise, the participation was heated with thousands of people coming in to sign up for the contest within the 15 days of registration period. Participants had to be between 18 and 25 years of age, unmarried, childless, without a criminal record, and so on.

The judging criteria embraced two parts: one was education and specialty and the other was appearance, talent and so on. The second also included requirements for the body, but it focused on overall performance.

"At the time, contestants also competed in swimsuits which were not as fashionable as they are now," Ning Xiaozhou said.

(Beauty Contest in China: from Dreadful Monster to Mild Pet, Xiao Mingdi and Gao Wei, published in *Chinese Business Morning View* on July 13, 2008).

Suits for rent

According to *Workers' Daily* on August 8, 1983, blazer shorts were all the rage in Shanghai. In the summer, it was fashionable for girls to wear white, beige or light green blazer shorts along with golden belt, knee socks and high-heeled sandals.

In 1984, a sign that read "Suit for Rent" was placed in the window of a photo shop in Shanghai to cater to people who liked to pose in a suit. It was in Wangkai Photograph, the most famous photo shop at the time that the wedding dresses and suits were available for rent. In the late 1970s and early 1980s when the Zhongshan suits still prevailed, it was hard to find a suit in an ordinary photo shop. Some bridegrooms were photographed wearing a suit made by his bride before marriage. Although the collar looked a little bit wrinkled, it had become a fashion.

Then there were suits with Chinese characteristics, which didn't have the shoulder line and collar ironed so wearing it felt like wearing a robe. Moreover, what's hilarious was that people in suit always kept the trademark on the cuff

 A suit

←

At that time a lot of clothes had shoulder pads.

←

Women suit

and wore a pair of cloth shoes on their feet.

After the First Plenary Session of the 13th Central Committee of the Chinese Communist Party held on November 2, 1987, five newly-elected members of politbure standing committees first made their appearance in suits, which soon led to a suit fever throughout the nation.

Zhou Changqing, the current director of *Fashion*, said that the reason why suit fever spreading from south to north, cities to villages could challenge the ever old Zhongshan suit, undress uniform and young men's jacket was the thirst for political restructuring. *Fashion* quoted an article title from *Tokyo Shimbun*: "Bye, Zhongshan Suit". (*Fashion* special issue in 1983)

Famous designer Guo Pei recalled that when she started the career in the field of fashion design in the 1980s, she had designed a white single button suit out of tablecloth in stock which was nine cents a meter. After the suits were launched to the market, she said: "They sold so well that selling fashionable clothes was like selling cabbages." People from all walks of life tended to wear suits from government officials to construction workers or vegetable sellers. "Everyone is like white-collar in society".

People at that time didn't know how or when to wear suits. Their suits were wrinkled and had shoulder pads. Due to the fact that there were fewer clothes off-the-peg and they were relatively more expensive, people generally went to the tailor shop to have their clothes made. As a result, various suits appeared in clothing stores. Every tailor shop could make clothes no matter what material was chosen, attaching a trademark and then it turned out to be a suit to wear.

At that time, men inclined to unbutton the suit and hung a bunch of keys on their pants.

Yu Zongyao, former general manager of China Apparel Industry Corporation recalled: "The design of Chinese suits at the time was really below average. In 1986 when I went to France, I brought two suits and a blouse with me. However, I felt I could wear neither of them for the material, design and details fell far short of that of the France. So I didn't have my clothes changed for many days. In the second year, I went with the model team. The leader of the female models wept backstage at the thought of the distinctive difference between them and the foreign models on the same stage. It was then we realized how outdated our clothes were."

Fake collar, production of the "face"

The invention of the fake collar is truly original.

Lu Xun once said: "Face is the spiritual guidance of Chinese people."

It was said that people in the fashionable city of Shanghai invented the fake collar because they cared much about face. The young would feel uncomfortable if they did not wear shirts. Especially in cold weather, they did not like to wear sweaters with ugly shawl collars.

Fake collar were real collar but separated from the shirt. They consisted of a front opening, back part, button and buttonhole, like the upper part of the shirt was cut out. One could wear it inside the coat to give others a false impression that he was wearing a shirt. Because the detachable collar revealed was completely the same as shirt collar, so it was called fake collar.

Made from remnant materials, fake collars were very cheap and didn't require cloth coupons plus they came in a complete range of sizes like shirts so they gained great popularity from the young people. Some people liked to collect collars with different colors to wear like white, grey and light brown. On work days, many people used fake collars in dark colors that did not show dirt. Standing in front of the mirror, a man would feel pretty good wearing a fake collar inside the sweater and a Zhongshan suit. At the time, if the fake collar was red-checked, it would impress people with its unique combination of color.

Moreover, fake collars had to be bought in Nanjing Road in Shanghai because that was where the resin collar, that was quite stiff, was found. With a fake

Dacron fake collar (left); Plaid fake collar (right).
Provided by the Ethnic Costume Museum of Beijing Institute of Fashion Technology

collar, a man would feel confident to go on a blind date or meet his girlfriend. But one thing to note was that if the room temperature was high, one could take off the coat but not the sweater because it was awkward to see a fake collar which had only two pieces of cloth on the front and one piece behind, with two or three buttons and two bands to fasten arms in case the fake collar would come out.

Now, people in Shanghai are willing to buy old fake collars at a high price. Unluckily, with the continuous improvement of material life, fake collars, a transitional product left behind, used. It has become a lasting memory of a generation, a topic of conversation and a witness of the times.

Jeans closed the door to college

In the late 1970s and early 1980s, young people in China got a crush on casual clothes like jeans and T-shirts and girls even began to take off their bras, all of which formed a street fashion against traditional culture.

Zhou Changqing, the current director of *Fashion* magazine clearly remembered: It was a day in 1980s when people were all dressed in the gray blue Zhongshan suits, he saw a girl wearing a pair of tight jeans on her way home. He became very angry at the sight of her legs wrapped tightly by jeans and ass waggling as she walked. In Zhou Changqing's view, any decent person would not wear jeans.

At that time, Zhou Changqing was not the only person with this view. In a recruitment of graduate students, a university in Shanghai warned a qualified student: If you continue to wear jeans, you will be rejected.

On February 24, 1985, *Life Weekly* published a letter from a reader named Xiao Zhou. In the letter he told a story about him and jeans: "I'm already 28 years old but still don't have a girlfriend. Lately, my teacher introduced a girl to me and told me secretly that on the day I met the girl, her parents would watch our every move from a distance, so I need to be well dressed. My neighbor A Xiang actively suggested: 'A worsted plaid jacket with a pair of washed jeans is in fashion. It can make you look lively and modern, what's more highlights the beauty of your body.' I took his advice. Unexpectedly,

Jeans

In the 1980s, a flood of global fashion made its way into China and quietly left an imprint on Chinese clothing.

Provided by the Ethnic Costume Museum of Beijing Institute of Fashion Technology

after the date, I got the response from the girl, saying that it was hard for her parents to accept my clothes so they feared I would not get along with their innocent daughter."

In the end, his first date failed.

Warm and light military coat

In the mid-1990s, we suddenly found that Chinese people, regardless of class, gender, job or age, almost all had military cotton-padded overcoat in dark green when the winter fell.

There were two reasons for this. First, when the young fashion followers went to the dance hall or other places of entertainment, they need to wear less. However, the main vehicle at the time was the bicycle, so the clothes worn indoor could not resist the cold weather in the open air. Plus buying a fur overcoat in that era was economically unfeasible for most people, the military coat then turned out to be a perfect substitute. Second, the emerging cotton wadded jacket was too short to keep the legs warm, therefore people preferred to buy an army green cotton-padded overcoat with excellent quality and reasonable price at the expense of nearly a third of their monthly wages.

Thanks to the young, the military coat soon became a fashion trend.

It may be due to the fact that the military coat was indeed warm and light with reasonable price or that Chinese people were deeply driven by conformity, work units used to distribute welfare products including military coats. In winter, when leading cadres at all levels visited factories or rural areas, they always wore military coats. In addition, from retired veteran cadres to middle-aged or young doctors and teachers, all regarded the coat as a symbol of modern, youth energy and the spirit of never being isolated from the masses.

The military coat had been popular for nearly a decade until the early 1990s when the leather coat was massively launched to the market. Because the leather coats were in all price ranges, which were affordable for people in different economic levels, they began to abandon the military uniforms including the military coat. (Hua Mei: History of Chinese Clothes, China Textile Press, in November 2007)

Military coat

Five stresses and four points of beauty

In February 1981, nine institutions including the National Federation of Trade Unions and The Central Committee of the Communist Young League jointly put forward an initiative targeting the whole nation, especially teenagers, known as the "Five Stresses and Four Points of Beauty". The five stresses were: stress on decorum, manners, hygiene, discipline and morals. The four points of beauty were: beauty of the mind, language, behavior and the environment.

Soon the "five stresses" and "four points of beauty" began to influence people's daily life.

According to the *China Youth News* on February 12, 1981, collage students in Beijing and aspirant youth across the county all began to divert their attentions to aesthetics study. Lectures about "the Essence of Beauty" were held everywhere.

At the same time, studies on western philosophy like the thoughts of Sartre, Nietzsche and Schopenhauer were also popular.

On May 1, 1981, *Beijing Evening News* reported: "The China Photo Studio in Beijing Wang Fujing Street has set up a photography studio this year specialized in taking five-inch color photos. In recent months, it has gained great popularity among the masses."

On February 18, 1983, *Shanghai Youth Daily* interviewed Professor Zhang Disheng, a famous orthopedic expert and also president of Shanghai Ninth People's Hospital about the problem of young people doing cosmetic surgery. Professor Zhang argued that beauty of appearance should be encouraged, but beauty of the mind was what we really need to pursue in life. Like an old saying goes: good sense and clever hands go hand in hand. Later, he still held the thought, saying: "Beauty of mind can be shown from eyes, facial expressions, manners, clothes, languages, attitudes and many other aspects. However, cosmetic surgeons may only guarantee your external beauty." Then he reaffirmed: "I still that sentence, 'Seek truth from beauty; beauty and truth are inseparable.' Only in this way, can we achieve mental and physical beauty."

According to *Shenzhen Special Zone Daily* on September 6, 1985, the medical plastic and cosmetic center in Shenzhen People's Hospital had attracted many male customers.

Say goodbye to dark yellow face

In 1983, after the Chinese people bade farewell to an era of black, grey and blue colors, the Ruby Beauty Salon opened at the crossing of Madang, Huaihai Road in Shanghai. At the time, the director of the Municipal Women's Federation sighed with emotion that Shanghai people would say goodbye to their dark yellow faces.

On opening day, there was a long queue outside the salon. People there were all young ladies who had heard the news. Reporters from Japanese NHK, American PBS, Swiss National TV Station, France, Netherlands, Federal Republic of Germany, Hong Kong and Macao all covered the news and couldn't help exclaiming: "Chinese women who like to dress in clothes made of blue cloth should wait in line to get facials!"

The Ruby Beauty Salon led a boom in the beauty industry across the country. As a symbol of the liberation of the Chinese women's lifestyles, it was one of the three elements marking Shanghai's reform and opening up, the other two elements were the Shanghai Stock Exchange and the Old Jazz Band Peace Hotel.

At the time, it cost RMB20 to get a full beauty treatment and RMB8 for a simple one, which was expensive in Shanghai. However, it didn't frustrate those who wanted to improve their looks. A lot of newly married couples came all the way from Zhejiang, Jiangsu and Northeast China to have facials, listing it as a part of their honeymoon schedule.

Writer Cheng Naishan recalled: "Having a haircut or facial in Ruby is a symbol of status. You can always hear some style-conscious girls say with pride 'I had my facial in Ruby!'"

According to statistics, the turnover and profit of the salon in 1984 was almost five times higher than they were in the year before. By 1988, Ruby Beauty Salon had already opened up eight chain stores across the country.

Ruby Beauty Salon was back in business on May 5, 2009 in Tongren Road. (Liwei: Shanghai's First Beauty Salon Reopened Today, published in *Oriental Morning Post* on May 8, 2009)

Short curly hair and wavy hair

In the early 1980s, most of the students still favored braids, which were popular in the 1970s. However young women workers had already cut off their long braids to get a short hair permed into waves. Some people spiked up their bangs with hair gel; some arched the front part of the hair and then fixed it with hairpins, which was considered as a good way to make them look taller and was well received by short girls.

At that time, some young girls didn't feel bad about cutting their long hair. They thought the popular short curly hair would make them look fashionable. When the short curly hair grew long, it turned out to be beautiful and mature medium hair with loose waves, also called "wavy hair". This elegant hairstyle was favored by many female stars. Film stars like Gong Xue always appeared with medium curly hair on the covers of magazines like *Popular Cinema*, *Movie World* and so on. Too deeply attached to wavy hair, some people even feared that the hair would be pressed straight while sleeping, so they often curled it before going to bed.

In 80s, perm was very popular. The hairstyle in Red Suspicion was greatly favored by young girls.

Provided by the Ethnic Costume Museum of Beijing Institute of Fashion Technology

⬅ —————————————————

Romantic and elegant medium hair with loose waves

To save money, many people preferred to do their own hair with curlers than going to the salon. In the street, people with curly hair could be seen everywhere, which created unique scenes.

With the broadcasting of Japanese dramas *Red Suspicion* and *Volleyball Heroic Woman,* the hairstyles of the two heroines soon prevailed and were frequently imitated by people. The hairstyle of Kojika Jyun (the heroine of *Volleyball Heroic Woman*) gave people an energetic image for she tied two small bunches of hair, one on each side of the forehead that facilitated movement as opposed to the hair flowing down to shoulders. For Sachiko (heroine of *Red Suspicious*), her short hair did not fall out of style till now.

In 1983, Mainland China aired the Hong Kong TV series *Huo Yuanjia* for the first time. Actors Huang Yuanshen and Liang Xiaolong had a hairstyle with bangs in front and hair extending to the neck, which became popular among the young.

In the 1980s, Hong Kong and Taiwan dramas were all the rage in Mainland

China. Lin Qingxia's center part straight hair, the classic hairstyle in dramas adapted from Qiong Yao's novel, left people a pure image and was still popular. Classical hairstyles at the time also include Xu Xiaofeng's hairstyle and Feifei's hairstyle, all provided reference to Hong Kong TV, which intended to have a vintage feel.

In the late 1980s, the perm became widespread and various hairstyles came into being. With the gradual disappearance of braids, Afros began to prevail. Because the afro looked like the hair had exploded, it was interesting to see people walking in street with the curly hair all over their head quivering in the air.

Noodles in Yuebin Restaurant fascinated foreign reporters

Yuebin (Pleasing Guests) Restaurant, the very first privately owned restaurant in Beijing opened to guest in 1980. Afterwards, more and more restaurants sprang up all over Beijing.

On September 30, 1980, Guo Peiji, who had worked as a chef in the Internal-combustion Engine Plant helped his wife Liu Guixian fire up the stove before going to work. When he came back home from work, he was shocked by what he saw. His house was packed with people and the waiting line stretched out of hutong to the Wusi Street. One of his neighbors pulled his sleeve and whispered: "You've already opened your restaurant, why do you still go to work? Go home and check out how many foreigners there are."

At noon, the stove fire was still burning. Liu Guixian spent RMB36, the only money she had left, to buy four ducks. She intended to cook some dishes and invite neighbors to have a taste. Unexpectedly, the news spread and drew many foreign journalists. When Guo Peiji entered the house, there were still three foreign journalists reluctant to go after missing the first meal of the opening day. Hearing this, Guo Peiji got some noodles from his neighbors and made several bowls of noodles with thick gravy to serve those foreign guests who later ate with great relish.

Long Buller, an American reporter of the United Press International (UPI), once wrote: "In the heart of China which is under the leadership of the

Communist Party, delicious food and private businesses are gradually back to life from the small and narrow hutong."

The Yuebin Restaurant got more and more famous. In the Spring Festival of 1981, the Vice Premier of the State Council Chen Muhua and Yao Yilin paid a visit to the restaurant, encouraging the couple to proceed boldly. Words from the two distinguished guests put the couple's minds at ease. To celebrate this wonderful moment, they happily bought a sack of firecrackers and set them off with children for nearly half an hour.

According to Owner of Beijing's First Privately Owned Restaurant Talked About Reform and Opening up (published in *Beijing Times* on November 25, 2008):

Chen Lin was a regular guest of Yuebin Restaurant. He had many favorite dishes like elbow pork in garlic and vinegar, fried duck, egg rolls served with pancakes, leeks and hoisin sauce, stir-fried cabbage and other recommended dishes. At the time, Yuebin Restaurant was ahead of other restaurants in Beijing with its various dishes and pleasant taste.

After reading the front page news of *Beijing Evening News* about the opening of Huibin Restaurant, senior high school student Chen Lin begged his father to try the food there. He still remembered that it was a snowy night in winter when he and his parents waited for two hours to get served. They squeezed in a narrow corner and ordered three dishes and a soup: fried duck, stir-fried cabbage, Yu-xiang shredded pork and roast duck bone soup with tofu. The portions were generous, so his father also ordered a bottle of beer for three dimes and nine cents.

"Never in my life have I eaten such delicious food," Chen Lin said, recalling the happy moment on that day and repeating the compliments he had expressed before. The meal cost them less than RMB4, which was four days' meal expense of his family.

After eating at the Yuebin Restaurant, Chen Lin had no appetite for home-cooked meals. In winter, cabbages, potatoes, carrots and sweet potatoes had always been the main sources of food in Beijing. At that time, his mother would think of ways to diversify the dishes, so they would have eggs twice a week and pork once a week.

"If I can open a Maxim's in Beijing, then I can also open it on the Moon!"

In September 1983, a humble French restaurant started its business in the No.2 Chongwenmen Xi Dajie, not far away from the Cuihua Hutong.

The restaurant was called Maxim's de Paris. It was the first Sino-foreign joint venture restaurant in China. The Chinese side was Beijing Second Service Bureau while the French side was Pierre Cardin Company, which made its first attempt to invest in China. At the time, Fectopah Mockba, Peace Hotel and Dadi Western Restaurant were the only western restaurants in Beijing and they all provided Russian food.

After nine months' of renovations, Maxim's in Beijing turned out to be exactly the same as that in Paris. He Zhifu, who worked in the Second Service Bureau, once noted that the paintings on the diner's wall were classic French style, many of which were nudes. The Chinese side later reported this problem to the Cultural Affairs Bureau and Public Security Bureau, but neither of them could give any instruction. Then the problem was reported all the way to the Central Government where it was finally solved by a vice premier who agreed to leave those painting as they were.

On the day of opening ceremony, Pierre Cardin said: "If can open a Maxim's in Beijing, I can also open it on the moon!"

The restaurant boasted a Parisian decor, taste and service. Guests felt they had

Maxim's de Paris now

been transported to a Parisian bistro. However, the food prices were extremely high (nearly RMB200 per person) and they discouraged many people with a monthly income of dozens of RMB at the time. (Owner of Beijing's First Privately Owned Restaurant Talked About Reform and Opening up published in *Beijing Times* on November 25, 2008)

Yili Fast Food Restaurant: Cups, spoons and straws of cold drinks were all disposable

On April 20, 1984, China's first western fast food restaurant "Yili Fast Food Restaurant" opened in Xirongxian Hutong, south of Beijing Xidan.

Many western journalists in Beijing came to cover the event. A journalist of the Associated Press issued a dispatch saying it was another round of implementation of reform and opening up.

"Beijing's first western fast food restaurant will hold its opening ceremony on April 20 and begin to serve Chinese and foreign guests," *Beijing Evening News* reported. The news attracted people's attention. On the opening day, the 150 square-meter restaurant was packed with guests enjoying hamburgers, sandwiches, coffee and more. People from all over the city went for the experience and those on trips to Beijing regarded it as a window to Beijing's reform and opening up through which they could learn about the new approach.

Wang Peng, office manager of the Yili Food Co., Ltd recalled: "The people who went to the restaurant most were intellectuals. Music, western food and dim lights were all the rage back then and immediately won the hearts of people. The restaurant was nearly fully packed every day since its opening. People who came mostly were celebrities, athletes, journalists and college students in stylish clothes. It was perhaps that those people who found it easy to accept new things."

To this day, Zheng Dejin, who worked in the Journalism Institute of Xinhua News Agency, remembers eating in the Yili Fast Food Restaurant for the first time:

"It was the day after the opening day. When I stepped into the restaurant, I was greeted by a beautiful sound of light music and fresh air sent by the air conditioner. The restaurant was elegantly furnished with a row of bright and big mirrors on the right, which visually widened the limited space. Looking around, you could see high-class decorative sheets with cream color and pretty patterns mounted on the ceiling and four walls, neat square table and exquisite chairs arranged in good order and adjustable lighting flowing on the bright and clean terrazzo floors, which created a warm atmosphere to the restaurant. There was a lot of new stuff: After the costumers washed their hands, a little hand drier placed beside the sink could blow the hands to dry in less than one minute; waiters made out the bill by an electronic computer which was quick and accurate; the food ordered was placed in a tray which was easy to be carried; the cups, spoons and straws of cold drinks were disposable."

People even hold wedding ceremony in KFC

According to the *Beijing Evening News* on April 20, 1985, Huaqing Chinese Food Restaurant in Dongcheng District of Beijing would sell six to seven thousand box meals from 9 am to 6 pm, about seven boxes every minute.

One day in 1987, people happened to find a restaurant located in Beijing Qianmen. On the sign, there was an image of an old man with white hair, short beard and suit. People later realized that the man was the American Colonel Harland Sanders and the restaurant was called Kentucky Fried Chicken (KFC).

On the morning of October 8, 1990, the first mainland McDonald's finally opened in Xihuagong, Guanghua building, Jiefang road in Shenzhen. The restaurant contained 500 seats. Now the mark of the yellow "M" can be seen everywhere in China.

On the opening day of KFC, Feng Enrong, who lived in the Chuiyangliu, went out with her son Zhang Shuang at 10 o'clock to have a taste of western fast food. They transferred twice and finally got to Qianmen. However, "when I arrived, I saw a lot of people waiting outside the door. The queue was so long that had it already extended to the road."

"Even though it was snowing that day, it didn't discourage passionate customers.

McDonald's Restaurant run by Beijing Sanyuan Group Co. Ltd. and McDonald's USA.

There were so many people waiting outside that the staff had to call the police to maintain order. Finally a police officer came up with an idea. He asked people to queue in a circle and let a few people in at a time." After standing in line for nearly two hours, Feng Enrong finally got into the restaurant.

Outside the door, Zhang Shuang became interested in the sculpture of the goatee bearded and kind-hearted Colonel Sanders. Curiously, he reached his hand into the bucket of fried chicken carried by this old man. Behind him was an endless queue of people mostly dressed in black and blue.

Zhang Shuang liked the packaging the most. For a child, the only way to let the joy continue was to take the box away with him. After dinner, he took the boxes as well as paper cups back home. When he went back to school, Zhang Shuang was proud that he was the first child who had eaten in KFC and even wanted to paint the three letters on his face. He excitedly told his classmates about it and brought a paper cup for them to see. All his classmates listened with admiration and couldn't help swallowing slobbers.

"Every time I see the beautiful packaging, the delicious taste of fried chicken will come to my mind. Looking back, it can be one of the funniest things in my childhood." (A Bite of Memory: Lining Up for Two Hours in the Snow Just to Try Western Fast Food, published in *Beijing Evening News*, on October 21, 2008.

The success of KFC also encouraged other western fast food restaurants to target this huge market in China. In 1990, Pizza Hut opened its first restaurant in Beijing. In April, 1992, the world's largest McDonald's started operating in Beijing Wangfujing, serving for more than 10,000 customers a day. In the next few years, western fast food restaurants developed rapidly with thousands of branches set up.

Going to KFC became fashionable among teenagers. There were even couples that chose to hold their wedding ceremony in KFC. After the ceremony they would take the packaging boxes back home and place them somewhere conspicuous in the living room.

I want good wine with coffee

In the 1980s, two songs aroused Chinese people's interests in coffee. Chinese, who were accustomed to drinking tea, began to try coffee and became deeply attached to it.

One of the songs was *Good Wine with Coffee* sung by Teresa Teng: "Good wine with coffee, I only want to drink one cup. Thinking of the past, I drink another. Knowing that love is like flowing water, why bother to ask who he loves. I only want good wine with coffee, one cup after another."

Another song was *Come by the Coffee Shop* by Taiwanese singer Pai Hui: "Every time I pass this coffee shop by, I could not help but slow down my pace. It is where we first meet and where our love begins. Now you no longer come there. I become lonely again. Don't know what makes us turn from lover to

Chinese pop music has come a long way. However, Teresa Teng's sweet voice and tender feeling still linger on people's hearts. Many years ago, a generation lost themselves in the sweet melody. Many years later, in the company of her songs, this generation stepped into middle age and even old age.

stranger. The sweet aromas of coffee filled this coffee shop, and my love for you still remains. Don't know when we can start over. Let me tell you how much I miss you."

The songs didn't merely talk about coffee, but related it to love that had gone with the wind.

China was a country with a long history of tea drinking, so the coffee there didn't sell very well. In order to encourage Chinese people to accept coffee drinks, Nestle launched a slogan in 1980s, saying "The taste is great!" It advocated a leisurely lifestyle of western countries, which was fresh and appealing to the young. Soon, Nestle coffee became widely known in China.

On March 31, 1985, *Life Weekly* published a report entitled Why Does Coffee Sell so Well from the journalist Dai Wenyan. He wrote: "Since the Spring Festival, coffee in Shanghai is always out of stock. Actually coffee drinking has not yet become a hobby for most Chinese people. However, with the development of economic opening and the continuous improvement of people's living standards, more and more people begin to drink coffee. It's no wonder that an expert from the business circle once said: 'It is a good thing. In a sense, it can reflect a country's economic and cultural level.'"

On August 30, 1987, Wei Zhixin, a journalist at *Life Weekly* reported:

"Coffee fever had already spread throughout Shanghai. It was estimated that the national annual sales of imported instant coffee topped 1,000 tons and

Shanghai accounted for half. As much as 70% or 80% of customers of coffee were middle-aged and young people.

For the young people, coffee was indeed a fashionable drink. Many liked to have coffee in a delicate cup and chose strong coffee with bitter taste for they thought it was the best way to drink coffee."

Bars there are quiet

Coffee became popular, so did liquor chocolate. However, chocolate centered with white wine was very expensive. "Life is like a box of chocolates, you never know what you're going to get." A lot of people remembered this classic sentence from the movie *Forrest Gump*.

On October 30, 1988 *Life Weekly* published an article by Yang Jishi who said that the bar had become a new part of the night-life:

Foreign wine (left). Laoshan spring water (right).

"The bar is quietly becoming a new pleasure in Shanghai's night-life. Bars had already moved from the upscale and luxury hotels to exquisitely furnished small restaurants along the streets of Shanghai. In downtown, bars from privately-owned restaurants were quietly emerging. To compete with them, Huaihaixi Restaurant, which was located in Songshan crossing, Huaihai Road also opened a bar whose business later became prospered. Although there were only 38 chairs in the bar, it attracted over 60 customers every day from 8pm to 12pm."

The article also pointed out five requirements for clubs: Dim light, quiet environment, long stays, high-quality wine and an elegant layout.

Bar-goers were mostly young and middle-aged people. They went there for one of five reasons: to do business, go on a date, make friends, enlarge business relationships or other reasons. Of course, all were private conversations.

In the late 1980s, privately owned bars were out of favor. According to *Life Weekly* on April 9, 1989, the reason was that the bars grew too fast and charged too much, thus resulting in few customers. At the time, the famous French wine Remy Martin XO could cost RMB60 to RMB90 for one ounce.

In 1989, the first bar in Beijing opened in Sanlitun.

Garrulous Zhang Damin faces housing tension

In the early 1980s in Beijing, the earthquake shelter-tents facing streets were gradually pulled down. However, the demand for housing continued to rise. People had no choice but to renovate, strengthen and enlarge earthquake shelter-tents, which were later transformed from self-saving facilities to kitchens that would ease the difficulties in housing.

The undisciplined growth of small kitchens further exacerbated the already severe living environment. Many originally messy warrens were so greatly occupied by kitchens that left only a few narrow and winding corridors for just one bicycle to pass through. Meanwhile, the linoleums, purlins and plastic sheeting of earthquake shelter-tents were piled up in each corner of the yard. Small kitchens disrupted the overall layout of yards. High-density living space and chaotic living environment all weakened people's self-restraint and led people's daily life in disorder. Neighbors frequently quarreled or fought for land to build a house. According to a police station, among the civil dispute cases, 85% were related to homestead disputes.

Zhang Damin was one of the people who were seriously bothered by housing. The novel *The Happy Life of the Garrulous Zhang Damin* told a story about a small house:

"The structure of Zhang Damin's house is ramshackle. It is like a hamburger dropped on the ground. You can still pick it up and eat, but the layer and content was somewhat in a mess. The first layer is the walls, door and the yard. Walls are not high and covered with morning glory, presenting a false image of pastoral scenery, which could fool people's eyes. The door was not solid for it is two old windows fit together with several curved plywood nailed on it. The numbers are still on the wood so every time there are visitors they will tell them that it's not a piece of normal wood for it comes from the back chairs of an auditorium. Pushing the door open, you can see a half-meter deep pit with an area of almost four square meters. On the left, there is a shed covered with linoleums. It is where piles and piles of honeycomb briquettes are placed. On the right, there is one bicycle on the ground and two hanging on the wall. Next to the bicycles is several heads of purple garlic and what under the garlic is a paint bucket filled with rubbish. Damin's family called this pit 'yard'.

The second layer is the kitchen, which also has a poor layout with one end of the room wide and the other end narrow, taking the form of a spiced pork shoulder. This is the rich part of hamburger. Windows, walls, ceiling and floor are all black and sticky which are hard to clean. A dusty bulb hanging by an electric wire is like a shriveled eggplant but will not rot. The threshold of the kitchen is nice. It is knee-high and very thick, looking like a dam. Through the kitchen, we come to the third layer - living room which is also master bedroom. It is a 10.5 square-meters' room equipped with a double bed, a single bed, a table with three drawers, a folding table, a washstand and several folding stools. The rear window is not big and faces northward. The room lit by the faint light coming through the window always reminds people of a vegetable cellar.

The last layer is the back room. It is six square meters with a single bed and a bunk bed, which makes the room look more like a sleeping car of train. There are no windows on the wall but one on the roof. With the white light directly shooting down from the top, the room looks more like the vegetable cellar. It is this multi-layered burger dropped on the ground, lost in the ashes of the city, ugly and distasteful, how could people eat it?"

The novel was later adapted into TV series. It described a family of eight living in a small house with only 16 square meters. Like a can of sardines, the house was so packed that people could hardly breathe, which showed, maybe a little bit exaggeratedly, ordinary people's demand for housing in Beijing. Zhang Damin and his younger brother had both got married but still had to share a room. Because the double bed could not be transformed into bunk bed, they all had to sleep in one bed with a curtain hanging in the middle. However, it was not a long-term solution. One day, Damin came up with an idea. He built a house around the tree in front of his house. When it was finished, he and his wife began to sleep in each side of the tree.

Stories about housing tension made audiences sad for this helpless life.

Urban residents can buy houses

The country stepped up the efforts in house building, especially the promotion of commercialization of housing.

On June 5, 1983, Xinhua News Agency reported that the State Council had approved the Administrative Measures on Individuals in Cities and Towns to Build Houses. It said that residents or staff members who had officially registered permanent residence in cities and towns and had housing problems could apply to the local real estate management authorities to build a house. The house area would amount to the average of their registered permanent residence. Generally speaking, each person should not have area exceeding 20 square meters.

Early in April 1980, Deng Xiaoping pointed out in a speech that urban residents could purchase or build houses individually; both new houses and old houses could be sold. One-off payments or installment that took 10 or 15 years to pay off were acceptable.

The first residence community built in Beijing after the founding of the nation. It was located in Xicheng District.

From Exhibition Catalogue of Beijing Archives Treasure

Xie Ranhao, a reporter at *Economic Daily* recorded the arduous course of housing reform in the 1980s.

Around the 1980s, public housings were sold at full price. Due to the fact that the income level of urban residents at the time was too low, it basically came to a halt by the end of 1981.

At the time, houses sold at full price were newly built. The local government was in charge of building houses and then sold them to individuals at cost.

The houses were sold at an average price of RMB120 to 150 per square meter. The total price of a house was roughly equal to 10 to 12 years of total income for a worker or 5 to 6 years of total family income.

At the beginning of 1981, a pilot project of public housings sold at full price expanded to more than 60 cities and numerous towns. Besides pilots for the sale of new houses, there were also pilots for the sale of old houses.

In April 1982, the State Council consented to a pilot project in Zhengzhou, Changzhou, Siping and Shashi for the sale of newly built public housing at subsidized price. The principles of the subsidy were as follows. The purchaser paid one third of the price; the unit where the purchaser works and the local government each subsidized one third. The house was still sold at cost price and the average price per square meters was roughly controlled between RMB120 to RMB150 yuan. After being subsidized by government and unit, the purchaser would pay for the house at a cost roughly equal to three or four years of income or two years of total family income. In addition, people who were willing to buy the house would enjoy a series of preferential policies. For example, a one-off payment would get a discount of 20% and the time limits of installment were extended to 20 years, etc.

The subsidy policy greatly aroused people's enthusiasm to buy houses.

To address the problems in the pilot project, in March, 1986, the former Ministry of Urban-Rural Construction and Environmental Protection clearly stated in the *Notice on the Relevant Issues Concerning the Pilot for Selling Public Housings at Subsidized Price in Cities and Towns* that, in principle, public housings should be sold at full price. Each local government should take actions to stop any reckless practice of selling old houses by cutting down prices at will.

With the promotion of reform, people's living conditions gradually improved. On January 31, 1988, *People's Daily* reported that in 1987, the year of "International Year of Shelter for the Homeless", cities and towns across the country had built houses with total area of 140 million square meters (excluding of houses for agricultural population) and there were over 8 million people moving to their new houses.

"I would rather have a bed in Puxi than own a room in Pudong"

On February 5, 1989, *Life Weekly* reported that there were two million households in Shanghai, among which 100,000 were eager to move. There were two main reasons. One was family conflicts and the other was inconvenient living environments.

"I would rather have a bed in Puxi than own a room in Pudong" was a concept that spread in Shanghai in the 1980s. At the time, Pudong had just started to develop. Even though there were many spacious houses newly established, its inconvenience still showed in many aspects like traveling, shopping and entertaining. What's more, there were no government agencies.

Puxi was quite convenient in every aspect but housing. A stone house with tens of square meters typically housed a family of seven or more. In the late 1980s, children of the "honorable mothers" should be married. However, housing became a big problem that always stood in the way. The Shanghai government advocated the development of Pudong and provided preferential policies to those who would like to move there. However, people still refused to go, saying "I would rather have a bed in Puxi than own a room in Pudong". It meant that as long as there was a place to sleep, one would not move to Pudong.

There was also a correspondent saying in Guangzhou: "I would rather have a bed in Hebei (north of the Zhujiang River) than own a room in Henan (south of the Zhujiang River)."

On October 13, 1992, Shanghai TV Station broadcasted that numerous Shanghai people moved eastward to Pudong. It was reported that in early October, the number of residents moving to Pudong had reached over 100,000 out of more than 200,000 and was the highest in years. People's attitudes had already changed. If there were two houses with same spatial areas in Pudong and Puxi, Pudong's residents would still choose the first one without hesitance. They said that the development of Pudong was promising and it would definitely surpass Puxi in the future.

In the Great Wall Hotel, only the dust outside the window was made in China

On June 20, 1984, Beijing's first joint-venture five-star hotel, the Great Wall Hotel, opened.

The American Christian Science Monitor reported on June 6, 1984: "Standing in the outskirts of Beijing, the Great Wall Hotel was a magnificent 20-story high-rise, which however, looked inharmonious with the surrounding environment at the first glance. The hotel was a symbol for nouveau riche to show off wealth, and also an example of western materialism trend. There, only the dust outside the window was made in China."

The course of the Great Wall Hotel's opening recorded the difficult start of China's tourism industry during the reform and opening up.

In 1984, China had golf in the Zhongshan Hot Spring Golf Club.

The Zhongshan Hot Spring Golf Club was about 23 kilometers south of Shiqi, Zhongshan City. Co-founded by Hong Kong celebrities Huo Yingdong and Zheng Yutong, it was the first golf club in China and also the first golf club with a standard golf course with 36 holes, qualified for tournaments. The most unique part was designed by famous professional golfers Arnold Palmer and Jack Nicklaus. Their work was unparalleled.

On May 5, 1987, the capital's first racecourse was set up in Daoxianghu garden, west of Beijing and opened to tourists. It was run by Benma (Galloping Horse) Economic Tourism Development Corporation in Sujiatuo Village, a suburb of Beijing. It covered an area of 75 acres and owned altogether 20 race horses and walking horses.

Tour guide borrowed a khaki Zhongshan suit

Before the 1980s, many Chinese people didn't have the concept of "tourism". After entering into the 1980s, domestic tourism grew. However, there were not many scenic spots to travel to. Beijing, Xi'an and other places rich in history became some of the few popular tourist cities. At the time, going to the capital

In this era, tourism was still a new thing.

to take pictures in Tiananmen Square or the Great Wall was an amazing thing admired by people.

In August 1982, the China General Administration for Tourist Industry changed its name to the National Tourism Administration.

The first administrative regulation for the tourist industry called *Provisional Regulations on Administration of Travel Agency* was issued in 1985.

A tour guide named Liu Zhi recalled: "When I became a tour guide, the whole country was poor, so were we. Before we met our first guests, we even had no uniforms. However, our manager asked us to put on our best clothes for it could show Chinese people's high living standards and at the same time upgrade the image of China. I hurriedly searched my closet but could not find a satisfying one. At last, I borrowed it from my friend and still remembered that it was a khaki Zhongshan suit."

At the time, the hotels and restaurants were fewer and the infrastructure poor. However, tourists travelling to Guilin basically returned satisfied. Why? One reason was that they were amazed and fascinated by the stunning scenery of Guilin and the other was that the environment back then was really nice. (I Became a Tour Guide in the Beginning of Reform and Opening Up published in *Guilin Evening News*, on November 24, 2008)

The first outbound tourism in China dates back to 1983. Since Hong Kong and Macau opened tourists to Mainland China, people in Guangdong area began to visit their relatives in Hong Kong and Macau, which marked the beginning of outbound travel.

On November 15, 1983, a group of 25 Chinese citizens set off from Guangzhou to Hong Kong to visit relatives and tour around. Hong Kong media called it "China's first group (outbound tourist group)."

Hong Kong tours conformed to the historical trend and finally promoted the development of related tourist industry. Tour groups gradually evolved from one group per day and 25 people per group to 12 groups per day and 48 people per group. It was estimated that there were more than 17,000 people coming to Hong Kong every month.

Huang Lejie, from Chaozhou, Guangdong Province, still remembers his first journey to Hong Kong 20 years ago. At that time, he went to Hong Kong to visit his aunt whom he had not seen for years. Many relatives and neighbors envied him for his trip and asked him to bring back some products made in Hong Kong.

"A relative asked me to bring a gold necklace back for her, a friend asked me to bring a watch and some people want some medicines." (Lai Shaofen: *From Luxuries to Elements of Life—Tourist Industry Witnessed the Change of People's Life*, posted in Xinhuanet.com, on November 3, 2008)

Riding a motorcycle is cool

In the late 1970s, there were eight things that always appeared in the rich families in Guangzhou. They were motorcycles, cameras, televisions, refrigerators, washing machines, tape recorders, sewing machines and watches. Bicycles had already been excluded. After 1978, private motorcycles appeared on the streets of Guangzhou. Two years later, even in the undeveloped areas like counties or even villages, one could find the trace of the Jialing motorcycle.

In 1983, the first imported motorcycle model was the CJ70.

It was not until 1980s that motorcycles began to gain the favor of people. At that time, the motorcycle was a symbol to show off wealth. Riding a motorcycle through roads and streets would undoubtedly attract a lot of envious looks.

"It is so eye-catching! I am the first group of people to ride motorcycles in Leshan," Li Yunsheng told a reporter. In 1980, he asked a friend in Guangzhou to buy a tax-free 50CC Suzuki motorcycle at a price of over RMB1,900.

"The feeling of riding a motorcycle at that time was even better than now driving Mercedes or BMW," Li Yunsheng said with a smile. "At that time, I thought I was rich, but now it looks that I was too easily satisfied."

From the motorcycle, Chinese people's modes of travel changed greatly. Around 1980, motorcycles gradually entered into ordinary people's life, which was a prelude to private cars. (Zhong Chengjia: Private Cars Driving into People's Homes, published in *Leshan Evening News* on August 12, 2008)

Electric motorcycles, a variant of motorcycle fed by electricity, were more environmentally friendly.

Electric tricycles appeared in the 1980s and soon became a hit in urban and rural areas. However, due to problems like poor security, they were abandoned. But the shaking associated with riding an electric tricycle was not forgotten.

Individuals can also buy cars

According to *Shanghai Automobile News* on July 28, 1986, national private car ownership had reached 290,000, of which 95 percent were trucks.

In the 1980s, the right of control on the country's automobile production fell to the State Development Planning Commission. The country's vehicle production back then was 220,000, but car production was only 4,000, a severe shortage.

In February 1984, the State Council issued *Provisions on Individual Farmer or Joint Household's Purchasing of Vehicle, Vessel, Tractors in Operating and Transport Industry*. It was the first time clarified the legitimacy of individual purchasing the car.

Against this background, on July 3, 1985, Shanghai held the first International Auto Show in China with the attendance of 73 auto companies. In the opening day, 20,000 spectators flooded into the exhibition hall, the first group of car fans.

However, some heads of related departments still objected. People in society also questioned: If individual could buy cars, how do we deal with oil shortages? How do we deal with road congestions?

"At the time, it was the billing provided by the Materials Bureau that could purchase a car, not money. The car should be affiliated to units and be bought in the name of the unit," Wang Changqian, a dealer of Cherry recalled. However, some people could buy a used car of foreign embassies through relationships.

Mr. Yang, from Zhenjiang, Jiangsu Province was the first to buy private car. Local police didn't know how to manage it, so they placed a motorcycle license plate on the car. When Mr. Yang bought a motorcycle in 1978, they gave him a bicycle number plate.

In the 1980s, even though people had cars, they still could not drive. Because driving education also depended on the unit. Without the certificate issued by the unit, one could not take the driving test.

In the late 1980s, a large number of educated youth returned to the city and hoped to become drivers, so they used every way possible to join units to learn to drive. Due to the sharp increase of learners, the vehicle administration office had to take restrictive measures. The number of drivers was determined by the number of cars the unit owned. One car would only allow for two drivers. Units without cars were not allowed to issue certificates. Because the learning boom did not fade, in the late 1980s and early 1990s, the professional driving schools came into beings. (Yang Kairan, Guan Nan, Shi Wenfu:

Evolution of Cars in the 30 Years of Reform and Opening up: from Luxury to Travelling Tool, published in *Beijing Times* on November 28, 2008)

The expressway was a main indicator of the modernization of transport. Expressways had become an index to measure the level of economic development. In December 1984, the Shanghai-Jiading Expressway began construction in Shanghai and opened to traffic on October 31, 1988. This was the first expressway with entire lanes open to traffic in China.

Cassette recorder invigorates family dancing party

In the early 1980s, recorder sprang up in China. On the road, there were many "new youths" with long hair and bell-bottoms carrying recorders. They were the fashion pioneers at the time and the earliest celebrity worshipers after the reform and opening up. In the late 1980s and early 1990s, recorders found their way into every family.

In 1980, dance parties held in the open air were everywhere in parks, squares, streets and other public places of provincial capitals with thousands of onlookers. Given that the recorder had just been introduced, few people could have it, so they tended to play harmonica, flute, guitar, erhu and other convenient instruments as accompaniment to dancing. As long as there was square, whether the ground was rough or not, there were dancers.

On June 14, 1980, the ministry of public security and the ministry of culture issued *Notice on Banning Commercial Dancing Party and Spontaneous Dancing Party in Public Places* and claimed that: "Gathering dancing is prohibited in parks, squares, restaurants, streets and other public places." The notice said:

Sanyo cassette recorder

"This kind of party will cause great trouble to social security. Some people's dancing is vulgar, ridiculous and tacky. The place for dancing is out of order with abominable incidents happening occasionally like gang fighting, indecent assaults on women, stealing and death from squeezing or falling. The masses have become greatly concerned with those phenomena and insist that dance parties be prohibited by the government."

After the banning order was released, dancing parties had to be held elsewhere. With popularity of cassette recorders, family dance parties began to prevail. People seldom danced in street but in homes that were spacious. Deng Lijun's songs and some so-called decadent music of the late 1930s and 1940s were well received by people and recorded a lot. At that time young people were generally home dancers and they danced cheek to cheek or under dim light. The older people still preferred to enjoy ballroom dancing in the streets.

Yang Jiawei in her the *First Ballroom Manager Was Once "Invited" to the Public Security Bureau* (published in *Yanzhao Metropolis Daily* in November 28, 2008) wrote: "Around the year 1983, a commercial ballroom prepared to operate out of a 1,000 square meters' hall on the third floor of a building behind the Yanchun Hotel, a top hotel which was one of a kind in Shijiazhuang then got into trouble on the day of the opening ceremony."

In the afternoon, the public security department summoned the manager of the hotel in for questioning and claimed that he would be held accountable for setting up the ballroom and was forbidden to start business. The manager Liu Shaoquan had been watched over after making explanation to the department. At that time, due to the fact that the public security department had not dealt with similar situations, could not determine the nature of the case. They hurriedly asked for instructions from their superior but got uncertain replies. Finally, when consulting the city leader in charge, they knew what to do for he said: Providing a place for people to dance can add vitality to their cultural life, what's the big deal? What we need is to do a good job in security measures. After hearing the reply, the department was reassured and released the manager at once. At 8 pm on April 8, 1983, the first ballroom held in Yanchun Hotel opened on time amid the sound of music with people dancing to their hearts content.

It's hard for young people today to imagine the scene of ballrooms when they were all the rage. In the morning, they were filled with people, much more jammed than crowed buses and sometimes people could barely dance due to the limited space. People who went to the dancing clubs were of all ages. Generally speaking, in the morning or at noon, the guests were relatively older, but at night, the young filled them up. They went to clubs to make friends, go on dates, get new experiences and so on. Many went there just to meet girls. Dancing in clubs helped many people develop relations and get married. However, people may have an affair due to dancing so it also destroyed many families. What's more, it always leads to fights for dance partners.

However, in those days, dancing in ballrooms was an upscale form of entertainment and a very fashionable thing. Bell-bottoms, pop music, long hair and other popular elements could all be seen at dance clubs.

The way of dancing had become the concern of many club regulators, so they made a rule for tens of thousands of dancing clubs in the nation that dance should not be done against the face, chest and body.

Disco in vogue

In the early 1980s, Disco became popular among young people.

Disco is derived from the African-American folk and jazz dance. The main point of the dance is to shake the knees with the beat, keep the middle of the body relaxed and use the power on the hips and the rapid bends and stretch of knees. It is more like self-entertainment with various and free moves. There are no fixed patterns, so either solo dancing or couple dancing is acceptable.

Someone recalled seeing the eye-catching sign that said "Millionaire Dishigao" (another Chinese name for disco), he thought it was "Millionaire's Shigao" for "Di" also indicates a possessive relation. So he couldn't figure out what on earth was that: "In senior high school I entered the world of disco. Liu Wei, my only roommate with a recorder gave us the chance to get exposure to that advanced culture. But until now I still believe that it is my deskmate who enlightened me. Without her voice that woke up my heart, disco may not have come into my life. 'Shout! Shout! Shout! Dance like a disco queen', 'wave your hands, shake your heads, all troubles will slip away from your feet',

Teach and learn from each other. Every morning, when the cheerful disco dance music is played, the retired elderly come from far or near to Binhe Park, south of Suzhou River, to dance. This is the scene of the old teaching and learning from each other after they finished dancing.

'dance the tango, dance the haso, not as good as dancing the disco for it has the most varying moves'. I have been a faithful fan to disco from its rise to its final decline." (Begin from Disco, published in *Employment Times • Leisure Magazine*, April 4, 2006)

In 1985, the Indian movie *Disco Dancer* was a big hit. Batwing-sleeved blouse, scarlet lips and crazy plastic earrings became fashion trend among the young in disco club. The scene of singing and dancing in the film were exciting, winning the hearts of the young. It was at that time the disco dance started. Disco was finally recognized by mainstream and the song of the movie impressed a lot of people.

Jimmy, come on! Jimmy, come on!

Let's hand in hand, to dance disco,

Love you in our mind, forget your sorrow.

Jimmy, come on! Jimmy, come on!

The youth time is more wonderful, we are passionate and happy,

Swing to follow in the rhythms, come on dance with me.

In 1987, an American movie named *Breakin* was introduced to China. The audience were immediately attracted by the rotating moves, which were different from the regular ones. Then in almost every street you could see a boy with leather mittens, batwing-sleeved blouse, cloth wrapped on the head and high top sneakers imitate the moves of window cleaning or aliens' walking over and over again. The two characters Ozone and Turbo in the film captured the hearts of more and more young people.

The batwing-sleeved blouse was in fashion at the time. It had flowing sleeves that looked like the wings of a bat. In detail, it has various collars and sleeves with seamless armholes, tapering towards the wrist. Now new styles are developed like batwing-sleeved coats, overcoats and jackets whose sleeves are very wide at the top and independent from the main piece.

Karaoke "changed the night of Asia"

In the late 1980s, thanks to the opening policy, the karaoke of Japan was introduced to China. When night fell, a television, two sound boxes and several microphones were placed on the street for people to sing. Outdoor karaoke became the most fashionable way for citizens to entertain themselves. One could sing a song by putting RMB1. Over a period of time, outdoor karaoke had also became a means of communication for men and women unfamiliar to express their affection.

On February 9, 1989, according to *Wenhui Daily*, after the Huanglou karaoke nightclub first appeared in Shanghai, karaoke won the hearts of people and quickly caught on.

On July 1, 1991, the first nightclub opened in Guangzhou and was named Guangzhou Golden Voice Karaoke Nightclub.

With the development of the economy, more and more luxury karaoke clubs sprang up like mushrooms and open-air karaoke gradually retreated to the edge of cities with the entertainers changing from urban youth to migrant workers.

In 1971, Daisuke Inoue, the father of karaoke, invented the first karaoke machine in the world. American magazine *Time* wrote: "Daisuke Inoue has changed the night of Asia".

Unforgettable "decadent sound"

In the late 1970s and early 1980s, mainland people got into Teresa Teng's songs through relatives abroad or by eavesdropping on Taiwan broadcasts. Her songs were so well received that were repeatedly transcribed.

Songs about family, love, homesickness and life experience were beautifully performed through Teresa Teng's tender voice. Teresa Teng's songs soon spread nationwide. However, Chinese officials criticized them as too "bourgeois" or "obscene".

But Teng didn't know her songs were so widespread in China.

When interviewed by an American journalist, she said primly: "I have no special feelings for my popularity in Mainland China for I sing to my compatriots." As for her songs being labeled as "bourgeois" or "obscene", Teng merely stressed that if people would be fined for listening to her music then "don't listen to it".

Teresa Teng's songs were wide spread through unofficial channels, but at the same time began to affect official artists.

At 8 PM on December 31, 1979, a TV program called *Legend of the Three Gorges* was broadcasted after the CCTV news. *Township Love*, a song performed by Li Guyi, a solo singer of central orchestra was unveiled to the audience along with the program.

The beautiful melody together with Teresa Teng's way of singing soon brought *Township Love* great popularity.

But *Township Love* was also criticized by Chinese officials. Some people said: "The song serves as a part of entertainment life of capitalist society like coffee house, bars, dancing halls and night clubs." Other problems were the distance from the mouth to the microphone while singing, the gasp frequency and the choice of musical instrument.

In the CCTV Spring Festival Gala Evening of 1983, Wu Lengxi, the minister of the Radio, Film and Television ministry, after hesitating, finally lifted the ban on *Township Love*. (Thousands of Letters from Masses for Supporting Decadent Music, published in *Beijing News*, November 10, 2008).

Wang Lei, a critic from Beijing once wrote that in a sense, Teresa Teng enlightened the original pop music of the mainland. In the 1980s, the brick single card recorder began to make its way into every family and tape had become a fashion product favored by the young. The songs of Teng, which were once labeled "obscene", became top music. They were covered over and over again even by the pioneer of original pop music of the mainland, whether male singers like Cui Jian and Tang Dynasty or female singers like Cheng Fangyuan and Zhang qiang. Teresa Teng taught mainland audiences what pop music was.

Most of Teng's songs were love songs with great tenderness. She decorated herself into a bunch of lovely roses with her songs; the roses bloomed and faded naturally. From *The Story of a Small Town* and *Your Sweet Smile*, people experienced another kind of feeling beyond revolutionary friendship. Those feelings were once disgraced and regarded as dross of the bourgeoisie. The songs didn't concern humanity but focused on the subtle and fragile feelings of individuals, which will eternally be engraved on people's hearts.

It is an unforgettable feeling and rebel attitude that forms a collective youth memory of a generation and from then on, they begin to explore the meaning of life as well as that of individuals.

The release of Cui Jian's song – *I Have Nothing*

In 1986, Cui Jian first performed the song *I Have Nothing* on the anniversary concert of the International Year of Peace along with hundreds of stars in Beijing.

The Father of Chinese Rock – Cui Jian

Cui Jian, wearing a long coat reminiscent of the Qing empire period, a battered guitar on his back, one trouser leg higher than the other, jumped on the stage of the Beijing Workers Gymnasium. At that time, the audiences still didn't understand what happened.

When the music started, Cui sang: "I had asked you endlessly, when will you go with me?" The audiences were silent. Ten minutes later, the song ended and in the warm cheer and applause, the first Chinese rocker was born.

Since then, Cui has become known as the "Father of Chinese Rock".

The song named *I Have Nothing* has been described as a milestone in the history of Chinese rock and Chinese pop music.

Abroad, rock was just a kind of the pop music but in China, a country with five thousand years of rich cultural background, rock was totally different from pop music. Mainstream abroad, rock was generally regarded as "weird" in China.

Cui Jian and the song *I Have Nothing* were symbols that told people China had world-class singers and rock. Since then, due to Cui's performance, rock presented a splendid sight.

Cui Jian said the spirit of the song *I Have Nothing* continued, which was a sensitive suspicion.

Nowadays, many people hope to be middle class; so the song *I Have Nothing* is not glorious any more. However, people still find it difficult to close their hearts when listening to *I Have Nothing*.

One critic said, in those days, Cui Jian's song was the only thing we believed in. It was his love that warmed us; it was his anger that represented our feelings; it was his obscurity that made us reserved; and it was his blandness that seemed to represent our voice.

The song *I Have Nothing* has been a symbol of the mentality in an era.

In 1987, "Northwest Wind" (a style of music) began to influence a generation with *Xintianyou* (a kind of Shanxi local melody). "My home is on the Loess Plateau; a gust always whistles away; no matter from northwest or southeast; they are all my songs, all my songs." *The Loess Plateau* was well known as a representative work of "Northwest Wind".

Focusing on the Loess Plateau where ravines crisscross and dunes are undulating, "Northwest Wind" has the spacious, untrammeled, resounding and melodious styles given by the nature. With the poor fields, low rainfall, and cold weather, it has been created in such hostile environment; thus it owns vast, dismal, vehement and deep feelings given by poverty. Like the broken poplar blossoms on our shoulders, these rough songs have gotten a generation's suffering unloaded and become a part of our life.

The Shaolin Temple causes Kung Fu fever

Taking three years, the Chinese mainland and the Hongkong Zhongyuan Film Company co-produced the first Kung Fu film. *The Shaolin Temple* was an unprecedented attempt. It not only gathered hundreds of martial artists but also brought the real ancient Shaolin Temple to the big screen.

With great repercussion, the classic Kung Fu film released to the public in 1982, in Mainland China, Hong Kong and Korea. The price of a cinema ticket

A propaganda poster of the film The Shaolin Temple

was only 1 *jiao* in the mainland. The film generated RMB100 million in the box office. Jet Li, starred and became famous. In the film, Jet Li, was less than 20 years old and fully showed his consummate military skills including Chinese boxing, swords and sticks, and soft weapons, which broadened people's horizon.

Thanks to *The Shaolin Temple*, Jet Li has become another famous Chinese action star after Bruce Lee and Jackie Chan.

People have shown special preference for *The Shaolin Temple* because they had seen a real entertainment film as well as the real military skills and the miraculous military gestures showed by Jet Li without any performing trace in the mysterious temple with the elegant and beautiful scenery. The film has achieved success.

Making a sensation throughout the country, the release of *The Shaolin Temple* caused fever of Kung Fu. Even many teenagers went to the Shaolin Temple to pay their respects to masters and to learn Kung Fu. It even triggered a public discussion on whether teenagers should watch Chinese swordplay films.

Someone could not bear the "Misty Poems"

The Misty Poets were a group of the 20th Century Chinese poets that were public idols in the 1980s. Many poems of Bei Dao, Shu Ting and others were published in publications across the country.

The Answer, a poem of Bei Dao, marked the beginning of the era of "Misty Poems":

Baseness is a passport for the base, honor an epitaph for the honorable.

In August 1980, Zhang Ming, a writer, published an article named *The Stuffy Mistiness*, in which such poems were partially called the "Misty Poems". That was how they got their name.

As a lucky one among the Misty Poets, Shu Ting had the most readers. *To the Oak Tree*, Shu Ting's first work for the public, has been a required reading in middle school:

If I love you –

I will never be a clinging trumpet creeper,

Using your high boughs to show off my height;

…

I must be a ceiba tree beside you,

Be the image of a tree standing together with you.

Many people read this poem with passion at their weddings to express their yearnings and pursuits for love.

At dusk of March 26, 1989, the famous poet, Hai Zi, ended his life by lying on the path of a train between Shanhaiguan and Longjiaying. However, his poem has been in the heart of a generation forever:

From tomorrow on, I will be a happy man

Grooming, chopping, and traveling all over the world

From tomorrow on, I will care foodstuff and vegetable

Living in a house towards the sea

Generally, people haven't paid much attention to the "Misty Poems" and other poems.

Chinese were proud of the women's volleyball team

In November 1981, the Chinese women's volleyball team competed in the Third World Cup Volleyball Match in Japan. After seven rounds of 28 matches, on November 16, China's team won the world championship on the basis of an overall victory.

Lang Ping, the "Iron Hammer" in the Chinese women's volleyball team.

Provided by Beijing Archives

All the Chinese rejoiced at the first world championship.

It was just a beginning. Over the next few years, the Chinese women's volleyball team got five consecutive championships. We can't remember how many people cheered. The Chinese women's volleyball team made people think of the famous saying "life can have several beats".

With an echo of the five consecutive championships, *Volleyball*, a Japanese TV series became popular in China. A group of female volleyball players, represented by Oka Junko, used magic skills such as "a bolt from the blue" and "swift action" to make volleyball all the rage. Many were moved by their consummate skills and the humane story of friendship.

On November 20, 1985, Nie Weiping, a Chinese challenger, continuously defeated Kobayashi Koichi and Masao Kato, the first-rate Japanese chess players. Finally, Nie triumphed over Hideyuki Fujisawa, the Japanese life honorary "chess emperor" and won victory of the first Sino-Japan Weiqi Chess Challenge Series.

It was Nie Weiping that Chinese were proud of in 1985.

The road of life becomes narrower and narrower

The "Pan Xiao's Discussion" in 1980 was "the first love of the Chinese young generation's thought", according to a later monograph.

A letter named *The road of life ah, how it becomes narrower and narrower* signed by Pan Xiao was published in *China Youth* No.5, 1980. Today, people are still moved by the depth, bitterness, gloominess, sincerity and indignation in the letter.

The road of life ah, how it becomes narrower and narrower; but I have been very tired ah, as if once giving a sigh of relief means a completely extinction. Actually, I once went to a Christian church and watched the religious service secretly; and I had an idea of being a nun; even I wanted to go to die... My mind was extremely confused and contradictory.

Nowadays, we all know "Pan Xiao" doesn't exist. In fact, "Pan" represents Pan Yi, a sophomore in Beijing Institute of Economy; and "Xiao" represents Huang

Xiaoju, a young woman in Beijing Fifth Woolen Sweater Mill.

At that time, the editor of *China Youth* separately made arrangements in advance with them for their contributions. Then they separately selected a word from their own names to make up the pseudonym.

"Pan Xiao's Discussion" made the summer "hot".

According to statistics on June 9, less than a month, the magazine received more than 20,000 letters.

Initially, many letters talked about the meaning of life as well as expressed the appreciation and admiration for the discussion itself:

"How many young people across the country are like Pan Xiao who hope for spiritual manna and yearn for a torch to light the youthful enthusiasm."

"It's the reality. Though it's ugly, it's more powerful than the false things glossed over by people."

"As an aspiration of an honest person, it can strike a responsive chord in the hearts of other honest people."

"Thanks to the person who braved to write it and the person who allowed to publish it."

Lots of money and packages came from all over the country to express the sympathy and love to "Pan Xiao", the "weak woman".

In July and August, the hottest months among a year, "Pan Xiao's Discussion" reached its peak: numerous readers' letters were brought every day. More and more readers called or went to the editorial department directly asking to meet Pan Xiao. There were even some people who pretended to be Pan Xiao. Reporters from various press units gathered around the editorial department to interview Pan Xiao directly.

On August 20, a special report about Huang Xiaoju was broadcast on CCTV after the *Network News Broadcast*. Huang Xiaoju explained the letter to hundreds of millions of audiences. In the end, her positive and moral declaration became a well-known saying widely read:

"We can't live as flies just due to the garbage in society!"

With high paraplegia, Zhang Haidi learns four foreign languages by herself

In 1983, Zhang Haidi, a youth with broken body but firm spirit, became a model.

At the age of five, due to a spinal cord tumor and high paraplegia, Zhang Haidi's body was two-thirds paralyzed.

She overcame the disease through willpower and strove for success that even healthy people couldn't achieve. She studied medicine and technology independently and treated more than 10,000 patients. Moreover, she learnt four foreign languages by herself and translated many works and materials.

Zhang was named one of the five most outstanding disabled people in the world by NHK television station and one of the 20 most powerful women

On April 10, 1985, Zhou Yinchang, Zhang Haidi and other comrades at the closing meeting.

Provided by Beijing Archives

On April 10, 1985, Zhang Haidi gave the closing speech of the "Seminar of the Youth's Ideological Education".

Provided by Beijing Archives

round the world by *Globe* magazine of Xinhua News Agency.

For Zhang Haidi, the day April 2, 1993, was unforgettable. After passing a series of strict tests and defending a high-level master's thesis at Jilin University, Zhang became the only master student that had not been to college among the hundreds of thousands of master students. She became a master of philosophy and finished her studies on a wheelchair.

There was a photo that Zhang standing at the age of five observably hanging in her room. She had not stood up since then. Once she sadly said: "If I have known I was only for five years of health, I would keep on running and never stop; if I had known I could feel pain for only five years, I would tumble more times to enjoy the feeling of the pain."

The frog sunglasses from Atlantis

As a kind of sunglasses, the frog sunglasses (also called oversized sunglasses), with large lenses and light colors, were designed to prevent the bright sunlight and strong wind from damaging or discomforting the eyes. They were fashionable in the 1980s among the young in cities. Fashionable men and women favored wearing frog sunglasses.

Why were they called frog sunglasses?

Due to the large lenses and light colors, people wearing them looked like frogs. Therefore, people called them frog sunglasses.

The *Man from Atlantis* was the first American science fiction television series

Frog sunglasses were popular for a time.

to be shown on CCTV in 1980. This American TV series created a great sensation across the country for the mysterious western world, the science fiction plots and the novelties that could be seen everywhere. As the leading character, Mark Harris with a giant stature and solemn look always wore a pair of frog sunglasses. Indeed, he was majestic looking and graceful. One moment, the image of Mark Harris was popular among the youths; and in today's catchword, they became the "fans" of Mark.

The body size of Mark Harris was innate; while it was impossible to have such a stature. But it was easy to wear such a pair of sunglasses. Thus, many fashionable youths tried every means to buy a pair of sunglasses like Mark Harris'.

One moment, no matter what shape their face, young people wore those sunglasses. In the street, many people's faces looked like the big eyes of frogs.

The actor You Yong recalled: "'Mark's sunglass' were an important symbol in the pop history of China. Known as 'frog sunglasses', this kind of sunglasses was the most popular element; however, people couldn't buy them at that time in China. Although the ones I bought were counterfeits, they were quite fashionable."

In those days, it was an outstanding feature to wear the frog sunglasses with the brands for showing that they were authentic "foreign goods". Because the foreign letters on brands could satisfy their vanities more or less.

In fact, few frog sunglasses were imported and most of them were copied by some factories. Compared with the old-fashioned sunglasses, frog sunglasses were fashionable and beautiful.

"Palm phones" as big as a brick

According to *Workers' Daily* on March 5, 1985, "a fever of private telephones" appeared in Shanghai from October, 1984. The average of household applying to install private telephones every day reached 1,500 from October to December.

Private telephones generally came into ordinary households throughout the 1990s. At the afternoon of June 24, 2001, Bian Jinkai, a lineman in Shanghai Telecoms, dismantled the communication equipments at a messenger call service station in Newbridge. Because almost every household installed telephones and nobody used messenger calls.

In 1987, Motorola Company launched a mobile phone as large as a brick whose name was mobile phone of 800M and ordinary people called it "palm phones".

Suddenly, "palm phones" became a status symbol; because prominent people of various circles including labor contractors, bosses and the first group of Chinese investors owned them. Holding the palm phones and speaking loudly on the road, a person would attract others' envy. Without doing anything or saying anything, the owner sat on a public place and put the palm phone on the table, which obviously was worth a thousand words for showing off.

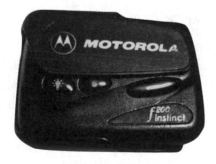

⊙ ───────────────
A VP of Motorola with a Chinese phone, which was a relatively better one.

At that time, the range of people's monthly income was RMB100 to several hundreds. A palm phone cost more than RMB30,000. Add the network access fee and the phone cost more than RMB40,000. In the black market, it was much higher reaching RMB50,000 . The call charges were very high as well. Thus, ordinary people couldn't afford the palm phone and use it. With high prices, the palm phones were insufficiently supplied and had to be imported from Hong Kong. Without strong abilities, people who had enough money couldn't always get one.

In those days, a person with a palm phone at the hand, needless to say was likely to have thousands of RMB or be very important. Other people envied, revered and admired them.

After the palm phone, pagers appeared. With the popularizing rate generally rising, the pagers upgraded from digits to Chinese demonstration.

Sometimes they were called "beepers".

At that time, it would cost more than RMB2,000 for network access for a pager. What was more, people had to request others with strong abilities to buy it.

A "call me" message was fashionable.

Civilians had the right to buy gold rings and gold necklaces

Since 1981, treasury bills have been issued at home; and the amount issued in the same year was between RMB4 billion to RMB5 billion .

On August 9, 1982, the People's Bank of China allowed the sale of gold products at home.

Pan Xinhua and Liu Kaiming, the reporters of *Xinmin Evening News*, came to the "Shanghai Arts and Crafts Service Department" in the west of the Grand Theater on Nanjing West Road in Shanghai in the early morning of September 28, 1982.

With the store opening, Pan found only three kinds of gold ornaments: rings, necklaces, and heart-shaped pendants of 14K at the price of RMB30 per gram, lying on the counters.

It was the first day that gold ornaments could be sold.

When Pan Xinhua gazed into the gold ornaments, customers were queuing up in the store.

Taking the lead, a woman, the worker in a woolen sweater mill and her son who especially accompanied his mother, bought a 14K gold ring whose price was RMB37.1.

"We make a good life; and everyone has his own job. Thus, we decide to buy a gold ring."

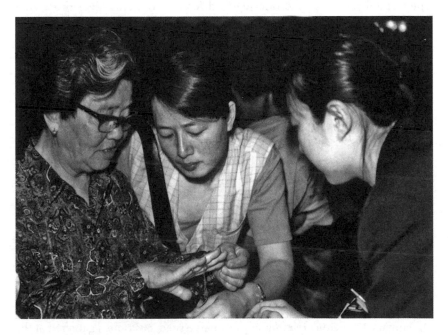

"Help me to choose one." An old woman who was selecting ornaments at Beijing Caishikou Department Store.

Provided by Beijing Archives

The son said: "My mother used her own money to buy it."

The manager of the store, Ye Hongnian, told Pan Xinhua that: "Today, the gold ornaments sold are of 14K; while, on November 3, the gold ornaments with higher purity will be sold."

On November 3, 1982, Pan came into the store again and found the types of gold ornaments increased. Moreover, the purity of some gold ornaments was 18K. At that time, the price of the cheapest one among the gold ornaments of 18K was RMB49.2, which was even higher than RMB42, the monthly wages of a worker at first level. Among the rings, some types the old people in Shanghai liked were added, such as glitter rings and flower rings; so did the necklaces. Rectangular necklaces and necklaces were added as well.

The Central Bank stopped offering gold for the gold and silver processing industry in 1964. Actually, after that, civilians couldn't buy gold ornaments in any channels until 1982, which lasted for 18 years. (*The Beijing News* on December 28, 2008)

Panic purchasing

On December 18, 1981, the State Council decided to reduce the prices of polyester-mixed cotton cloths and raise the prices of tobacco and wine. People couldn't adapt themselves to the prices rising.

In January 1983, the Central Committee of the Communist Party of China and the State Council decided to substantially reduce the prices of chemical fabrics and properly raise the prices of Cambodian textiles from January 20. Meanwhile, the State Council also decided to reduce the prices of partial light industrial and electronic products including watches, alarm clocks, cotton rubber shoes, roll films, color television sets and partial electric fans and so on.

On January 17, the day relevant notifications issued, customers gathered at the counters selling cotton textiles at the Department Store as well as the counters selling towels and children's garments. On that day, customers rushing to purchase didn't leave until 11 pm.

In November 1983, Ministry of Commerce announced that cotton cloths and

Panic purchasing in 1988. The young man gave all his money to purchase gold necklaces.

bat wools would be sufficiently supplied without limits and coupons would be temporarily suspended from December 1. Due to some worries, customers rushed to purchase cotton fabric.

Throughout the 1980s, buying sprees like the one in 1983 happened at all times and places because of the shortage of commodities as well as people's urge to improve their quality of life. Department stores were the first target where people rushed to purchase commodities. Commodities people purchased included leather shoes, fur caps, down jackets, suits, refrigerators, electric fans, radios, televisions, chemical fabrics, seersuckers, and woolen yarns and so on. In the first few years, people rushed to purchase new products including new styles, new design and colors, and new species; in the later years, people were not so crazy and just rushed to buy famous-brand products.

The guardrails were applied around the counters for the security of customers. When stores opened, customers ran to the counters as if they were in the race. Therefore, people called it "business is war".

In 1988, China's reform entered a critical stage. The prices of a few important commodities and labor services were controlled by the government and prices of most commodities were regulated by the market.

Rush to purchase! Rush to purchase! In 1988, rushing to purchase made a strong impression on people and swept through the whole country.

Prices began "making a breakthrough" in Shanghai. In March 1988, the Shanghai government adjusted the retail prices of 280 kinds of commodities that belonged to petty commodities and daily necessities with the price-rise between 20% to 30%. Soon, the prices in other places were out of control, which caused a panic purchasing in summer.

According to the newspaper: "People are so crazy that buy everything they see. They rush to buy not only the commodities that can retain their values, but also the consumer goods as well as the dead stocks."

The national government decided to open the prices of the 13 kinds of cigarettes and wines in the market on July 28. After that, it was in just a few hours after the openness of stores in Beijing, Tianjin and Shanghai that the cigarettes and wines prepared for selling in one day were snapped up. On the afternoon of that day, more than 30 points of sale in Beijing concertedly raised the prices. What was more, the prices were regulated separately on 29th and 30th in big cities, so that the situation generally was stable.

In August, there were many rumors going the rounds that the prices would generally rise on September 1. So, in the mid-August, the forebodings of panic purchasing appeared. On August 17 and 18, it was obvious that the panic purchasing would happen in Shanghai. Matches, soaps, washing powders, towels, coverlets, and aluminum pots were hot in the market. On August 19, buying spree swept across the country.

Taking Shanghai for example, commodities people rushed to buy included leather jackets, eiderdown quilts, camel hair quilts, woolen blankets, toweling coverlets, woolen yarns, bed covers, cotton sweater and trousers, singlet vests, washing machines, vacuum cleaners, range hoods, high-grade sound recorders, video recovers, and gold ornaments and so on. So many people withdrew cash from banks that Shanghai Bank was in an emergency. Hualian Department Store in Shanghai sold one washing machine every two minutes and it sold 500 washing machines one day. On August 27, cash sales amount reached RMB2.3 million, a record.

On August 28, the buying spree in Shanghai went into climax. Thus, the Shanghai Government had to take emergency measures. People bought salt and matches within the limits of coupons and bought new aluminum pots with the old ones relying on marriage certificates or residence registrations.

From August 29 to 31, not all commodities' prices rose so the purchasing spree generally disappeared.

After the 1990s, this phenomenon went down in history.

The villages owning televisions

In the late 1970s, black-and-white televisions with several channels appeared. At that time, the televisions were in short supply. However, a lot of families wanted to have one.

In February 1980, *In Enemy Camp for 18 Years*, a nine-volume TV series broadcast on CCTV, had remarkable significance. As the first TV series in China and the first melodrama, it aroused extensive attention.

In 1981, more and more Chinese were attracted by *The Garrison Dare-to-die Corps*. When it was broadcast, even the thieves wouldn't work because of the empty streets. Through it, people acquainted that there was no precise point between good people and bad people.

The Spring Festival Party was broadcast on CCTV for the first time on New Year's Eve of 1983. Since then, many Chinese would make dumplings, play with firecrackers and watch the Spring Festival Parties on every New Year's Eve.

The first Chinese production line of color televisions was built in Tianjin Wireless Factory on October 22, 1980 by the Victor Company in Japan. It could produce14-inch and 21-inch color televisions and 150,000 sets per year.

↑

The Hitachi color television.

It was difficult to buy a color television throughout the late 1980s.

According to *Workers' Daily* on January 3, 1984, 80% of families in big cities owned televisions and more than 360 villages owned televisions just in Hebei Province. Some villages owning color televisions were built in Shandong and Heilongjiang Provinces.

According to *People's Daily* on August 26, 1984, in the end of 1983, there were 35 million televisions throughout the country, among which 8 million were in villages.

According to Xinhua News Agency, on August 13, 1985, there were 3,000 villages owning televisions across the country.

Girls asking for too many things for the marriage

From the 1980s, people would say "*tan lian ai*" (they fell in love).

Before that, as for "*tan lian ai*", people usually expressed it in words – "*chu pengyou*" (being girlfriend/ or boyfriend) or "*gao duixiang*" (being a true love of one's).

In the 1980s, weddings grew grander and grander and dowries changed considerably: "*Laosanjian*" (three valuable articles in the past) including watches, bicycles and sewing machines were replaced by "*Xinsanjian*" (three valuable articles in the later period time) including black-and-white televisions, refrigerators and washing machines.

Shen Jian, the manager of Chunshenji Collection in Shanghai recalled:

Shen Jian made preparation for his wedding in 1988. According to the tradition in Shanghai, he needed to prepare "*Sandajian*" (three valuable articles), a sewing machine, a bicycle and a color television. After their discussion, they decided that the bride's family prepared the first article and they regarded a "phenix" bicycle of half new as the second one; while it was difficult for Shen Jian to get a color television.

In several twists and turns, Shen found a friend who had friends in high places. With cups going gaily round, his friend confidently said to solve his difficulty. However, in the three days before wedding, the friend informed Shen that, sorry, he couldn't get a color television. Shen was depressed immediately.

 ———————————

Wedding pictures in the 1980s.

Provided by the National Costume Museum of Beijing Institute of Fashion Technology

Returning home from work, he passed by a Xinhua Bookstore in Xujiahui and read an advertisement – "buy books to win a color television". Grinding his teeth, he bought the books with two thirds of his monthly income. Fortunately, he won the prize – a ticket of Kaige television.

"I immediately felt so well that I brought the television back by bicycle at that night; and I focused my eyes on it until the screen was snowy." Shen Jian smilingly said. (Zhang Juncai: *The Vicissitudes of Coupons* published in *China Economic Weekly* No.42, on November 17, 2008)

In those days, modular furniture was popular throughout the country. The "*Sidagui*" (four cabinets) referred to a TV bench, a wardrobe, a decorative cabinet and a bookshelf that were almost necessities for marriage in Shanghai, while the requirements of a marriage in other places were much lower.

At that time, an ordinary family only owned a chest of drawers. Though people didn't have many clothes, they always wore the wrong clothes because entire families used one chest. The mother comforted her daughter: "When we live in a better life, everyone will own a chest." Therefore, unlike the "*gaojia* girls" (girls asking for too many things for the marriage), some ordinary girls only requested a three-door wardrobe with a dressing mirror.

"*Hai Lu Kong*" was a characteristic word in the 1980s. It was a mate-selection criteria by smart Shanghai girls. The word "*Hai*" meant a man with overseas relations. The word "*Lu*" sounded like "*Luo*", which actually meant a family of policymaker. And "*Kong*" meant a family that owned an empty house. This showed how young girls in those days chose mates based on concrete needs.

At that time, another mate-selection criteria Shanghai girls used was "*Wudayuan*" that meant "a man who was a party member with a physique as strong as sportsmen, an appearance as handsome as an actor, salaries as high as seamen and wit as quick as drivers".

There was a jingle about choosing a mate that said: "First, one set of furniture, second, two dead parents, third, three machines as well as a ringing things (bicycles, sewing machines, watches and a music machine), fourth, four seasons wearing suits and standing straight, fifth, regular features, sixth, disowning all his relatives and friends, seventh, seventy yuan (wage), eighth, being capable of dealing with all men, ninth, no drinking or smoking, tenth, being perfect in every respect."

In those days, the bride's side, especially, some wife's mothers asked for bride prices so high that the bridegroom often could not afford them. The "*gaojia* girls" in many places, especially in Shanghai, caused public criticism.

In 1981, fourteen female workers in the Shanghai Third Bulb Factory proposed "setting up a right view-point of love and not being '*gaojia* girls'". The luxurious wedding was not necessary. Girls shouldn't ask for "*Hai, Lu, Kong*" or "*Quanji Quanya*" (referring to color televisions, radio recorders, washing machines, eiderdowns and down-pillows, etc.) or show off their dowries. Girls should choose a man with desire to advance and pleasant character as their husbands. After marriage, they could create a better life by themselves. With a response of many girls in Shanghai, the proposal was widely supported.

"Honeymoons" and "marriage trips"

On February 20, 1980, the State Labor Bureau and Ministry of Finance announced the *Notice About the Marriage, Funeral and Distance Leave of the State-owned Enterprise Workers*, which indicated that marriage leave of workers marrying at a mature age would extend to 15 days. Thus, "honeymoons" and "marriage trips" swept through the country. When people took trips, they would take photos that reflected the fashion and trace in an era.

In October 1980, the Communist Youth League of Bureau of Public Utilities in Tianjin organized a group marriage trip for young people, which was novel and popular in those days.

In the 1980s, the typical wedding involved a great meal and a fun gathering. When it was time for us to get married, we yearned the capital and wouldn't like to follow the traditional marriage. Thus, singing the song *I Love the Tian'anmen Square in Being* and heading north, we started our cherished honeymoon trips. Actually, most people chose a city for their marriage trips in the 1980s.

In August 1982, we had just graduated from college. After taking a rest, we started our trip to the capital. Carrying certificates provided by our work unit, college diplomas and a marriage certificate, we boarded a train in the Beijing-

The photo of marriage trip in the 1980s.

Guangzhou line. It was the first time for us to go to Beijing without any tasks. What made us confident was the RMB400 in our pockets that our parents gave us. Our parents separately gave us RMB200 to prepare for our wedding. At that time, people's monthly salary was about RMB30; so the money equaled to a year of income.

As industrious farmers, we went out in the morning and had a rest in the evening. Starting from Tian'anmen Square, we visited all scenic spots that were allowed to visit. The money at that time seemed to be more valuable than today. We spent only RMB10 eating and visiting in one day. All tickets including entrance tickets and bus tickets could be included. In my memory, the scenic spots were not like the gardens within gardens today. Having the entrance tickets, we had to buy another ticket for subordinate scenic spots. The price of the entrance ticket was five *jiao*, which was expensive. Generally, the prices of tickets were five fen or one *jiao* at most.

We took a marriage trip just after it started to be popular. (Recall: My

Honeymoon Trip – Visiting Beijing in the 1980s published in *The Great Wall On Line* on December 22, 2004)

"The firstborn is allowed, while the other babies are forbidden"

In 1980, Central Committee of the CCP published *An Open Letter to Party Members and Youth League Members about Controlling China's Population Growth*, in which it said that "we shall try our best to control the China's population within 1.2 billion during this century" and solemnly appealed for "a coupe having one child".

In September 1982, the Twelfth National Congress of the CPC made family planning one of the basic national policies of our country and explained its meaning, policies and guidelines and targets in detail. In November, the new constitution passed in the fifth session of the Fifth Standing Committee of the NPC clearly stipulated: "The family planning policy shall be carried out in China… Both husband and wife shall have the duty to practice family planning".

Family planning policy is the best; and one child was the best.

Propagandizing family planning policies in the villages.

Provided by Beijing Archives

The one child policy was the reflection of times. As a basic national policy, the family planning policy that a couple should have one child was extreme and strictly implemented in cities in the 1980s. During this period, a large number of single children were born. "The generation after 80s" and all its problems were the product of that period.

Nowadays, people think the slogans of the family planning policy are ridiculous:

"Proud of family planning, ashamed of son preference";

"Proud of having sex with a condom, ashamed of carelessness";

"A man again, whole village ligation";

"One person ligation, whole family honor";

"A person isn't ligatured as required, others will catch him";

"After ligation, a woman will fall ill; while a man well be fine!";

"Having a certificate to be pregnant and holding a certificate to birth!";

"Forbidding birthing the second baby";

"Popularizing one child, controlling two children and eliminating three children";

"Break the family rather than destroy the country";

"The firstborn is allowed, while the other babies are forbidden".

More ridiculously: "If a person isn't ligatured as required, his house will collapse; if a woman doesn't have an abortion as required, others will demolish her house and lead her cows away". Through these, people discovered how strongly the family planning policy was implemented.

At 8:56 am on March 10, 1988, the first test-tube baby was successfully born in Beijing Medical University third Subsidiary Hospital, which was a major breakthrough in reproductive medicine in China. After the invention of condoms, it was another success in separating reproduction from sex.

"Incompatibility" was a legal reason for divorce

In 1980, "incompatibility" was a legal ground for divorce according to the second Marriage Law in new China, which ensured people's right to divorce according to the law. This also eliminated stable marriages.

What's more, the traditional marriage value that people should be loyal to their spouse until death was totally shaken. Since then, "incompatibility" has been a common legal basis for divorce and the saying of Engels' has been often cited that "a loveless marriage is immoral".

Article 25 in the new Marriage Law stated: "People's Court shall carry out mediation; divorce shall be granted if mediation fails because mutual affection no longer exists".

The Marriage Law of 1950 was the first law as well as the first marriage law in New China. The Marriage Law in 1950 did not provide legal grounds for divorce.

To confirm the standards of divorce, the Supreme People's Court made the appropriate judicial interpretation from 1950 to 1980. Through the judicial interpretation, we know that the legal grounds for divorce included no contact between husband and wife, the unknown whereabouts of a spouse, the illness of a spouse and one party being less than the legally marriageable age. The principle of divorce was included in the *Opinions on Implementing the Civil Policies* issued by the Supreme People's Court on August 28, 1963.

It pointed out that whether a couple divorced or not, the court should first consider the basis for the marriage (free courtship or arranged marriage), the emotions after the marriage and the grounds for divorce and should check

A group wedding in the 1980s

on whether the couple could remain together. Second, the court said it had to consider the impact on the children and the social impact. The judges called the standards of divorce "considering three points and referring to one point"; that's to say, the basis for marriage, the emotion after marriage and the grounds for divorce should be considered; and the children's benefit and social impact should be referred to. In the standards of marriage, the "emotional" factor appeared but was not obvious.

Although the state amended the Marriage Law several times, it was the Marriage Law in 1980 with the word "incompatibility" that went down in the history of reform and opening-up. The significance of it was that people couldn't regard divorce as a punishment.

Many people at the time thought that the Marriage Law in 1980 was the reason for the divorce rate increasing in 1981. According to *The Record of Home Affairs in Shanghai*, the number of divorces was 883 in Shanghai in 1980 and 1304 in 1981.

Yang Dawen, a professor at the Law School of People's University and director of Marriage And Family Law Institution, participated in the revision of the Marriage Law in 1980 and didn't agree with it. Yang said: "In the past, it was too strict to divorce; so part of the divorces in 1981 solved problems left over".

Divorce agreement for a merry parting

Eating a "breaking-up meal" was popular in Beijing in 1987.

If paid much attention, people would find that some couples respected each other like guests and took their children to have meals in some famous restaurants in Beijing, such as "Peking Eastern House", "Peking Duck Restaurant" and "Xinqiao Western Restaurant". Actually, after finishing the divorce proceedings, the couples had a "breaking-up meal" in those restaurants. In the "Cuihua House" restaurant, a divorced couple took their six-year-old son to a "breaking-up meal". They told the reporter that due to incompatibility they had been living apart for two years. The wife proposed a divorce and the husband agreed. After finishing the divorce proceedings, to avoid hurting the child's feelings, both of them agreed to gather to give suggestions and wishes to each other.

Nowadays, many couples have divorced with fewer insulting words and quarrels during the division of property. Three characteristics of the changed divorce concepts are as follows:

First, the ratio of agreements in divorce has increased. Fewer couples ask the court for divorce sentences. Most of them divorce by mutual agreement in subdistrict offices without quarrel.

Second, both sides keep calm in regards to family property and child custody. They make allowances for each other with lofty stance and reasons.

Third, they wish each other well and separate peacefully.

In 1989, the caseload of divorce cases the court at all levels across the country reached 750,000, three times higher than in 1980. More amazingly, among these cases, the plaintiffs of 70% to 80% were women. Sociologists called it "the phenomenon of repudiating one's husband".

The passionate prediction of *The Third Wave*

Transnational enterprises would prevail. The invention of computers made SOHO (working from home) possible. People would be free of the shackles of nine-to-five jobs. The nuclear family would crumble. The rise of DIY (do it yourself) was visible...

This was all part of *The Third Wave* written by Alvin Toffler, an American futurist, in 1983. Nowadays, we find that the prediction came true and still feel the passion behind them.

In those days, Toffler and *The Third Wave* had an impact on China, which had just opened the door. In his book *The Third Wave*, Toffler described three types of societies. The first wave was the agricultural stage from 10,000 years ago. The second wave was the industrial stage from the late 17th century. The third wave was informational (or service industry) from the late 1950s.

The third wave was another revolution of human thought that we call the "information age". Information technology and social needs created strong impetus for its development. As the world integrated, people who pursued cooperation broke national boundaries.

Perhaps, Toffler didn't directly bring us wealth; but he gave us a dream. After a few years, young people who read Toffler's books became mainstays of Chinese economic construction. They were guided to "create the future" by Toffler's thoughts, more or less.

After a year, in 1984, Wen Yuankai, who suggested to Deng Xiaoping to resume the college entrance exam, launched the book *Megatrends in China* that swept through the country. Wen became known as the "Chinese Toffler".

No.001 Doctor Ma Zhongqi

On January 1, 1981, the degree system was implemented nationwide. The State Council stipulated that academic degrees should be of three grades: the bachelor degree, the masters degree and the doctor degree. University graduates would be awarded the bachelor degree. Postgraduates would be awarded the masters degree. And postgraduates who studied for a doctorate should be awarded the doctor degree after graduation.

In the afternoon of May 27, 1983, the first congress to grant doctorates and masters degree was held in the Great Hall of the People in Beijing. There were 18 masters and doctors who were known as the "18 warriors". On the day, Ma Zhongqi was awarded the No.001 doctor's degree. To show the importance to this first group of postgraduates, the sponsor specially chose the Great Hall of the People as the place where the congress was held.

It was the first time Ma Zhongqi entered the Great Hall of the People. As the representative of the students, he made a speech on the platform. Ma dressed well for this congress. His unit gave him RMB200 to buy clothes; although he earned less than RMB100 a month at that time.

"Not very open-minded, I thought it was right to wear Chinese style clothes," Ma dressed in blue casual dress. "At that time, there was no doctoral gowns or doctoral hats."

Doctors began wearing doctoral gowns and doctoral hats in the middle 1980s, which were designed by teachers in Central Craft Art College.

The doctor's degree certificate Ma Zhongqi acquired was signed and issued by Qian Sanqiang, the famous scientist and director of physics department in the Chinese Academy of Sciences.

Ma Zhongqi was 43 years old when he got the doctorate. Among the 18 people, there were nine people of more than 40 years. The youngest, Wan Jianpan, was 34 years old. (Guo Shaofeng: Recruiting the Postgraduate Again: from "Privileged Class" to "Academic Warriors" published in *The Beijing News*, on May 27, 2008)

People were afraid of telling others that they were RMB10,000 a year household

The buzzword "*Wanyuanhu*" was a title many farmers admired at in the early 1980s. As the name implied, it meant a household with an annual income of RMB10,000 or a household with savings reaching RMB10,000. At that time, in villages *Wanyuanhu* stood for the people who became prosperous first. It meant a household had huge wealth.

On April 18, 1980, a news report titled *The Spring in Yantan* was published by Xinhua News Agency, which said that as a farmer in Tanjianzi production brigade of Yantan commune in Lanzhou City, Li Dexiang with another five laborers in his family earned RMB10,000 from the production brigade at the end of 1979. Therefore, other commune members called his family "*Wanyuanhu*". Li was the first household with an annual income of RMB10,000 made public.

On November 17, 1980, Xinhua News Agency published a photo by Li Jin, a reporter. It showed Zhao Rulan, a commune member of Bachalu commune in Zhaotatou Village, Linqing County, who had earned RMB10,239 in a year from the cotton fields and was the first household with an annual income of RMB10,000 in Shandong Province reported by media. Zhao Rulan was the first Shandong Province *Wanyuanhu* to appear in the newspaper. About 51 news media ran the photo and the report and the word *Wanyuanhu* became popular.

Zhao Rulan passed away in 2004. Wang Lifen, his wife, looked back: "The children's father and the children were busy in the cotton fields in those days. At the end of the year, we sold the cotton and earned RMB10,000. We became a household with an annual income of RMB10,000. Since then, our family didn't have to worry about clothing and food. With the money we earned, we bought five bicycles, three sewing machines, two watches, one desk clock and two radios."

Zhao Guangze, the first son of Zhao Rulan, recalled: "When leaders asked about our annual income, my father was 'scared' and hesitantly answered little money". (People Were Afraid of Telling Others That They were "Wanyuanhu" published in *Qilu Evening News* on October 16, 2008)

Wanyuanhu turned a new page of prosperity in China.

The first group of individual households

In the late 1970s, most educated youths were heading back to cities increasing the pressure for employment, which created a class of youth waiting for employment.

In 1979, Yi Shengxi, a leader of the supply and marketing cooperative in Dashilan sub-district office in Beijing that lead 20 youths, sold tea at a stall at Qianmen for RMB1,000. Starting from the Big Bowl Tea for RMB0.02 and getting larger and lager, they set up companies in Beijing, Shenzhen and Hainan. The Big Bowl Tea stood for reform and opening-up and hard work and an enterprising spirit.

On June 21, 1980, the Beijing Administration for Industry and Commerce said that: The youths waiting for employment and the retired workers forbidden from running individual businesses before were allowed to operate them. The range of individual businesses included: shoe repair, bicycle repair, haircuts and sewing that were allowed before as well as house repair, shoeshine, three-wheel transport, letter writing, newspapers sales and tea sales that were added later. As for the businesses requiring high technology and needed in society, such as tailoring and fluffing cotton, a retired worker with one or two youth in a small team was allowed to manufacture and process them.

At the end of November in 1979, Zhang Huamei, a nineteen-year-old girl supported by her father, became "the first to eat crab" among the seven brothers and sisters selling cheap daily commodities at a stall in front of her house. At that time, it was illegal. Her commodities could be confiscated by the staff in the office if they cracked down on speculation. However, without jobs, Zhang relied on the stall to live. It was good to earn RMB100.

Why didn't the staff in the office crack down? Because the reform and opening-up policy had spread around the whole nation. One result was that the office shifted from cracking down on speculation to managing industry and commerce. According to the regulations, it informed Zhang Huamei to get a business license. (Qian Jiang: Zhang Huamei, the First Individual Household in the Mainland published in *People's Daily Overseas Edition* on December 8, 2008)

A self-employed salesman who sold clothes snatching a little leisure from the rush of business to eat noodles on the counter in the street of Wuhan.

Without hesitation, Zhang applied for the license. On December 11, 1980, the management of industry and commerce in Gulou issued the business license No.10101 with the seal of Wenzhou Administration for Industry and Commerce to her, the first business license for individual business in Mainland China.

Later, Zhang Huamei recalled: "In those days, people who did small business not only were despised by others but also worried about being caught by staff in the office for cracking down the speculation. Therefore, the stalls were small to easily pick them up. When the staff appeared, they immediately picked them up. We were nervous to do the business. These staff not only fined us but also confiscated all the commodities. We also feared the staff managing the market from the Industrial and Commercial Bureau."

Township enterprises, a new force suddenly rising

After the implement of the "all-round contract" with the enough food, some farmers had new ideas. Some ran transportation businesses, sold cobblestones or weaved woolen yarn. Some even established enterprises in the valleys. They were filled with fear and afraid to save money they earned in banks.

At that time, there was no final conclusion on whether a private person could buy tractors and cars, whether a private person could run a transportation business, whether a private person could buy a share of a fishpond to share profits according to contributions or whether commune and brigade could run enterprises.

In 1983, the No.1 document from the Central Government suggested loosening control on industry and commerce in villages. In 1984, the document encouraged communes and brigades to run enterprises and specialized households to develop production for rich as well as allowed farmers to work in cities, do business and establish enterprises.

In the Pearl River Delta, South Jiangsun and Wenzhou, township enterprises, used to be "tails of capitalism" and spread like sparks of fire receiving hundreds of millions of farmers... Huaxi Village in Jiangyin City, Jiangsu Province, generally became the "telephone village", "color television village", "air-condition village" and "villa village". The village was completely changed by the South Jiangsu mode, Wenzhou mode and the South China Sea mode.

The predecessor of township enterprises was the rural handicraft industry as well as the commune and brigade enterprises. From 1978 to 1983, the commune and brigade enterprises were widely established across the country. In 1983, rural labor received by commune and brigade enterprises reached 32.35 million and the total value of output increased from RMB49.3 billion in 1978 to RMB101.7 billion in 1983.

In 1984, the No.4 document from the Central Government decided to change the name of commune and brigade enterprises into township enterprises and emphasized that the only road to promote the rural economy was to develop township enterprises with preferential policies in terms of loans and revenues and so on. In 1987, Deng Xiaoping regarded the township enterprises as "the greatest gain beyond expectation" and "a new force suddenly rising" in rural reform.

Suspension from duty without pay

Suspension from duty without pay was common in China in the early 1980s.

The suspension from duty without pay meant that surplus staff in enterprises were allowed to leave for individual business while retaining their office in the original enterprises.

According to the *Ministry of Labor and Personnel and National Economy Commission's Notice about Suspension from Duty Without Pay*: the period of suspension from duty without pay should less than two years. During the period, staff shouldn't promote or draw benefits, subsidies and labor insurance and welfare; the staff that lost the capacity to work as a result of disease or disability should be handled as if they had resigned from office. When the staff took leave without pay and took other jobs, they should pay labor insurance of not less than 20% of their original salary in the original unit on a monthly basis.

Suspension from duty without pay was a bridge between the "iron rice bowl" in the planned economy and "going into business" in the market economy.

On March 3, 1983, the Ministry of Labor and Personnel started to actively carry out the labor contract system. It pointed out that the policy of "new recruitment and the new system" should be in transition for a period. New recruits would be hired under the labor contract system. Original employees would still enjoy the existing system and reform step by step. Eventually the labor contract system would apply to all staff.

In the respect of China's employment system, the labor contract system was a significant reform.

On September 9, 1986, the State Council issued four temporary provisions of the labor system reform: *Temporary Provisions of State-owned Enterprises' Implementation of Labor Contract System, Temporary Provisions of State-owned Enterprises' Recruitment, Temporary Provisions of State-owned Enterprises' Dismissal of Workers with Violations*, and *Temporary Provisions of State-owned Enterprises' Workers' Unemployment Insurance*.

The four temporary provisions focused on the reform of employing and recruiting workers; that was, it would carry out the labor contract system for new recruits in state-owned enterprises and it would cancel the privilege of children taking the place of retired parents and internal recruitment. Facing society, recruitment would be public. Considering moral, intellectual and physical aspects, recruitment would be selective. According to the new provisions, state-owned enterprises could break original limit of the unit to make full use of worker's strong points, wishes and job needs.

The reform basically made Chinese farewell the traditional "iron rice bowl".

"Let's go into business"

Someone said, people in 1984 were uproarious and enthusiastic; some even called 1984 "the starting year of a company", "the first year to go into business" and "let's go into business" as these ideas spread among young people.

It seemed that the Pearl River Delta was the brightest area in 1984.

In 1983, Wang Shi arrived at Shenzhen and took a minibus to Shekou. At the T-junction of Shennan Road to Shekou, he saw several large white iron cans standing in the north of the road as well as another three mental cans like those on the Shekou wharf. People around there told Wang Shi who was curious about the use of cans that the cans were used as corn storages in feed mills. Chiatai Conti Group, a feed enterprise invested by Chia Tai Group in Thailand, the Continental Grain Company in America and the Chicken Farming Company in Shenzhen, was at the T-junction; and Shekou Far Eastern JinQian Flour Feed Enterprise, a flour and feed mill invested by Far Eastern Group in Singapore, was located on the Shekou wharf.

After making inquires, Wang Shi found that Hong Kong had to import a large amount of corn it needed from other places. He wondered why not directly transport the corn from the northeast to Hong Kong?

Wang Shi started his business of corn. In several twists and turns, he reached a deal with Chiatai Conti Group and earned RMB400,000 "with nothing", which was his first bucket of gold.

With his first profit, Wang created the Shenzhen Exhibition Center of Modern Instrument of Science and Education.

 The book about Liu Chuanzhi.

It was the predecessor of Vanke Limited Company.

Locating in the special economic zone and adjoining Hong Kong and Macao, the enterprises in the Pearl River Delta could find opportunities to develop.

In Zhongguancun Science Park, prosperity emerged. After leaving the Chinese Academy of Sciences, Liu Chuanzhi started the "Lenovo Group" by selling electric watches and roller skates and wholesaling running pants and refrigerators. After 20 years, he purchased IBM's PC department form US$1.25 billion.

For business experience, Liu honestly said, they received investment of about RMB200,000 at the start of the business in 1984 but were unexpectedly cheated by a woman and that led to a loss of RMB140,000 in less than a month. It was hard to imagine such a huge blow.

The generation of entrepreneurs started inconceivable business stories that they achieved self-transformation in soft or extreme ways.

Follow Me: the fever of learning foreign languages in China

From the beginning of 1982, Chinese audiences could watch *Follow Me* on television at 6: 20 pm every Tuesday, Thursday and Saturday and at 8:30 am every Sunday.

At that time, *Follow Me*, an instruction program produced by the British Broadcasting Corporation (BBC), spread all over the world. Katherine Flower, an anchorwoman of a French program became the anchorwoman of *Follow Me* in Chinese on CCTV.

In Chinese, Katherine's family name "Flower" is Hua and she gave herself the Chinese name Hua Kelin during her work in Chinese.

Hu Wenzhong, the deputy director of the English department at the Beijing Foreign Studies University, was invited by CCTV to host *Follow Me* with Hua Kelin.

Hu Wenzhong recalled that the morning following the broadcast of *Follow Me*, "I drank soybean milk on a restaurant and found many people looked at me;

Follow Me to Learn English was popular for a time. It still has a very good market.

but I had no idea what happened. An idea suddenly came into my mind that *Follow Me* had been broadcast yesterday. How fast the influence was!"

Television was not very popular in those days and it was the first time many people watched foreigners speaking English on television.

After the broadcast of *Follow Me*, *New Nation*, a magazine in Singapore reported that it was a red hair girl in London who spoke slowly rather than a worldwide leader, a sports star or an artist that was the most famous foreigner in China in the 1980s.

Never stopped talking with a foreigner at the English corners

In the 1980s, it was common to learn English and English corners appeared everywhere.

A well-known one was in West Street in Yangshuo, Guilin. With the foreign guests' increasing, people in West Street no matter what gender and age spontaneously learnt English to deal with and communicate with foreigners. In 1993, a young man named Owen came to Yangshuo. Attracted by the atmosphere of learning foreign languages, he thought of it as an optimal place to establish a foreign language school. Making unremitting efforts, Owen established the Barco Business Foreign Language School.

Most businessmen in West Street knew English. People there always did business or chatted with foreign guests in fluent English. Even old women more than 70 years old or children around 10 years old could talk with foreigners. After inspecting West Street, some authorities regarded West Street as the largest natural "English corner" in the mainland.

Due to the famous Foreign Language Bookstore on Hubin Road, an English corner appeared around the Sixth Park in Hangzhou in the 1980s. Around 8 pm in summer, a boisterous crowd gathered at the English corner. People including workers, bosses, teachers and students, communicated with others in fluent or faltering English. It was said that, the park was the largest English corner in Hangzhou with three or four hundred people gathering.

At that time, a few foreigners were in Hangzhou. A lot of them gathered at the English corner. People actively learnt English and never stopped talking with foreigners at the English corner. Sometimes, there were some "masters" at the English corner. The word "master" had two meanings: first, it meant people with solid English foundation and fluent oral English who aroused admiration; second, it meant people who were enthusiastic about English and brave to speak it. It was said that Ma Yun was once there.

Statistics suggested that the male to female ratio at the English corner in the Sixth Park was 2:3.

The Foreign Language Bookstore also became a place for an indoor English corner, along with English debating competitions of middle school students, lectures on English translation and autograph sessions by singers or writers.

The pencils and erasers used by TOEFL candidates came from America

The first mainland TOEFL test began simultaneously in Beijing, Shanghai, and Guangzhou in December 1981.

In some aspects, it was a first examination in the mainland: it was the first time an American standardized test was introduced to China, to use machine readable cards and to test English listening. Moreover, the TOEFL test provided a reference for the reform of the college entrance examination.

What was funny was that the pencils, erasers and pencil sharpeners as well as the materials students used were transported from America. The reason was that people were afraid that Chinese pencils were not bold enough to ensure the accuracy. The yellow pencil was marked "TOEFL" with an eraser on the top, which was better than the eraser in China. It would not leave a mark on the paper. There were two invigilators in every examination room who sharpened the pencils before the examination. Two pencils were put on every desk. If something was wrong with the pencil, a teacher would change it at any time.

Besides the two invigilators, there was a maintenance person who specially maintained the headsets in the examination room. Ten minutes before the examination, students tested the headsets. If there were problems with a headset, the maintenance person would change it immediately.

The TOEFL test had strict requirements. For example, students couldn't change their answers to the listening test. If an invigilator found the change, the students would be punished according to the regulations. At the end of the examination, the pencils would be regained and used in the next year's test.

As the TOEFL test was introduced, the standardized reform was conducted in the college entrance examination in China in 1985. Objective items were added and some subjective items were reserved. Such a reform not only drew lessons from the TOEFL test but also made innovations.

According to a media report, there were 732 persons participating in the first TOEFL test. In 2009, there were 130,000. (Wu Peng: TOEFL Test Brought Objective Items into Chinese College Entrance Examination published in *The Beijing News,* on December 17, 2008)

Time is money, efficiency is life

Approved by Deng Xiaoping in 1984, the slogan "time is money, efficiency is life" was the most famous to show the spirit of reform and opening-up. The slogan was put forward by Yuan Geng, director of the Shekou committee at that time.

When the slogan appeared, Yuan had been under intense external pressure because some thought the slogan was capitalist. On January 2, 1984, Deng Xiaoping inspected Shekou. On the boat named "Sea World", Yuan Geng braved to talk about the sensitive topic with Deng. Deng gave a positive response and said: "It was right." Yuan Geng was reassured.

On February 24, 1984, Deng Xiaoping had a conversion with the central leadership and said: "The construction in Shenzhen sped up with the slogan 'time is money, efficiency is life.'"

With Deng's approval, the slogan "time is money, efficiency is life" spread through the whole country and generally became a common view and a code of conduct for people. It was praised as "the first heart sound to break through the mind control". (*Shenzen Special Zone Daily* on March 3, 2008)

On National Day 1984, the grand military parade and mass pageant were held in the capital Beijing. In two floats belonging to Shenzhen, a float of Shekou Industrial Area hanged the slogan "time is money, efficiency is life". From Tian'anmen Square, it spread throughout the whole country; and it became an intellectual impetus that encouraged Chinese to make full use of every minute for reform and innovation.

It is convenient for people to carry resident identity cards

On April 6, 1984, according to the *Proposed Regulation of Resident Identity Card of People's Republic of China* promulgated by the State Council: Chinese citizens who live within the territory of the People's Republic of China, except for children under 16 years old, enlisted army, armed polices, prisoners serving a sentence and people undergoing the education-through-labor program, shall apply for resident identity cards.

The items to be registered in a resident identity card included name, sex, nationality, birth date, address and validity.

People shall take the resident identity card as evidence of identity to handle civil rights issues such as polities, economy and daily life.

Before the implementation of the resident identity card system, the household register was used to identify residents. After the reform and opening up, people's involvement in policy, economy and daily life greatly increased. As a result, more activities required cards such as voter registration, children entering a higher school, employment, notarization, extraction of remittances and mail in the post office, sales on commission, travel tickets, visiting relatives and friends in other places, tourism and staying in hotels and so on.

Staff in government agencies and organizations, enterprises and public institutions could use employee's cards to confirm their identities and residents could use the residence booklet as well as the recommendation to confirm their identities. However, without any legal effect, employee's cards and recommendations were only available in some situations. Even worse, it was easy for lawbreakers to counterfeit or replace them. The residence booklet at that time was available only locally and was inconvenient for people to carry it.

It is convenient for people to carry resident identity cards and people can show their resident identity cards when necessary. It not only offers convenience for people but also simplifies the procedures to increase efficiency.

When Deng Xiaoping met Masayoshi Ohira, the Prime Minister of Japan, on December 6, 1979, he proposed a concept of the well-off, which became widely known in China. In the 1980s, people's lives changed rapidly so that food, clothing, shelter and means of travel – the four basic needs of life – made qualitative leaps due to the goal of being fairly well-off. The goal in the 1990s was to continue to be well-off.

MEMORIES OF
CHINESE LIFE IN THE

1990s

In the 1990s, food coupons ended.

This was a big event for the Chinese people, because they didn't need the coupons to buy food any more.

Behind this phenomenon was the proposal and acknowledgement of the "socialist market economy". People realized that market economy and planning economy, regardless of whether it was socialist or capitalist, were just the means of allocating resources and could serve to improvement people's lives.

The deeply promoted reforms profoundly affected people's daily life. In the 1990s, the housing reform had a substantial startup and people started getting used to buy commercial houses. Moreover, the stock market attracted more and more enthusiastic people to the pursuit of wealth.

The deliberate holes on jeans

In 1997, Lee Company exhibited the 23-meters-long Lee 101Z giant jeans in Beijing and Shanghai, which won the Guinness World Record and was a feast for the eyes of Chinese people.

Mending, torn salvaged, scratched, repairing lines, placing... In fact, it's very common and acceptable that jeans had one or two small holes on them. These one or two small holes attracted people's sights and implicitly flaunted the wearer's personalities and sex appeal and increased the degree of fashion of jeans.

On the streets of Shanghai in the 1990s, a fashionable youth wearing ripped jeans would cause others to look with disfavor.

When walking leisurely, a young woman with a ponytail, wearing a pair of sunglasses, carrying a drum-sized bag, coming from the opposite direction, suddenly attracted my eyes. Her dress was not very special, but her jeans with five holes, three on left knee and two on right, were so striking that all the passersby casted glances at her. Even though there were five holes on her jeans, the color was really very new. According to its color, I deduced that the five holes were deliberated opened. The bottom of her jeans legs had tassels which seemed like the people's dresses in a beautiful movie named *Water World* in that the ragged people living at the end of the century had no clothes to change in a long time. I thought she was wired and was going to walk away dismissively, she took out a mobile phone from her waist pocket and began to communicate in a soft tone using some English. I suddenly felt in my heart that she was a beautiful white-collar woman! (The Theory of "New Aesthetics" published in *Xinming Evening News* on May 13, 1998)

In the 1990s, the jeans shifted the old appearance and became more and more diverse in color, shell fabric and style. Many consumers were fond of Cutty sarks, jackets, skirts and pants, and printed denim and thin denim were no longer fresh .

The brand apparel shop

Since its appearance in apparel retail, the name of the mainstream business model of the exclusive apparel shop changed several times. Behind these changes was the rapid development of the apparel industry. In the mid and late 1980s, the exclusive shop appeared in the industry, they were mainly "clothing stores". Then, in the early 1990s, these shops changed their names to "suit shops", "skirt shops", "trousers shops", "women's clothing shops", "sportswear shops" and so on. In the mid and late 1990s, these detailed apparel shops shifted as exclusive brand shops, such as "Youngor shops", "Shanshan shops", "Kaikai shops", "Li-Ning shops", etc.

In the mid and late 1990s, the exclusive brand shops became very popular in the big cities. In order to attract female consumers, some foreign trade shops also sold exports at very cheap prices. At that time, the consumption patterns became much diversified and the women who ruled household finances became the main force of shopping and dressing. The clothing counters in stated-owned department stores, which dominated the Chinese consumption for decades, became tourist souvenir shops.

Even the students began to seek out brand clothing. Some casual clothing shops affiliated to foreign brands, such as the "Jeanswest" or "Baleno" and so on, begun to occupy business centers and pedestrian streets in the big cities.

Expensive brand shops and the cheap foreign trade shops polarized the

Film still of Shanghai Fever.

clothing purchasing of the young Chinese women in the 1990s.

According to the report of *Wen Hui News* on November 10, 1991, the men's taizi pants, a fashionable style of trouser, and women's fashion pants were very popular in the early autumn of Shanghai. Wearing these clothes had become a kind of fashion, style and enjoyment.

Self-employed entrepreneurs, government officers or bosses all liked to wear silk, cotton or polyester short-sleeve shirts with lower hems in the trousers and belts with huge leather phone sets, and carry leather briefcases under their arms. No one knew where these popular fashions came from but everyone followed because that was the fashion at that time.

Cultural T-shirt
– with slogan printed on the chest

In the late 1980s and the early 1990s, the cultural T-shirt became part of people's memories.

It seemed like all the teenagers in the cities put on white T-shirts without collars and sleeves overnight. This kind of T-shirt was special with popular slogans printed on them. These slogans, of course were not political slogans, influenced by Wang Shuo's writing (Wangshuo, a famous Chinese writer) but were rebellious, sarcastic, non-lofty slogans.

"Leave me alone, I'm upset!" "I'm a rogue, nothing to be afraid of!" "Go with feeling!" "I eat the apple, you eat the peel!" "It's hard to make money!" "It's bitter to have no money!" Such slogans were printed on T-shirts.

In the early 1990s, T-shirts with slogans influenced by Wang Shuo's writings had become the mainstream culture.

At the beginning of 1989, Wang Shuo, Mo Yan, Hai Yan, Su Tong and some other Chinese writers established the Haima Film Studio and appealed to sell the literature products according to their quality. The media called their appeal of pricing by quality the "Haima Phenomenon" and their studio finally lived up to the public because of the hot TV plays such as *Expectation* in 1990.

This TV plays was the first indoor play in China and the director, Zheng Xiaolong, said that according to the Ministry of Public Security's statistics, during the period of this TV plays broadcasts, the crime rate had obviously dropped and there was an incident that the phone of Wuhan city's leader had been ringing off the hook because an area in Wuhan suffered a blackout and the residents couldn't see this TV plays.

Then, Wang Shuo and his rascal culture gradually entered people's daily life.

In 1984, Wang Shuo published his first novel *The Air Hostess* in the journal *Dang Dai*, and in 1989, published the novel *Half Flame, Half Brine*, which caused a stir in the society. Later, he also created a series of novels, such as *Mortal Transfer, Ferocious Animal, The Trouble Shooter, I am Your Father*, etc.

As time went on, Wang Shuo, considered a cultural freak, gradually became a cultural hero of that era and took up a mainstream position. He arrogantly shouted out "I'm a rogue, who do I fear!" and "Innocence Abroad!"

People wearing cultural T-shirt to join the 50ᵗʰ National Day Celebration.
Provided by Beijing Municipal Archives

Underwear-style dress

Underwear-style dress was a new fashion of using underwear characteristics for outerwear design. The main character was that in order to give people a special impression, the short-front and the lace-briefs had been used as elements for outerwear design. In the 1990-1991 spring and summer women's conference in Paris, this style of outerwear design appeared many times and was very popular throughout the 1990s.

Underwear-style dress derived from the inspiration of fashion designers who were never satisfied and broke the traditional ways dressing. Even though this type of dress was not always approved of.

According to a report in *Wen Hui News* on July 15, 1992, the wind coat was not only used to keep warm. At present, the thin-type of wind coat made of flax-yarn or soft-yarn is more attractive than the common skirt in summer.

In the summer of 1994, popular styles in Shanghai streets, such as the strapless or the backless dress, the jacket with short skirt, the long coat with short shirt, were all very modern.

In the summer of 1998, the suspender skirt, a typical example of underwear-style dressing, was very popular. A tanned-skin girl, wearing the suspender skirt, looked like her original white skin was covered with a transparent black veil and was charming and fascinating.

The open and bare clothes gradually became widely popular in China, especially among southern girls. They claimed that "if you don't have a beautiful face, show your chest; if you don't have a beautiful chest, show your shoulders; if you don't have beautiful shoulders, show your legs". The new trends were of hiding what did not need to be hidden like hands and shanks, showing what did not need to be shown like the waist and navel, sandals without heels, shoes without socks, toenails painted with colors or pasted with plastic flowers, toe rings, and more. Even handbags were transparent and mechanical movements of the wristwatches were totally revealed. The anti-traditional character of modern people was reflected in all these new trends.

Fashionable casual clothing

The clothing of the 1990s began to return to its nature with no more ornaments and decorations. The shell fabric of the clothing became thinner, lighter and softer and people preferred to choose natural shell fabric and blended fabric, such as cotton, flax, silk, wool, etc. The color, pattern and style of the clothing were all from the association and expression of nature.

Throughout the 1990s, casual clothing was most fashionable dress style.

According to the memories of Yu Zongyao, the former general manager of China Clothing Industry Company, during the development period in the 1990s, the development of China's business suit was pretty fast. Until then, the result of development was just the suit, including the female business suit. After the suit's rapid development, the development of casual clothing followed. "Casual clothing" referred to clothes used in daily life.

A kind of attractive casual-style suit quickly became popular in Shanghai. Even though its design had some casual clothing elements, its appearance and style still belonged to the suit type. The design of this casual suit was very special. It had an open front that was long and casual, the middle usually had one delicate button, and the lower was small square shape. The waist part was rather loose and the line of its whole appearance was simple and smooth. This kind of suit usually used thin cloth materials of middle or top grade quality.

The casual-style suit.

Cosmetics & skin-care products

In the early period of the 1990s, the cosmetics and skin-care products of Zheng Mingming brand became very popular in China and the founder, Zheng Mingming, was awarded the title of "International Beauty Godmother" because of her products. In 1995, Zheng Mingming, the Chinese beauty leader, published her new work *Beauty Hotline*. Due to the backward situation of Chinese beauty-related knowledge, the Beauty Hotline became the most targeted and practical way to solve any beauty questions.

Some people jokingly called 1995 the "beauty year", because professional beauty parlors begun to provide diversified services. You would find that a small beauty parlor with only 50 or 60 square meters could not only provide skin-care services, but also weight-loss services and had two chairs and two hairdressers providing hair services.

In 1996, the international brand L'OREAL began to enter into China. Its various bright colored dye hair creams showed Chinese people that their hair could also be dyed in other colors. At that time, the most popular hair dye color was wine red.

At that time, thick eyebrows, black eyeliner and red faces were all very popular makeup looks. In order to look more beautiful and whiter, people preferred to tattoo eyebrows and eye lines and "change skins" in beauty parlors. Thus, people's eyebrows became more and more like broadsword, eye lines like black caterpillars and faces like drinking wines. Some people jokingly changed Wang Fei's song lyrics of *I'm Happy Because You're Happy* to "your eyebrows become thicker, your eyes look darker…"

In October 1998, Wang Fei showed a very eye-catching wound-looking makeup on the cover of her new released album *Sing & Travel*. The makeup was so popular that it appeared frequently on fashion magazines and a lot of beauty editors set up special sections to teach people how to do it.

After the emergence of tattoos, there were a number of injuries due to the immaturity of this technology but people's pursuit of beauty was not stopped.

Japanese fashion fans

In the early 1990s, Japanese fashion entered China and more and more boys and girls became its fashion fans.

Akana Rika was the character of the Japanese TV plays *Tokyo Love Story* and her bright and sincere personality, her strong smiles and her tearful eyes were all impressive. Her mannerism and attitude towards love catered to modern women's fantasies. This TV plays promoted not only Rika's image, but also her dressing style, for example, the half-long wind coat became fashionable among most urban white collars. Since then, famous stars, such as Lao Lang, Gao Xiaosong, Huang Lei all kept half-parted long hairs like Mikami Kenichi in *Tokyo Love Story* during the first few years of their fame.

The manifestations of the Japanese fashion trends have been summarized as the follows: "It was very popular among those born after the 1970s, the trends' fans liked skateboarding, wore hip-hop clothes and garish headscarves, they were fond of Japanese animated cartoons, like *Chibi Maruko Chan*, *Doraemon*, *Sailor Moon*, *Slamdunk*, *Meteor Gardon*, etc. and Japanese TV soaps, like *Love Letter*, *White Book of Love*, etc. They wore the platform shoes and short-tassel skirts, and always permed their hair. The journal *How* offered spiritual food

⊕ ────────────────

Film posters of Miyazaki Hayao's Spirited Away.

for them and Noriko Sakai, Namie Amuro, Utada Hikaru, Kimura Takuya were their favorite Japanese stars." (Yu Ping's Long Vacation and the Japanese Fashion Trend published on No.316 of *Sanlian Life Weekly*)

When Japanese fashion prevailed, people started to call the box lunch "bento" and felt that this name was more fashionable than the previous one. *Liangfan*, derived from the Japanese words and meant wholesaling, gradually became popular and had great influence on Karaoke hall's or KTV's names and a lot of shops changed their names according to this Japanese-style word. It seemed that *Liangfan* all of a sudden, existed all over the street. Of course, among all these new words derived from the Japanese, the most popular one was "Liaoli" which had become a kind of psychological suggestion to the consumers as its high qualities.

The Japanese fashion trends lasted to the new millennium without fading. In 2003, when *Spirited Away* won the Academy Award for best animated feature, more and more Chinese people became crazy about Japanese animation. At the same time, the Japanese TV plays *White Tower*, which had been called a great immortal TV play, also attracted lots of fans.

The Korean fashion mania

The resounding shout of "We are the future" from the HOT team rocked a lot of teenagers in Asia. Korean fashion culture swept the nation overnight and young people, influenced by this fashion trend, wearing baggy pants with blond cool hair, were all over the street. Korean pop culture became quite trendy in China in the late 90s.

Some Korean-style hair colors and dress styles catered to teenagers' tastes and fashion trends.

Korean and Japanese fashion fans dyed their hair with colors and wore long pants that swept the floor. Many people thought that they were freaks and never knew why they were so seriously enamored with Japanese and Korean idols. Some people even saw them as a decadent generation with lazy habits and no cares.

But Korean fashion fans claimed that the reason why they were enamored with Korean songs was that their songs could encourage them rather than the songs of Mainland China, Hong Kong and Taiwan.

In the early 1995, Sorabol, which had been considered as the most authentic and expensive Korean restaurant, opened in Beijing. Dining in Sorabol became a symbol identity, status and taste.

Sassy Girl was a very hot Korean movie in 2002 and the image of this movie's "girl", played by Gianna Jun, was so vivid that she had became the dream lover in many boys' hearts. Her beauty when she was in silence and her insufferably arrogant when she was arguing all gave us a very deep impression.

In 2005, the Korean TV plays *Dae Jang Geum* became very hot in China. This TV play promoted not only healthy and positive attitudes, but also the Korean clothes and foods. After watching this play, many men sighed with emotion as to why they had not married a woman like Lee Young-ah, who could cook good meals.

Korean food became more and more popular.

Korean fashion not only referred to clothing style but to a shockwave containing Korean music and films. After the prevalence of the Korean music and TV soaps, more and more people began to praise the Korean beauties and handsome men. For example in clothing, the first stage of the dressing styles were baggy pants or sleek fabric splicing color pants, round-collar T-shirts or baggy jackets, irregular edged holes on the elbow part of the cloth or the knee part of the jeans. The most interesting style was that on the double-shoulder leather bag or the front part of the cloth, it must be full of tourist souvenir medals or costume-trademarks. All those styles contained a lot punk elements, but through performances by Korean stars, these elements were more likely to be accepted by Chinese youths. At a later stage, the style were that neat dresses with gentility, dashing dresses and foreign flavored dresses with a little of Asian implicit features. The pronunciation of the Korean fashion trend in Chinese was much similar with the Chinese weather forecast term "Han Liu", so it became prevalent very quickly.

In the 1990s, hip-hop culture began to spread in Asia and quickly became prevalent in Japan, Korea, China Taiwan and other places. Along with the spread of the "Korean wave", hip-hop quickly became a symbol of fashion and more and more young people began to pursue and learn it. Due to this fact, hip-hop, originally a cultural term was defined as a musical term of street dance in a narrow sense.

Food coupons quit historical stage

In May 1993, Beijing was the last city to stop using food coupons and food coupons became historical relics. This was an iconic event during the transition of the planned economy to a market economy and deeply influenced people's lives and habits.

Food coupons were a kind of worthless security, but for more than 10 years after the reform and opening up they had been known as a second currency and, for some years, were even more useful than the RMB. They could be used in farmers markets, business streets and business locations to buy anything one wanted, such as the staple or non-staple foods, fruits and vegetables, articles of daily use, clothing, flowers and birds, insects and fish, all kinds

Food coupons, which played an important role in the history of new China, no longer in use.

of furniture, and more. They could also be used to pay the cost of repairing watches, leather shoes, bags, and other items. Some even used them to hire temps or babysitters.

In short, the functions of money were all reflected by the food coupons and in addition to the RMB, they had become "China's First Coupon", widely used and stable in value.

After the implementation of Guangdong's open food price policy (on April 1, 1992), Zhejiang (on January 1, 1993), Jiangsu, Anhui, Fujian and Jiangxi provinces and Shanghai (in April, 1993) followed. They opened food purchasing and sales prices as well. Food coupons totally exited the food market. On May 1 in the same year, Beijing also joined this reform. By the end of 1993, 95% of national cities and counties had completed the open food price reform.

Since the 1990s, the food supply and demand gradually oriented to the market and the disappearance of food coupons became inevitable. Several years later, food coupons had become a kind of popular collectible.

The "vegetable basket project"

In the late 1980s, with the improvement of people's living standards, the contradiction between supply and demand of fresh agricultural products, such as vegetables, meats, dairy products, aquatic products, fruits, etc., became more and more obvious.

In order to alleviate the nation's strained non-staple food supply, in 1998, the Ministry of Agriculture put forward the project of "vegetable basket". The first phase of this project was to construct meat, eggs, dairy products, aquatic products and vegetable manufacturing bases and stock breeding and feed processing service systems, which were supported by the central and local governments to ensure that residents had fresh vegetables to eat year round.

The "vegetable basket project" had instant effect. Since the 1990s, dining tables had gradually changed. Common winter foods of northern residents, such as radish, cabbage and potato – which had been called the "three treasures" –

The "vegetable basket project".

were gradually replaced. The sale of products in farmers markets, including all kinds of fresh meats and vegetables, had become diversified.

The rich "vegetable basket project" obviously improved the quality of food consumption in urban and rural areas as well as the nutrient structure of Chinese people. In 2000, the per capita consumption of grain was 206 kg, vegetable was 110 kg, edible vegetable oil was 8.2 kg, sugar 7.0 kg, meat was 25.3 kg, eggs 11.8 kg, milk 5.5 kg and aquatic products 11.7 kg. Most of them were higher than the international average.

The rich "vegetable basket project" introduced peasant household gardens into the market, promoted the adjustment of agricultural structure and created a big industry. In Shandong Province, Shouguang City became known as " China's first basket", many new vegetable cultivation technologies, such as soilless culture, music cultivation, gaseous fertilizer and so on, were widely used and produced many vegetable varieties.

The "vegetable basket project" enriched the Chinese dining table and improved nutrition for Chinese people.

"Fried bean curd and beef with cayenne pepper"

In the 1990s, people were no longer parsimonious about dining out because earning money had become easy.

The cheap and affordable Sichuan restaurant had become their first choice.

Sichuan restaurants, when they appeared in people's view in the first few years, were commonly small and unsophisticated. Some were simple and shabby, decorated with materials and elements that were full of Sichuan regional characteristics and gave consumers strong feelings of appeal and affinity. The food prices were also very cheap, so consumers loved them.

People finally had the opportunities to eat authentic Sichuan hot pot and taste the Sichuan spicy flavors. They discovered "Fried Bean Curd and Beef with Cayenne Pepper", "Duck Blood", "Cattle Stomach" and "Huang Hou".

Of course, there were other special foods such as "Yuan Yang (mandarin duck) Hotpot" that was half spicy and half clear. The hotpot was divided into two sections with an S-shaped baffle which made it look like a Ying-Yang symbol, half red and half white, half spicy and half clear and half soft and half strong. Someone said the red part looked like the setting sun, while the white part looked like snow. Foreigners who ate Yuan Yang Hotpot described it more vividly: the red soup was boiling like disco, while the white soup was soft like the waltz.

In 1992, Chen Lin decided to start his own business, so he borrowed some money from his friend and opened a restaurant in Beijing's Che Gongzhuang. His main business was Sichuan and home-style dishes. In order to ensure authentic tastes, he entrusted his friend to find a Sichuan chef.

In 1995, Chen Lin was mentally and physically exhausted and transferred the restaurant to others, something he regrets to this day. He said that if he could have persevered for two or three years, maybe his restaurant would have caught the recovery of Sichuan cuisine. In fact, the most important thing was that as time went on, more and more people became very glad to spend money to dine out.

Fresh seafood becomes common air freight

From the late 1980s to the early 1990s, restaurants of Cantonese cuisine opened around the nation and each of them introduced "fresh seafood" as a specialty. Thus, eating Cantonese cuisine became a fashionable way of life.

The prevalence of Cantonese cuisine was not an accident. With strong southern-oriented trends in China, derived from the "Pearl River Delta" which ahead in China's reform and opening-up, Cantonese cuisine with its leading specialty of fresh seafood quickly occupied the market in Beijing, where popular restaurants were traditional Shandong cuisine. Quickly, Cantonese and the Teochew cuisines became very popular in the North and eating dim sum, drinking Canton soup, tasting snake gall or snake blood liquor, sending Cantonese mooncakes, and other traditions became common in the north.

The advertisements of fresh seafood could be seen everywhere and it seemed suddenly, big aquariums were built in every seafood restaurant. An insider said that previously, the Shanghai food service market was dominated by frozen raw materials, but after the prevalence of Hong Kong Cantonese cuisines, which took fresh seafood as raw materials, the situation changed and more and more people flocked to Cantonese restaurants to taste their "fresh" flavors.

As it became fashionable, Cantonese cuisine made northern bosses, who were lavish and sensitive about their reputations, spend money without hesitation on these high-grade dishes to show their status. These dishes included Australia lobsters, Australia scallops, Mexico abalone, Thailand birds' nest and Madagascar shark's fins.

People still remember that at the time in Beijing, the most famous Cantonese restaurant was "Shun Feng". Besides, the Hong Kong Food Palace, Da San Yuan and other Cantonese restaurants were also very hot.

In the 1990s in Shanghai, seafood restaurants emerged in Zhapu Road and Huanghe Road (between the Nanjing West Road and the Beijing West Road) and at that time, due to their incredible popularity, these two roads were hyped treasures.

Buffet made many people "hungry in, full out"

In the 1990s, buffets gradually became popular in China, and this meant people had more choices.

Facing the lavish buffet filled with numerous delicacies, many Chinese people who had experienced the famine years would feel a little panic. When they came in the restaurant, first they would look around to see what dishes were expensive and which were cheap and easily filling. After that, they would pick up all the expensive dishes and eat eagerly until they felt a little full, maybe for half an hour. By this time, a lot of dishes remained on their dishes and pots. That made them full of regret, because the rule was: "Don't waste food, we will charge according to the weight of the food left."

Usually after the eating "fight", many people would feel very uncomfortable when they got up, because they were too full to stand straight and if they wanted to sit back, they couldn't bend over any more. A writer said that the feeling of hunger was similar to the feeling of being full. After eating at a buffet, people found that overeating was also a painful thing.

"Hungry in, full out" was a typical slogan that many people identified with. In fact, there were still a lot of people eating buffets with the mentality of "eat back the money of the cost". But as time went on, people's living standards improved and they began to realize that some buffet eating habits such as "only eat the expensive dishes rather than eat what's right", "to eat back the money of the cost", " empty the stomach before eating at the buffet", "drink less, or even don't drink", and others were not very healthy.

Zhang Cungang could not help laughing when he remembers his first experience of eating a buffet. He said: "To celebrate my birthday, all my family went out to eat at a buffet. Because it could not only get a feast for our appetite, but also celebrate my birthday, but when they thought about the high price of RMB30 per person, we all decided to eat back the money regardless of how our stomachs felt. So after the eating, the whole family's bellies bulged. We had to walk around to digest. From this event, it can be seen that at that time, people still preferred economical and affordable ways for dining out."

The event of Starbucks in the Forbidden City

On January 11, 1999, at 9 am, the first Starbucks in Mainland China opened at the Beijing International Trade Center.

On January 12, 2007, a host of CCTV wrote in his blog that Starbucks, "as the unpresentable symbol of food culture" had opened in the Forbidden City. This was an insult to traditional Chinese culture. The host also lodged a personal protest to the CEO of Starbucks, Jim Donald, and asked him to move the shop out of the Forbidden City.

This article caused a sensation on the Internet and the click rate broke through 500,000 very quickly.

On January 19, the *People's Daily* published this article, quickly then, hundreds of domestic media paid attention to this event and some mainstream media such as *Guangming Daily*, Xinhua News Agency, CCTV, and others covered it. Internationally, more than 250 foreign media including Reuters, CNN, BBC, *Financial Times, Forbes, Wall Street Journal, Business Week, Time, Washington Post*, all reported on it as well.

At the time, there was a lot of debate on this topic. Some agreed that Starbucks should move out. The reason was not Starbucks' disrespect, but the lack of self-respect at the Forbidden City. Some said Starbucks should not profit from the Forbidden City. Some thought that there was nothing wrong with Starbucks it should be kept there to show China's confidence and inclusiveness.

In July, 2007, Starbucks moved out of the Forbidden City.

The trademark of Starbucks.

The night market

In the late 1980s and early 1990s, the state-owned and collective shops opened during the day and were vacant at night. Some shrewd individuals spontaneously formed the night market, usually consisting of some mobile booths, opening at dusk and closing at midnight.

Shopping at the night market became popular.

Whenever night fell, many people and their partners went to the night market to buy all kinds of clothing and goods and eat all kinds of snacks.

The advantages of the night market were convenient shopping, various kinds of goods and cheap prices. But at the same time, there were also had many problems, such as garbage, unhealthy food, fake goods, noise and so on. Many big cities began to set standards for night markets or ban them.

Articles of luxury

In 1992, it seemed that a group of foreign luxury goods entered the Chinese market simultaneously.

In June, Hennessy XO, entered the Chinese market once again and chose

Shanghai, China's largest city, as its landing port.

Afterwards, someone made a joke to mock stammerers, but in fact mocked the expensive XO, too. The joke was: In a nightclub, a waitress recommended XO to a stammering guest. The guest asked: "How much is it?" The worker answered: "18,000, open one to have a try?" The guest stammered: "A, A, A..." After hearing this, the worker quickly opened one very skillfully. With the sound of "Pang", the guest finally broke out: "A ...Are you kidding me!"

In April 1992, the Chinese flagship shop of LV opened at the Beijing Peninsula Palace Hotel. A lot of international luxury brands such as Armani, Chanel, Gucci, Dior, and more followed. Guided by female consumers, the Beijing International Trade Shopping Mall, specially selling international high-grade brand products opened. In addition to foreseeing that the fashion taste of the Chinese people were improving along with their wealth, luxury brands also manifested that Chinese women were present at the important social and business occasions with more independent status.

In 1992, Dunhill opened its first Chinese shop in the Beijing International Trade Shopping Mall. Armani, Chanel, Gucci and CD followed after that.

In April 2, 2009, the *Yangcheng Evening News* reported:

In March of this year, a report in the *New York Times* attracted our attention. It said that "China is now the world's fastest growing luxury consumption market."

According to the released report of the World Luxury Association, to January of this year, China's luxury spending totaled US$8.6 billion, which accounted for 25% of the global market. It overpassed the US for the first time and made China the world's second largest after Japan.

"Did you buy a house?" becomes a common greeting

In the 1990s in Beijing, commercial residential building was not yet hot and a lot of people still lived in welfare housing allocated by their work units. At that time, there were only several modern buildings, such as the Blue Island Building on Chaowai street.

In the early 1990s, Beijing started to build its first overall planning residential community, Fangzhuang Community. This community in Fengtai district, was located in the southeast area of Beijing's Second Ring Road. The community's residential floors were strewn at random and looked very peculiar. The place was known as Beijing's "rich people's region" at the time.

Around 1993, the Exchanging House Conferences became hot among Beijing residents who were still allocated welfare houses.

On October 17, 1991, the Housing System Reform Leading Group of the State Council issued the *Opinions on* Comprehensively *Promote the reform of Urban Housing System*. This meant that housing policy, which had lasted for decades, would be fundamentally changed.

The Opinions proposed that the reform should be started from the system of low rented public houses that would transform the system of welfare allocation to the system of buying. The residents should, through commodity exchanges (buy or rent), get the ownership or use rights for their own housing. This reform brought housing into the consumer market and created a benign circle for housing fund input and output.

In July, 1998, the State Council issued the notice on further deepening the reform of urban housing system and speeding up housing construction and demanded that in the second half year of 1998, housing distribution should be stopped and the reform of housing allocation monetization be gradually implemented. After stopping housing distribution, newly built affordable houses, in principle, could be sold but not rented.

In 1998, commercial residential building suddenly became very prevalent as working units would not allocate housing for their workers and workers had to spend money to buy them. If one did not have enough money, the banks would be very glad to lend.

That year, housing exhibitions in Beijing were busier than temple fairs. People flocked to all kinds of housing exhibitions for fear that they would miss a piece of information. "Did you buy a house?" became a common greeting. Residents, it seemed, could not eat, but would buy a house.

That year, Beijing finished constructions of 19 affordable housing projects at once. The development of Huilongguan and Tiantongyuan districts let many ordinary Beijing residents realize their housing dreams. Gradually, residents got used to the phenomenon that people needed to queue all night to qualify for economical housing.

In 1999, public housing that had already been bought could be resold in Beijing. Residents, in order to consult the policies, flocked into real estate transaction management halls in all districts and counties.

It seemed that all of a sudden, terms like mortgages, loans, monthly installment payment and debtors all became common.

Property management company and owner committee

From the 1990s, China's housing privatization rapidly developed, which made property management a business industry.

In the early 1980s, property management was introduced from Hong Kong. On March 10, 1981, the first professional foreign-related commercial housing management company in Shenzhen, the Shenzhen Property Management Company, was officially established. The company began to apply unified property management to Shenzhen foreign-related commercial housing, which marked the birth of this emerging industry.

In April 1994, the Ministry of Construction issued order No.33, the *Management Approach for the City New Residential Districts*. It clearly pointed out that the residential area should gradually introduced socialized and professional management and uniformly implement professional property management by property management companies.

On September 1, 2003, China's first property management regulations came into effect which provided important legal basis to standardize the property management, safeguard the legitimate rights and interests of owners and property management companies and improve the people's living and working environment. In the sketch *House Renovation* at the 2005 Spring Festival Gala, a detail impressed people: An contractor played by Huang Hong, and the owner, played by Gong Hanlin, were pounding the wall, suddenly, someone shouts outside the window, "what are you doing!" After hearing this, the contractor said: "This rude voice must come from the property management staff!" The owner said angrily "What's the matter with them, I have handed over the decoration security payment, and I can decorate my house as I want!"

At Nanjing Xinjiekou, there were a lot of tall buildings. The Yangtze River trade building shaped as a matchbox looked very inconspicuous among them. But the first owner committee of Nanjing was established in this old-fashioned building and made the first event that owner fired the housekeeper in Nanjing.

On November 26, 1996, 11 units including Ping An Insurance Company launched the organizing team. On January 10, 1997, the team elected the property management committee of Yangtze River trade building.

The event of firing housekeepers happened in November 2000. The Yangtze River trade building was managed by the developer's property management company when it came into use. But after that, the two sides split. The owners' committee fired its original property management company due to bad services and employed the Huamingyuan property management company. But beyond the committee's expectation, the Huamingyuan property management company wasn't qualified and unable to manage the building. Fortunately, the committee quickly responded and dealt with it properly, without causing a disorder.

After the establishment of the owners' committee of the Yangtze River trade building, some buildings and residential districts followed.

The state encouraged individuals to buy cars

According to the data of State Statistics Bureau at the end of 1991, Chinese private cars had already reached 960,000.

After Deng Xiaoping's Southern Tour Speech, the limitations that affiliated units should use coupons to buy cars were loosened. In 1992, Ferrari held a sales exhibition at the Asian Games Village Convention and Exhibition Center, and on the last day of this exhibition, Beijing's former richest man Li Xiaohua bought one for US$138,880 and became China's first Ferrari driver.

In February 1993, China's Ministry of Finance decided to cancel the approval process of buying cars and buying estate cars, off-road vehicles and tool cars wouldn't not require approval any more. At that time, among the seven kinds of exclusive controlled goods, the car had become the first good that didn't need any approval formalities.

Then, on July 4,1994, the State Council published the *Automobile Industry Development Policy* and said: "The State shall encourage individuals to buy cars... no localities and departments shall intervene, with administrative or economic means, with individuals to buy and use the legitimate cars. On August 30, 1996, the State Council issued a notice to cancel local government restrictions on economic car purchases. Since then, Jettas and Fukang cars became very common." (Changes of Cars in the 30 Years of Reform and Opening Up: from Luxury Goods to Means of Transportation, written by Yang Kairan, Guang Nan and Shi Wenfu, published in *Beijing Times* on November 28, 2008)

Wedding in the air

In 1990s, the wedding ceremony gradually became more and more various in style and wedding photography studios and wedding planning companies became more and more prevalent. Wedding pictures, festooned vehicles, formal dresses and banquets gradually became essential elements in wedding ceremonies.

The dishes at wedding banquets at the time were similar to present dishes and the difference might be the amount of the cash gifts. In the mid 1990s, cash gifts were almost RMB50 and RMB100, but today the amount is several times that.

In the late 1990s, young people advocated individual characters and wedding ceremonies became more and more diversified, such as tricycle weddings, outdoor weddings, antique weddings, western weddings, group weddings, undersea weddings, air weddings and so on. It was believed that there was nothing people could not do.

On January 28, 1990, the *Modern Newspaper* reported on a novel and unique air balloon wedding ceremony between Shang Xiang, an artillery lieutenant in Xinjiang, and Zhu Rong, a Chinese girl of the Han nationality. They held their wedding ceremony on an air balloon without a wedding banquet or gifts. It was the first case in China and the third case in the world of holding a wedding in the air.

On October 2, 1995, jointly organized by Jiangsu Youth League Committee, the provincial Women's Federation and the China Eastern Airlines, a new type wedding ceremony was held on the flight from Nanjing to Beijing.

On October 29, 1995, in Taiyuan of Shanxi Province, a wedding motorcade formed by Chaalis cabs in uniform red, with six or eight hanging red balloons and draping colored silks, became a new sight.

Parents hate the Internet cafe

In May, 1996, China's first Internet cafe named Weigaite opened in Shanghai. Quickly, this high-tech form of recreation became popular among young people. Their parents, on the contrary, hated these Internet cafes because their children always played truant to play games. Violence was also common.

A corner of the internet cafe

On May 14, 2009, the China Youth Research Center released a study on "*Youth Network Damage Problem Research*" which showed that the average online time of youth was 5.3 hours per day, and nearly half of them had contacted inappropriate websites.

According to an investigation, the treatment for teenage internet addiction had little effect, so public internet sites might be an exploratory measure to find effective ways to solve the problem of teenager's internet addiction. It was reported that Changsha had seen 150 public internet sites for underage teenagers.

Public Internet site could filter some websites and games and teenagers had two hours of online time on the premise that all their homework was they had parental permission. Teenagers who had already surfed the Internet in a public site could not get online in another internet cafes. (Seventy Percent of Children Reduce Their Pressure through Network, written by Zhou Yimei, published on the *Beijing Times* on May 15, 2009)

Personal handy-phone system (PHS)

In January 1998, the first Chinese "PHS" came out in Yuhang district (the north part of Zhejiang Province).

The "PHS", also called personal access phone system, made the traditional fixed telephone no longer fixed in a certain position and could make the free mobile calls within the scope of the wireless network coverage. In addition, it also provided roaming service within the scope of different base stations and as a supplement and extension to the local telephone network. It could be charged and used to call just like a fixed telephone. It was portable, cheap and very convenient for people to use, so this environmentally friendly wireless telephone was vividly called the "little smart phone".

Consumers gradually became aware of the good features of the "PHS": cheap price to enjoy wireless service; low radiation; environment protection; little and smart with fashion design; long standby time; able to send and receive emails and short messages; surf the Internet; read the news; download all kinds of pictures and ringtones; and more.

⊙———————————

*The PHS used set-card separation
technology.*

However, it also had some drawbacks. For example, sometimes the signal was not very good; it could not provide national roaming service like mobile phones, it was just a supplement and extension to the fixed telephone. In some local places, the phone calls were not very good. All in all, it was still different from traditional mobile phones.

In February, 2009, CMCC (China Mobile Communication Corporation) announced that government departments required the elimination of all PHS wireless access systems by the end of 2011. This meant that the PHS, which had been developed for 12 years, would disappear.

QQ and MSN
– keeping the secrets of work offices

In 1997, the Tencent Company named their new software OICQ (Open ICQ). People could use the OICQ to communicate and receive instant messages. It was very convenient and fully functional. It could instantly send and receive messages, page networks, chat rooms, transfer files, send mobile phone short messages and more. It also offered value-added services for traditional wireless paging and mobile communication.

In April 2000, Tencent decided to change the software's name to Tencent QQ. The Tencent mark, a penguin, became very familiar.

In August 1995, Windows 95 attracted the attention of the IT industry. At that time, MSN was just a popular instant messaging software in many people's eyes.

Quickly, MSN became very popular among many people, such as office workers, when the white collars were unwilling or unable to talk to their neighbors, they would bow their heads and typed on MSN.

A lot of signatures of MSN were very special and among them there were a lot of Han Han's well-known sayings (Han Han, the representative writer of the generation after the 1980s), such as the famous signature of MSN in 2007, "being talented is just like being pregnant, only it takes a long time to see it".

China becomes the 145th country with five-day workweek

There was a song named *I want to go to Gulin* which reflected the people's desire for leisure:

"I want to go to Gulin, I want to go to Gulin, but I have no money when I have time.

I want to go to Gulin, I want to go to Gulin, but I have no time when I have money."

Busy for thousands of years, Chinese people finally had the opportunity to enjoy leisure times.

China had become the 145th country in the world with a five-day workweek.

From the foundation of New China foundation to the 1990s, China had been practicing the six-day workweek and eight hours per day working system. The total working hours were about 2,448 hours in a year.

On April 10, 1995, the notice on the implementation of *the Provisions of the State Council About Worker's Working Hours* was released by the Beijing Municipal Government. (Beijing Municipal Archives)

With the development of the economy and society and the reform and opening up, the nation started to consider the problem of leisure. Being fairly well off meant more income and leisure time, higher living standards and more recreation. On May 1, 1994, the nation started to practice five and half-day workweeks with an extra day of rest every other week. In May 1995, it started a five-day workweek system, with a two-day weekend. This event became a symbol of improvement of people's living quality and the increase of social civilization.

After that, people's lifestyles dramatically changed. Before, people were able to rest only on Sunday. But instead of rest they had to busy themselves on household things, such as cleaning, shopping and visiting friends and relatives that made them feel more tired. Thus, people called the Sunday as "fighting Sunday" just like the saying in Feng Gong's crosstalk: "On Sundays, who not to be the houseman to help the mother-in-law carry the gas-jar?"

After the implementation of the two-day weekend, people had an extra 52 days of rest per year and more time to deal with odd things. The "fighting Sunday" gradually changed and happy Friday appeared. Saturdays were set aside for housework and Sundays for rest. The benefits to the people could not be counted in terms of days.

White-collar and petty bourgeois

On January 26 and 27, 1995, the *Shanghai Youth Daily* published the First Public Survey on Mainland White-collar, after that, the word "white-collar" quickly attracted people's attention.

On April 14, 2002, the *Shanghai Youth Daily* introduced the survey research report of Shanghai Academy of Social Science, The Development of Shanghai White-collar. The word "white-collar" was first written in the annual blue paper of Shanghai's development. The blue paper also believed that the problem of white-collar had gradually attracted people's attention and been understood and accepted.

The features of high-income and high-rank made white-collars become more influential in social and economic fields. They also played an irreplaceable role in promoting urban political, economic and social development.

It was generally recognized that "white-collars" were a group of people leading fashion trends and their life-styles demonstrated society's lifestyle choices.

According to the survey, the incomes of the white-collars were higher than general members of society. Nearly 60% of white-collars positioned themselves in the "secondary consumer class" and although they had high incomes, their consumption consciousness was rather rational. About 55.8% of the white collars laid their emphasis on the quality of goods and their practical function.

The survey also showed that Shanghai white-collars tried to live a kind of high grade and high style leisure life, such as watching TV (70.5%), surfing the Internet (61.8%), reading journals and newspapers (57.3%), listening to music (56.3%), reading books (53.1%), etc. All these were favorite recreational ways among the white-collars.

"If my family name is Bai, and if I have a child, I will name him or her Bai Gujing." A recent college graduate, who was in charge of the copy machine, jokingly thrashed as the "best actor" or "best actress" in order to become the "Bai Gujing" at an early date.

In the 1990s, the petty bourgeois became very popular

Petty bourgeois, transliterated as "*bu er qiao ya*" in Chinese, referred to those young people who yearned for western lives and pursued the inner experience and the material and spiritual enjoyment. This term also expanded as Daniil Simkin in the meaning, which referred to people who pursued the life taste.

The petty bourgeois often liked coffee, households, wine, tea, laptop computers, etc. They liked traveling. In terms of dress, they didn't pursue the most expensive, but pursued their own style. They could speak fluent English. They believed that the spirit was more important than the flesh, ideals higher than reality, and personal character higher than common character. They liked to go Dutch.

DINK

DINK meant couples who had double incomes, but no kids.

The DINK family formed in the 1980s and populated European and American countries. In the 1990s, DINK families appeared in China's big cities.

The DINK families reached 12.4% of the total in Shanghai, according to a survey of family by the Shanghai Women's Federation. The survey also showed that with the appearance of single families, late-marriage families, single parent families and empty nest families, traditional big families of three generations under one roof gradually decreased, the structure of Shanghai families became more diversified. The experts noted that the important reason of this phenomenon was the changes of Shanghai family culture concepts.

According to the statistics, the average permanent resident household had dropped from 4.06 people 20 years earlier to three. Families of three and families of two already accounted for more than 80% of the total. Traditional families paid more attention to birth, consumption, raising children, supporting the elderly, etc. while among Shanghai's young, the notion of fertility had gradually faded, more and more young couples preferred to enjoy life as two people.

According to a social survey by the Horizon Research Consultancy Group in February, 2002, China's large and medium-sized cities, DINK families added up to 600,000 and nearly 70% of the people surveyed thought DINK families would increase.

With industrialization and modernization, the new generation of Chinese families faced an awkward choice. Relatively new research targeting Chinese higher education classes for master degrees or above showed that this class still had a positive attitude toward fertility, but this survey also showed that factors like "involving energy" (25.4%), "influencing work" (16.7%), "economic ability is limited" (18.6%), "affect two-people's lives" (13.6%), etc. made having children more and more daunting.

On October 12, 2007, the *Morning Post* reported that after the prevalence of DINK families, pets-only DINK families once again attracted attention.

The pets-only DINK families referred to those DINKs who were reluctant to raise children but wanted to enjoy the parental warmth and fun so they kept pets and took them as their "children".

Psychologists reminded citizens to correctly measure their attitudes to pets to avoid suffering from pet dependence.

The foreign blockbuster vs the New Year movie

In mid and late 1990s, foreign blockbusters were first introduced to China.

Especially in 1998, *Titanic* stepped onto the big screen on the mainland and unexpectedly won the box office at RMB320 million, accounting for 20% of the annual national movie box office revenue of RMB1.44 billion.

In 1999, movie audiences had fallen to 450 million, which meant that on average each audience saw a movie every three years. This was the present situation of the Chinese film industry.

On December 24, 1997, the first New Year movie named *Party A and Party B* took to the big screen after careful advance publicity. The marketing was similar to that of foreign blockbusters and the movie earned RMB11 million in Beijing alone. This movie first showed the charm of New Year movies and made the director, Feng Xiaogang, more popular. Seen another way, in the fourth year of the entrance of the foreign blockbusters in China, the movie was really the successful "work" of domestic "students".

The posters of the New Year movie Cell Phone

The "Adam and Eve" sex shop

On March 23, 1993, a shop named "Adam and Eve Healthcare Centre" opened at No.143, Zhaodengyu Road in Beijing.

This was the first sex shop in China.

The shop owner, Wen Jingfeng, opened the left-handed supplies shop and a specialty weight reduction shop before, but both failed. In a country where speaking of sex publicly was still regarded as indecent, he decided to open a sex shop.

At that time, when he told people of his plan, everyone thought he was a "rogue" and no one was willing to rent to him.

In those years, condoms were provided by the Family Planning Committee. Fortunately for him, after a long talk with the Committee, the leader finally agreed and said: "Harmonious sexual life is the foundation for good birth and good care, we will fully support you to break through this forbidden area."

When he applied for the business license, another problem appeared: sex products had not been included in the scope of business stipulated by the state, so which category should they belong to? For this problem, the Industrial and Commercial Bureau had a fierce debate until someone came up with an idea that classified sex products into the category of articles of daily use and health food. So this problem was successfully solved.

After the business license application, the next was to recruit employees. Wen Jingfeng went to the career fair and put up signs. Among the dozens of resumes, he finally identified three interview candidates. But in the final stages of the interview, a girl first asked about his shop's business scope and Wen Jingfeng answered frankly. After hearing this, the girl stood up to leave and said: "Isn't that selling an aphrodisiac?" The other two followed her and also left.

Seeing from the shop sign, ten bright red Chinese characters " 北京亚当夏娃保健中心 Beijing Adam-Eve Healthcare Center", no one knew what the business was. The shop, with 30 square meters, looked like a clinic. In it, there was a gynecologist wearing a white coat, he also helped shoppers. The counters stood against the walls and displayed condoms and impotence drugs provided

A sex shop in Beijing

by the Family Planning Committee. Next to them were manuals.

Most of the young people came to this shop to buy contraceptives, while the middle-aged people were mostly concerned about sex harmony. As many as 90% of customers were middle-aged males, while women often called the center hotline for counseling.

After the "Adam and Eve" sex shop, more than 100 sex shops opened in Beijing in 1995 alone.

From 1997 to 1998, Viagra was listed in the U.S. This quickly caused "Viagra mania" around the world. This news also caused a stir when it spread to China.

On July 1, 2000, Viagra officially entered China and a lot of Chinese reported the news.

On July 1, Viagra came to Guangzhou's big hospitals and caused intense response.

On June, 29, the First People's Hospital in Dongshan district was the first hospital to stock Viagra in Guangzhou. It stocked the first batch of Viagra with 50 boxes, each box with one pill was worth RMB99 and each pill had 50 mg. The next day, the first pill was sold to a Guangdong patient of about 52 years. At first, this patient was reluctant to register in the outpatient department, and wanted to buy Viagra directly. The pharmacist explained to him that only after the doctor's check and prescription would he be able to buy it. So he had to let the doctor measure his blood pressure and check whether he had heart disease. After these checks, the doctor opened a prescription for Viagra.

After that, the man explained that he had no sexual dysfunction but wanted to try different aphrodisiacs. After taking the pill, the man threw the pill box and specification paper, leaving only the blue pill in his pocket. He also told the pharmacist not to say the medicine name so loudly, because it would make the patients very embarrassed. (The Fourth Edition of *Jiangnan Times* on July 4, 2000)

Stock exchanges return

On November 26, 1990, approved by the People's Bank of China and authorized by the State Council, the Shanghai Stock Exchange was established. This was, since the founding of the People's Republic of China, the first stock exchange on the mainland.

Before this, Chinese people knew a little about the stock exchange through Mao Dun's novel, *Zi Ye*, and the movie adapted from it.

On the opening day of the Shanghai Stock Exchange, 25 stocks from Shanghai, Shandong, Jiangxi, Anhui, Zhejiang, Hainan and Liaoning, etc., became Exchange members. They were divided into several different business types, such as brokers, dealers, regulated brokers, regulated dealers, etc. The Exchange adopted spot trading rather than the futures trading and at the initial opening period, its business was mainly bonds trading, including treasury bonds, corporate bonds and financial bonds. After a period of transition, it paid equal attention to bond and the stock trading.

On December 19, in the morning, the Stock Exchange held an opening

The "Yang Millionaire" after trading stocks

ceremony and after half an hour when the former exchange trading was closed, the number of trades reached 49 with a value of RMB5,879,008.

In the same day, Shenyin Securities opened an account at the Shanghai Stock Exchange and became China's first individual securities investors.

On July 3, 1991, the Shenzhen Stock Exchange officially opened and realized centralized stock trading.

This was China's second stock exchange.

Yang Huaiding resigned his job on March 23, 1998 and quickly became a well-known "Yang Millionaire" after investing in stocks.

Before that, he was a worker at a Shanghai ferroalloy factory with 6,000 employees. With cultural degree of junior high school, his monthly salary was only RMB60.

In 1990, when stocks boomed, Yang sold his shares for RMB850 per 100 shares. At the end of the year, on the opening day of the Shanghai Stock

Exchange, with the opening quotation of RMB374 per 100 shares, Yang bought 100,000 shares. When the share value increased to RMB2,300 per 100 shares, he sold them again.

When he dealt in treasury bonds at the beginning, a lot of people called him "Yang Millionaire", but in fact, after trading stocks, he was worthy of the name.

The formal family name of his grandson was "Yang Xian" and the pet name was "Zhang Tingban". He had said that he would pay all his attention to stock trading all his life. He even jokingly said that after death, he would scatter his ashes at the gate of the Shanghai Stock Exchange.

The supermarket revolution

On March 26, 1994, the Malaysian retailer Parkson entered China and the supermarket emerged.

In the next year, a swarm of other retailers, like Carrefour and PriceSmart, followed this trend. As time went on, the supermarket gradually evolved into the Chinese people's favorite shopping place. At first, they were counter-style supermarkets, afterwards, they gradually became large warehouse-style supermarkets.

On March 12, 1996, the *Xinmin Evening News* published an article: "On Zhongyuan Road, which was less than a hundred meters long, there were 17 supermarkets, such as Hualian, Sanjiaozhou, Jinjiang, Zhenyuan, Liannong, Xingdi, Liming, Weimin, etc. While in Pudong District, the competition between the supermarkets was also very fierce: near the Dezhou store of Hualian supermarket, Baijia, Yuyuan, Baxie, Jinzhong, Hengdapingjia, Changchun, Jiajiale were all gathering."

Being different from the traditional ways of shopping, the supermarket had great influence on people's life.

With a wide variety of goods, the visual effect would made people want to buy.

This shopping mode could give customers the biggest option because they didn't need to care about the shop assistant and they could choose and pick the goods they wanted, if they changed their minds, they could put them back at any time.

The cereal & oil goods shelves in Huarun Supermarket

Provided by Beijing Archives

The yogurt in the supermarket cooler

Provided by Beijing Archives

At the early stage of the prevalence of the supermarket, theft was common. It was a test of morality to resist the temptation to steal.

In the 1990s, there was a front-page report on the *Southern Weekend*:

"Yichulianhua Supermarket opened in Shanghai with low-price propaganda. On its opening day, its 16,000 square meter sales space was jammed with people. The excited consumers immersed in the wide variety of commodities like a carnival. When the staff checked the inventory after the supermarket was closed, the scattered chicken bones and the empty cans of beers and beverages on the ground stunned Mr. Kevin, an American vice president of this foreign-owned supermarket. Purportedly, on that day, the supermarket had 'sold' more than 600 chickens, but only 200 chickens were paid for at the cash desk, so the other 400 chickens might have been 'digested' by consumers on the spot."

Nowadays, the supermarket has become very popular in China and people are accustomed to it.

The hard life of non-local female job-seekers

In the early 1990s, the popular proverb in the society was "no matter it was in the north and south, east and west, the richest place was in Guangdong". During those years, Cantonese was the most popular dialect among government officials and young women and the southern areas had become the first choice for university graduation and talent.

According to statistics, since 1992, the number of migrant workers from other provinces to Guangdong reached more than 10 million per year and by the late 1990s, the number even reached 15 million. If adding the people moving from Guangdong to the Pearl River Delta and urban areas, the number might

Still of the TV play Non-local Female Job-seeker

be 26 million. In the eyes of many migrant workers, Guangdong meant dreams, opportunity and success.

"I don't want to say, I am very kind…" this song comes from the TV play *Non-local Female Job-seeker*. This TV play was very famous throughout the country in the early 1990s.

But in fact, the life of the female job-seekers was much more difficult than on TV.

In 1993, the 8th edition of the *Democracy and the Rule of Law* published a long article titled The Death of the Non-local Female Job-seeker, written by Mei Jianhua and Pi Guangzhou. This article discussed the death of Shu Jingfang, a female job-seeker at a Sino-foreign joint venture named Libao Bedding Article Company in Shangtou, Nansha City in Guangdong Province. On February 10, she suddenly bled profusely from the head and fell to the ground and was dead when she was taken to the hospital.

Her factory said "gastrorrhagia" caused her death but her family didn't accept that, so after the second autopsy, it was confirmed that machines had caused fatal injuries.

After this event, the treatment of job seekers attracted public attention and along with the social progress, this situation would be gradually improved.

China's first directly elected township head

On December 31, 1998, after an intense campaign speech, China's first directly elected township head appeared in Buyun Town, Suining City in Sichuan Province. This event demonstrated great progress in China's democratic political construction.

Because of this, Yunbu town was called "the first township of China's direct election".

According to the introduction from Tan Xiaoqiu, the first directly elected township head, the electoral committee used various ways to propagandize this election campaign, issued more than 3,800 copies of publicity materials and received a lot of people's consultations. The committee not only sent open letters to all town voters, but also mailed open letters to the more than 4,200 voters working outside the town.

Seeing from the later results, the voters' enthusiasm was peaked and more than 500 voters returned to their hometown and took part in the election.

Finally, the town elected 15 people as candidates. Five were party officials. On December 15, 1998, the town held a primary election meeting that included 161 people, including the township cadres, each village cadre and the villagers' representatives. After the 15 candidates were elected, they were required to deliver a policy speech on the theme of "based on the actual situation of Buyun, how to develop Buyun's economy". After that, they would answer questions raised by each district representative.

Then, through secret ballot, two formal candidates were elected. They were Zhou Xingyi, the middle school chemistry teacher of Buyun, and Cai Yunhui, the director of the village committee. Tan Xiaoqiu, as the party nominated candidate, bypassed the primary election, and directly became a formal candidate. Starting from December 20, all these formal candidates would deliver their policy speeches to the whole town. They had held a total of 13 speeches each in ten villages, the residents' committee where the township government was located, the township middle school and the township market on the marketing day.

According to the statistics, the entire town had 11,347 voters, including 3,700 migrant workers, and issued 6,236 ballot tickets and took back 6,212 of them. The election result was that Tan Xiaoqiu won 3,130 votes which accounted for 50.19%, Cai Yunhui 1995 votes and Zhou Xingyi 1017 votes.

On December 31, 1998, in the afternoon, the electoral committee announced that Tao Xiaoqiu had won.

On January 4, 1999, under the supervision of the chairman of the township people's congress, Tan Xiaoqiu, holding the corner of the national flag, solemnly swore to the whole town people.

Essay Revival

In 1992, the book, *Cultural Journey*, written by Yu Qiuyu, was successively published in Mainland China and Taiwan. Its publication caused a big stir in the literary world.

This book's vigor, knowledge and language were all far beyond the "poor and weak" essay works at that time. Yu's essay works had been called "another peak in the history of Chinese modern essay", and he was renowned as "the last essay master of this century, and is the first poet who ushers the fresh air of the essay."

Yu had created a new social mood of the cultural essay.

In the mid and late 1990s, the pirated books of the Yu's essay, *Cultural Journey* and *Poem Note*, could be found at any bookstall in big cities. Yu not only spread his essays, but also spread knowledge of the culture and history inside his essays. The more important thing was that his essays trained a large number of essay lovers and cultural followers which contributed to a national essay revival.

The book Cultural Journey. The essay revival, triggered by Yu Qiuyu's essay led more and more people to pay close attention to and appreciate the essay.

In 1993, *Fei Du*, written by Jia Pingao, was serialized on the journal *October*, and then was published by Beijing Press with a first print of 500,000 copies. The book, at that time, caused a lot of controversy because there were too many spaces and entire parts were substituted with the words "here delete many words".

Of course, those deleted words were all sexual descriptions. This intentional or unintentional pruning attracted widespread attention from all walks of life. According to the incomplete statistics, the formal and semi-formal published versions of *Fei Du* sold more than one million copies but sales of pirated copies reached 12 million.

At that time, the booksellers had hyped this book as the "modern *Jin Ping Mei*" (a pornographic book in ancient China).

Chinese Football League A

On April 17, 1994, in Chengdu, with a whistle, the Chinese Football League A started.

The rival of green Guoan was the Guangdong team. At 61 minutes in the game, Yang Chen scored the first goal in Guoan's first professional league. At 71 minutes, Xie Feng kicked the second goal. Guoan beat Guangdong 2-0 and helped the team achieve their first professional league victory.

Da Lian Wanda Team won the annual champion of the Football League A.

Since then, Chinese people on one hand watched the game of Football League A, on the other hand were saddened with the disappointing of Chinese football.

Some 14 years after the "5-19" football event in 1985, a Yugoslavian named Milutinovic became the head coach of the Chinese football team. On October 7, 2001, he led the Chinese men football team and realized the World Cup dream of several generations. On the World Cup in Japan and South Korea in 2002, the Chinese football team was totally failed.

On the Spring Festival Gala, Song Dandan and Huang Hong had satirized Chinese football in their sketch *Going Home*. Later, during the 2008 Spring

Festival, Song Dandan and Zhao Benshan satirized football in their sketch *Torch Bearer* again:

Liu Liu: Which game gives you heartache?

Song Dandan: Football.

Liu Liu: Which game gives you more heartache?

Song Dandan: Chinese football.

MEMORIES OF
CHINESE LIFE IN THE

21ST CENTURY

In the new millennium everything changes fast and there are more and more personalized requirements. So many choices and such quick transformations are part of the basic necessities of life. The credit card is used for payments. "Mortgage slaves" and "living paycheck-to-paycheck" (penniless by the end of every month) have overcome people's consumption pattern and short messages have altered the way people communicate. Above all, the introduction or perfection of a variety of laws and regulations, including property laws, gives more attention to safeguarding the legitimate interests of individuals. Chinese people are proud of the Beijing Olympic Games and have learned from SARS and the Wenchuan earthquake to face disaster and pursue a wonderful life.

Bellyband on the street

Since the late 1990s, enchanting skirts with shoulder straps have emerged. However, only young, sexy and slim ladies with fair skin deserve to wear them. Here is a good way to wear the skirts in public. A T-shirt can be worn inside or with a small chiffon shawl outside the skirt. In this way, ladies can avoid over-exposing themselves and the effect of obscure beauty can be achieved.

In the spring of 2000, a baby tendency surfaced among young women in Shanghai. They styled their hair with two small plaits or topknots and wear "foot shaped" baby shoes with big round toes (black cloth shoes with the lace on one side, shaped closer to the feet). They were usually dressed in varicolored tights or overalls with an embroidered bag or small leather bag, decorated with a fluffy teddy bear or a little dog on the strap and slinging it across the shoulder. In addition, female college students drank from milk bottles, made themselves up with baby lotion, and spoke in babyish tones. The women nearly 40 years old would put on children' garments as well. It was really a fashion.

On January 8, 2002, Xinhua News Agency reported that a national costume fashion of women wearing bellybands had again emerged in Beijing. Quite a number of dazzling Chinese-style bellybands could be found in Xiu Shui street stalls – cotton, silk, linen, classical, improved, outwear, underwear, and so on.

During the Cannes Film Festival Award Ceremony in 2001, Zhang Ziyi wore a tailored long red bellyband dress, just like what an ancient Chinese lady would wear. As a result, bellybands became the love of a number of Chinese and foreign celebrities and among fashionable women at the time.

Without a pair of leather shoes or slippers, bellybands on the street can be seen as swimsuits. Bareness is fiercer and fiercer and people became gradually accustomed to it. Later,a well-known expression suggests that meat prices rise fastest, stocks fall furthest and women's clothes shrink the most.

Foreign girls with bellybands on the street in Hangzhou.

APEC Summit makes Tang suit famous

In October 2001, 20 national leaders in red and royal blue Chinese-style Tang suits opened in front participated in the APEC summit in Shanghai. For some time after that, the Chinese Tang suit rapidly grew in popularity.

As one of the main designers of Tang suits for APEC leaders, Yu Ying said that designers decided to call them "Tang suits" because in many foreign countries Chinese people lived in places called "Tang People Street" or Chinatown. Their clothes were naturally named Tang Suits. In addition, some overseas Chinese also call Chinese style clothing Tang suits. "So it is an international nomination," she said half-jokingly. She believes that the Tang Suit is a general term used for Chinese style clothing. (*Beijing Youth Daily*, February 3, 2002)

Front-opening Chinese-style Tang suit.

After 2004, a "Han Dynasty clothing fever" emerged among college students. That meant holding activities in dark clothes or robes from the Han Dynasty. They think it is a real Chinese costume or distinctive traditional dress. Although the "Han Dynasty Clothing Fever" has not been recognized by the mainstream, it is still popular with young students where different opinions are common.

In the film *In the Mood for Love* directed by Wong Kar-wai, Maggie Cheung dressed in Qipao (Chinese robe) is very sexy and elegant and added to the popularity of the traditional dress style. Some in the audience have confirmed that there are some 30 different robes that Maggie Cheung wears in the movie.

Xiushui Street in the north, Xiangyang Road in the south

Anyone who loves clothes in the new millennium has heard of the Xiangyang Road market in Shanghai.

Xiangyang Road Market in Shanghai.

The Xiangyang Road market started in the year 2000, when some vendors left the neighboring Huating Road clothing market that was demolished. Initially, the market had little business. To attract more customers, a few illegal vendors began to sell fake goods with brands like Louis Vuitton, Hermes, Chanel, Prada and others. Surprisingly, Chinese and foreign consumers that could not stand the high prices of the real thing swarmed to these markets to buy fake top brands with relatively high quality. In the market, there would be a number of foreign customers shopping at almost wholesale scales. In many people's minds, the Xiangyang Road market became "the fashion landmark for civilians". At 9:30 p.m. on June 30, 2006, the Xiangyang Road market was shut down.

In Beijing, Xiushui Street became "the landmark" of the reform and opening up policy and the so-called "Riverside Scene at Qingming Festival of 20ᵗʰ Century".

Xiushui Street in Beijing, affectionately referred to as OK Street by many foreigners.

Starting in 1982, some vendors sold clothes and small articles in Xiushui East Street. By 1985, the small Xiushui Street was occupied by a variety of goods. From 1995 to 2001, the original street specializing in silk sales began to be filled with counterfeit goods. With the departure of the original vendors, many businessmen from all over China came to Xiushui. Many were shrewd southerners selling knockoff clothes, leather belts, glasses, and so on.

From 2006, famous brands targeted the Xiushui Street Market in succession. Five European manufacturers including LV and Chanel jointly prosecuted sellers of counterfeit products at the Beijing Xiushui Street Clothing Market. The manufacturers won RMB20,000 each. After that, a great number of famous international brands started filing lawsuits against Chinese retailers.

At 11:30 a.m. on January 7, 2005, a bulldozer pulled down the long-standing signboard of the "Xiushui Market" and the market itself was torn down. The new Xiushui Market was set to open on March 19, 2005.

The shutdown of the Xiangyang Road market and the transformation of the Xiushui Street market have reflected China's determination to maintain the intellectual property. At the same time, they have set two examples for similar markets in the domestic markets.

Residence permit replaces temporary residence permit

In 2001, an ordinary cobbler in Shijiazhuang changed his registered rural permanent residence into the urban residence certificate in Shijiazhuang for a cost of just RMB3.

In the past, the story was generally seen as a fable. With the development of the market economy, the special function attached to registered permanent residence has gradually faded. The market economy needs to allocate market factors through market means and, accordingly, the residence "hedge" between cities and towns and between different cities has started to fade.

Temporary residence permit issued by the Beijing Municipal Public Security Bureau.

As of June 30, 2003, the barriers to apply for a Beijing Work & Residence Certificate were drastically lowered, bringing about hope for non-local people that they could become residents of Beijing .

During two hours in the morning of July 1, as many as 50,000 people visited the website of the Beijing Municipal Bureau of Personnel. Prior to that, residents from other places could only live in Beijing temporarily.

On June 15, 2002, Shanghai launched the first residence permit system in China. From October 1, 2004, users of the Shanghai residence permits expanded to "domestic people living in Shanghai, without permanent residence of Shanghai".

According to the Shanghai Residence Permit Rule, the external population can enjoy some of the rights of Shanghai residents. For example, children with recognized talents can attend the university entrance exam. They would also be provided with other benefits such as unemployment insurance, comprehensive insurance, social insurance, and so on.

At the end of 2006, Shenzhen began to provide residence permits. Shenzhen residence permits focus on the dilution of household registration concepts and the inclusion of hospitals, schools, work and life in the scope of "residence permits". When a person changes jobs in Shenzhen, the number of residence permits remains the same. If the holder leaves Shenzhen, the permit "goes to sleep". Once the holder returns to Shenzhen, the permit is "activated" once again.

From 3G telecommunications to 4G

According to a report in the *Beijing Evening News* on February 27, 2000, digital cameras, digital video cameras, digital music players and audiovisual products became more and more popular with the young digital generations. About the size of a traditional tape, an MP3 music player can store more than ten pop songs with CD quality that can be downloaded free from the Internet. Many young buyers bought them enthusiastically.

The *People's Daily* reported on November 6, 2000 that the recently launched Siemens 6688 smart GSM cellphone was the first one with a built-in MP3 player and with an interchangeable media card. Thanks to the built-in MP3 player, one could listen to music by plugging in headphones into the cellphone. A specially made synchronous adapter could be connected to the computer to exchange files. In the new millennium, major items can't cover the rapidly evolving electronic products. The *Beijing Daily* reported on February 12, 2002, that carrying a small removable storage disk hanging around one's neck had emerged as a new fashion.

Mobile phones are becoming cheaper and cheaper, but call charges made many consumers unhappy. Fortunately, short messages emerged as a common means of communication. On May 17, 2000, China Mobile Communications formally launched the short message service (SMS) and sent the first message in China. That year, more than 1 billion short messages were sent in China.

A PC was used to send the first short message in the world to a mobile phone in 1992. That message was sent through the British GSM network. No one could have imagined that many years later inexpensive text message services put forward by telecom operators to tackle high charges would have huge influence on people's economic and cultural lives, even on politics. According to official China Mobile figures, 800 million short messages were sent through the company during the seven day Spring Festival in 2002.

In 2002, ordinary urban residents were more concerned about another matter. At the beginning of that year, China's simulation mobile communication network was comprehensively closed and China Mobile Communication entered into the "digital era".

On April 9, the CDMA network of China Unicom began to operate and the number of CDMA users hit 800,000 in five months. All Chinese mobile phone producers were doing the substantial business. Mobile phones made by international brands such as Motorola and Nokia hit store shelves one after the other and many were produced in China. Lenovo, Amoi, Waveguide and other domestic brands began to compete in the market.

At 14:30 on January 7, 2009, the Ministry of Industry and Information Technology granted three licenses for third generation mobile communications (3G) to China Mobile, China Telecom and China Unicom, marking the country's entrance into the era of 3G.

On the afternoon of December 4, 2013, the Ministry of Industry and Informati on Technology granted licenses for fourth generation mobile communications (4G) to China Mobile, China Telecom and China Unicom, with the three companies obtaining TD-LTE licenses. China's telecom industry formally entered the era of 4G.

SOHO, BOBO, or IF: Which group are you in?

The *People's Daily* reported on November 29, 1995, that working from home had emerged as a trend in contemporary society, a trend that appeared along with the ideal of the information highway and reflected higher efficiency and more conservation.

The *Beijing Daily* reported on June 21, 2001, that they might engage in website design, publishing books and cartoons or participate in building brand images. All this work could be done from home. A great number of individual studios have emerged, particularly among the fashionably called SOHO generation, a group of people who rarely show up in the office.

SOHO is an acronym for "Small Office Home Office", meaning that there is a separate office and a home office. SOHO is another name for freelancers, or a free, flexible and new way of working.

BOBO group is the combination of Bohemia and Bourgeois. To be a BOBO, one must earn a middle class income and have a decent job. Besides, one should have the "homeless" complex to wander all over the world and often put it into practice. Of course, this group definitely chooses five-star hotels wherever they go.

Before the middle class established a stable base in China, another life concept, namely, the IF group (International Freeman) also appeared. IF refers to people who freely select their place of work, living and travel based on their personality. The prominent characters lie in their ability, extra money and interest to take a trip in foreign countries. Fluent in at least one to two international languages, they own varied dress styles, integrating eastern and western fashion elements, for which other people are so eager.

Property income structures an olive shaped society

In the beginning of the new millennium, the middle class activated Chinese dream of a future life and the new push towards self-status. The creativity source of all bold positioning for ideal lifestyles can be found in the concept of the "middle class".

In October 2007, the Report to the 17th Party Congress put forward the idea of "creating conditions for more people to gain property income". It attracted plenty of attention.

Experts say "property income" refers to income from movable family property (such as bank deposits, securities, etc.), and real estate (including houses, land, collections, etc.) It also covers interest, rents and patent income by remising property rights and bonuses and incremental benefits of property gained through its operation. The proposal of "property income" also coincides with the push towards a majority of people being "middle-income earners" put forward in the report, and the push is interpreted as an "olive shaped society".

There was a saying popular in the new millennium: "Even though we can't win Liu Xiang, we must surpass the CPI".

Compared with CPI data, the bank's interest return must be negative. As a result, many people began to manage their money, believing in the advertising words that "if you don't manage money, you won't win money." They invested in stocks, funds, futures, foreign exchanges, gold, and other fields.

The theme of China's social wealth is changing. In the past, people were used to accumulating wealth slowly through honest work, keeping expenditures within the limits of their income and through thrift. While many people have found that in addition to labor, other elements, for example, capital plays a great role in wealth growth. With the "magic cube" of capital, wealth accumulation is faster than income growth simply relying on labor.

Artificial beauty

Since the new millennium, tattoo fever has been heating up. By 2007, tattoo rooms could be found in the streets and alleyways of nearly every city, regardless of size. Tattoos are generally seen as symbols of primitive societies or marks for gang members. However, "white-collars" are now getting tattoos, many small and hidden.

As cosmetology developed, "artificial beauties" appeared in society with eyes, nose, lips, chin, ears and even their face beautified through surgery. This kind of "artificial beauty" has led to some controversy. Some believe that it is a personal thing and others have no right to intervene. While some others think that the prevailing trends can only bring about the false and artificial fairness.

In 2004, Hao Lulu, "China's first man-made beauty" made her formal appearance after a process of 200 days and RMB300,000 with more than ten plastic surgeries.

In a public activity, Hao Lulu said her goal was to march towards the entertainment industry. She wanted to act in movies and television shows and become famous by writing books. Influenced by the prevailing trend of artificial beauty, many young people undertook plastic surgery and solemnly "ordered" "Kim Hee-Sun's nose", "Zhao Wei's eyes", "Shu Qi's lips" and "Brigitte Lin's chin".

In May of that year, the "artificial beauty" Yang Yuan's was disqualified from the finals of the 2004 Miss Globe Intercontinental Beijing competition, followed by a much-hyped legal rights safeguard for "artificial beauties".

Along with the disturbance of numerous "artificial beauties", was the emergence of the "ugly girl" Zhang Jing event in Tianjin. After 1000 failures looking for a job, Zhang Jing lost her confidence and blamed her ugly face. Finally, Zhang Jing chose plastic surgery to change destiny. It seemed like a reasonable choice.

"Harvard Girl" moving parents holding high hopes for children

In April 1999, a widely reprinted news report generated attention among numerous readers. Four famous American universities, including Harvard University, had admitted Liu Yiting, a Chengdu girl, at the same time. In all four cases, the costs of tuition and living expenses were covered.

In August 2000, *Liu Yiting, the Harvard Girl's Quality Cultivation Documentary* was published by the China Writers Publishing House and gave many parents hope that their children could follow in their footsteps.

Starting from Liu Weihua, the mother's feelings and experiences of early education theory learning while she was pregnant, the main body of the book completely records and narrates Liu Yiting's growth from zero to 18 years of age. The use of a large number of original data accumulated in the 18 years gives the book a large dose of realism. The narrative form is unique. The author gives narration is mixed in with comments in a friendly narrative tone, bringing about a characteristic appeal.

Of course, there are also some queries. Does the "Harvard girl" display a quality-oriented education? Is Harvard admission the single standard to judge excellence? Must children meet the expectations of their parents?

Later, the "tiger mother" and "wolf father" arrive.

The "Tiger mother" is a Chinese professor at the University of Yale, formerly known as Amy Chua, who published a book *Battle Hymn of the Tiger Mother* that caused a sensation in the United States. In the book, she introduced her Chinese approach to education for her two daughters. She calls her daughters "garbage" and requires them to get "A" in every subject. They are not allowed to watch TV, and they are forbidden to eat if they don't practice the piano attentively. Her education method stirred the American educational world and has generated great discussion on the educational methods of China and the United States. The story of the "tiger mother" appeared on the cover of *Time* magazine.

Xiao Baiyou is a Hong Kong businessman that claims to be "China's wolf father". He claims to "beating" his three children to educate them and all three have been admitted by Peking University. At the same time, he is ranked among successful parents. *Therefore, Brothers and Sisters in Peking University*, his parenting book, was published to introduce his experience raising children.

Who moved my cheese

In 2001, CITIC Publishing House published *Who Moved My Cheese?*, a book by the American writer Spencer Johnson. Since then, "Who move my cheese?" has served as a pet phrase for many people.

The book has sold more than 20 million copies worldwide. Through a seemingly simple fable, it tells people of a great way to cope with changes and succeed in today's changeable age. By utilizing this approach, you can embrace the things you want most in life, which is called "cheese" in the book. The "cheese" in the book is a metaphor for the goals we seek in real life. It may be a job, money, a sweet love, or a wonderful life.

In 2003, the book *Rich Dad, Poor Dad* told readers that assets and liabilities should be distinguished to calmly face the changes in individual wealth, to make money work for us, to not be a slave for money and to ultimately achieve financial independence. This book fundamentally shifted traditional Chinese values, concepts of money and outlooks on life.

"Not refusing any little soil, Mount Tai has its height. Not selecting streams, rivers make its depth." Therefore, great rites start from little things, and details determine success or failure. In China, too many people want to do great things, but there are very few people willing to focus on every detail. We lack executors making perfection more perfect, not resourceful strategists. We have formulated all kinds of management rules and regulations, but the strict execution is urgently needed. We must get rid of impatience and superficial touching, and advocate the attention to details.

Cover of Who Moved My Cheese?.
This book is the best-seller in 2001.

In January 2004, the book *Details Determine Success or Failure* was published. In the book the author put forward the idea of an age of fine management with details determining success or failure. The idea is described as "a needle plunging into the acupuncture point of fickleness in today's society". Subsequently, "details determine success or failure" became a buzzword for the year.

Homosexuality is no longer seen as a mental illness

Cui Zi'en, a lecturer from the Department of Literature at the Beijing Film Academy, revealed his homosexuality during a class in 1991. He became the first person to become openly homosexual in Mainland China. Because of this decision, he was removed from his post as an instructor by the Beijing Film Academy.

Over time, social tolerance for homosexuality has grown.

In Anhui Province, there was a case of lesbians living together. Since the local public security organ found it hard to determine the nature of their relationship, the case was reported to the national Ministry of Public Security. Here was the response: "Currently, no clear stipulation has been provided in Chinese law. As for the problem you reported, you can choose not to handle in principle and it is better not to give the security punishment in the name of hooliganism." The first official judicial interpretation of homosexuality has shown the attitude towards decriminalization of homosexuality, which was considered a historic sign.

In 1997, the new *Criminal Law* took effect and the "crime of hooliganism" used to punish some homosexual sex behavior was deleted.

In 2001, the third edition of *Chinese Classification and Diagnosis of Mental Diseases* was released. It outlines the diagnostic criteria for "homosexuality" as follows:

(1)Conforming the definition of sexual orientation disorders.

(2)Under normal living conditions, continuous eroticism towards same-gender people from teenage years, including thoughts, feelings and sexual behavior.

(3)Although normal sex can be realized with the opposite sex, the sex tendency is weakened or absent obviously. As a result, it's hard to establish and maintain the family relationship with members of the opposite sex member.

(*Chinese Journal of Psychiatry*, No.3, 2001)

From then on, the sexual activity of homosexuality is no longer seen as abnormal psychology and gays and lesbians are not treated as a mental disorder any more. This is undoubtedly social progress and tolerance.

The lawsuit for sexual harassment

In July 2001, Ms. Wang, a company worker in Xi'an, sued the company's general manager in the Lianhu District People's Court, asserting that the manager often harassed her by spooning.

The Lianhu District People's Court accepted the case.

No case like it had been heard in China before. Ms. Wang became the plaintiff party of "the national first sexual harassment case", which also caused the extensive concern of all sectors of society, especially legal professionals and the masses of women.

Because of personal privacy, the court was very careful on this case. To protect the parties' privacy, a closed trial was held on October 24, 2001, with only two to three people from the court knew the court session took place and only a handful of people learned of the result of the first-instance judgment. (Privacy to Sue "Sexual Harassment" Is a Secret, *Sanqin Daily,* December 23, 2001)

The court rejected the prosecution due to lack of evidence but the case marked the emergence of cases of sexual harassment in the courts.

Wang said: "Although I am the first one to sue for sexual harassment, I will not be the only one. I believe the violated will stand up bravely like me."

On August 28, 2005, the 17st meeting of the Tenth National People's Congress Standing Committee approved in a vote the "National People's Congress Decision on Amending 'Law on the Protection of Women's Rights and Interests'", which entered into force on December 1, 2005. The revised law on the protection of women's rights and interests stipulated that sexual harassment on women shall be banned and affected women have the right to complain to their units and relevant agencies.

This was Chinese laws' first clear opposition to sexual harassment, showing the increasingly strong protection of women's rights and interests.

New marriage law limits "having a concubine"

In April 2001, the new Marriage Law of the People's Republic of China was modified during the 21st meeting of the Ninth National People's Congress Standing Committee, which covered several hot issues.

First, marital rape was not stipulated. At the time, rape was believed to be a criminal issue, following under the scope of criminal laws. The Marriage Law is part of civil law, regulating civil legal relations. As a result, provisions of marital rape cannot be stipulated.

Secondly, a "husband and wife should be faithful to each other" which meant they should be loyal to each other when it comes to sex. An added item in the new Marriage Law regulates that the husband and wife should be faithful to each other, which is associated with spousal right. Spousal rights are the integration of rights and obligations produced by the identity of spouse, inclusive of rights on personal and property areas.

Loyalty is one aspect of spousal rights. It is one-sided to interpret spousal rights as the right to sex. Loyalty requires both parties to be faithful in love, including sex. Disloyalty means the betrayal of love and non-exclusive feelings for sex, prescribed in the marriage law of many countries. Love is the condition for the existence of marriage. Without loyalty and love, divorce follows. Faithfulness is a basic requirement.

Third, does the new Marriage Law include provisions for "a concubine"?

Together with the provision of prohibiting bigamy in the new revised Marriage Law, there is a clause that states that "the person with a spouse is forbidden to live together with another person", which actually bans having a concubine. Having a concubine is complicated and in some cases the man even holds a wedding with the concubine. Yet living with a concubine as husband and wife constitutes bigamy, and there is a responsibility to prosecute it according to the Criminal Law. Living together but without the name of husband and wife should be curbed. Therefore, the newly revised Marriage Law prohibits this kind of behavior. A married person cannot live together with another opposite person of the opposite sex without breaking the law. In the newly added chapter of legal responsibility there are corresponding provisions, namely, if a person with a spouse lives together with someone else, he or she will be responsible to compensate the party not at fault for compensation. As for bigamy, there are both criminal and civil liabilities.

In fact, the new Marriage Law focuses on property, family violence and divorce. Marriage difficulties like a concubine, fault compensation, and others are also stipulated.

Annotation of Marriage Law of the People's Republic of China

Marriage without unit proof

No marital status certification, no letter of introduction, no premarital check-up proof. The implementation of Marriage Registration Statute on October 1, 2003 replaced the Regulations on Marriage Registration Administration that had been effective for nine years. The removal of the word "administration" made it clear that marriage is a purely personal matter that that the parties involved are responsible for themselves, which shows the spirit of humanized management. Chinese citizens have more freedom on their personal life and enjoying a more tolerant social environment.

The biggest change in the new regulation is the clear stipulation that China's mainland residents only need to bring valid identity certificates, namely, household register and identity card when they apply to be married. In addition, a signed statement is also needed, declaring that the signatory has no spouse and no direct blood relations or collateral relation within three generations with the other party (commonly known as an affidavit of single status and no close relation statement). The long-demanded marital status certification by the work unit, premarital check-up proof and other formalities have all been eliminated.

There is much controversy associated with canceling the compulsory premarital check-up.

Many people believe that canceling the compulsory check-up does not mean a relaxation in the requirements for a quality population. The reason for the cancelation is that the requirement existed in name only and had lost any relation to its original intent. However, the premarital check-up is necessary to ensure the health of husband and wife and ensure the quality of the population in the future.

On November 20, 2002, the *Beijing Youth Daily* reported that a woman college student and her boyfriend were expelled from university after she was found pregnant in the school hospital for their "vicious conduct and immoral behavior". The couple believed the university had violated their privacy rights and were ready to sue.

Since September 2005, students in China's general institutes of higher education can get married at school in accordance with national related laws and regulations without agreements from the school.

The controversial provision of universities "forbidding marriage and fertility" has been finally abolished and the issue of whether undergraduates can get married during the period of school or not has been settled. Undoubtedly, new regulations for colleges and universities are adapting to the development of the social legal system.

"Super Girl", sing as my pleasure

In 2005, PK was all over in China. Someone has interpreted PK as Player Kill in traditional games and network games, meaning to kill players in computer or other ones. Another explanation is Point Kick in play, which means the penalty sport in football.

The Super Girl singing competition in 2005 made the word popular.

On December 30, 2005, *Shanghai Youth Daily* published the article "Li

Yuchuan – One Second from a Girl to a Queen" by Min Hui and Chen Li.

That year, the connotation of the word PK was that P for people, civilians, and girls, and K for the king.

Li Yuchun created a miracle. Because of her, the emotion of millions of Chinese collapsed in the summer of 2005 in a good way. In 2005, she changed from ordinary girl to a star in an instant. At one point, text messages to support her reached 3.52 people at home and abroad. She became an Asian heroine gracing the cover of *Time* magazine. It only took a second to fall in love with her.

Thanks to "sing as my pleasure", entertainment changed. Instead of stars entertaining civilians, civilians are entertaining civilians. Stars are no longer that unattainable.

F4, the idol group from China's Taiwan. F means "Flower and Friend". These flower-like handsome boys have built a pure and earnest image.

There was a mass-election. PK became known as the final election, corns as fans of Li Yuchun, box lunches as fans of He Jie and jelly beans as fans of Zhang Liangying. "Super Girl" words had the highest click rates on the Internet. On the powerful and complicated language platform, there is a great need for a leader to unify all corners of the country. At this time, Li Yuchun emerged.

In this carnival, all participants were kings.

Plastic limit an order against "white pollution"

A thin plastic bag given for free, costs nothing and weighs nothing. It is easy to fold and carry and can hold many things—liquid, solids and fresh things. That's why it is called a "convenient bag".

When "convenient bags" are used, they become garbage and are extremely difficult to deal with. A large number of discarded bags, plastic sheets and other plastic packaging products have caused increasingly serious harm and posed hidden dangers. Since these waste is mostly white in called, their impact is known as "white pollution".

The environmental protection bag designed by Ray Magazine

White pollution should not be ignored and people of vision have been calling on China's to say "no" to convenient bags.

Finally, on December 31, 2007, the General Office of the State Council issued the "General Office of the State Council's Notification on Limiting the Production, Sale and Use of Plastic Shopping Bags".

This notification referred to as the "plastic limit order" stipulates explicitly that "Since June 1, 2008, plastic shopping bags with the thickness less than 0.025 mm are forbidden to be produced, sold or used nationwide." And "in all supermarkets, shopping malls, marketplaces and other retail places, a compensation system for plastic shopping bags is to be implemented and no fee plastic bags are to be provided for free."

Xinhua News Agency reported on August 4, 2008, that during the two-month implementation of the "plastic limit order", only 20% plastic bags were provided in the supermarkets of Beijing, where people became accustomed to "carrying reusable bags, shopping baskets, and simple nylon cord string bags".

900 million farmers bid farewell to 2,600 year old tax on grain

The royal grain tax is said to have originated during the Shangyang Reform. For 900 million farmers, the best news of New Year's Day of 2006 was the abolishment of agricultural tax. The cancellation of the agricultural tax categories relived many farmers.

People who have lived in rural areas are familiar with the history of "agricultural tax paid in grain", which is the priority after farmer "rush in harvesting and planting crops".

On April 8, 2004, the Ministry of Agriculture issued the "Emergency Announcement on Spring Grain Production", requiring that agricultural departments at all levels promote and implement policies including direct grain subsidies, subsidies to improve crop strains, subsidies for the purchase of farm equipment, agricultural tax reductions, minimum price systems for buying grain and basic farmland protection, with the purpose of arousing the enthusiasm of general farmers to grow grains.

On December 1, 2007, the Ministry of Finance and the Ministry of Commerce launched a policy of sending home appliances to the countryside. Based on the rural consumption rate and demands, the highest price of home appliance products for the countryside is no more than RMB2,000 for a color television, no more than RMB2,500 for a refrigerator (or freezer), no more than RMB1,000 for a mobile phone and no more than RMB2,000 for a washing machine. The highest terminal retail price of each type of product shall not be higher than the winning bid.

China is paying increasing attention to problems facing agriculture, rural areas and farmers, to protect the vital interests of farmers, which is the inherent requirement of building a new socialist countryside.

In the new millennium, it is common for private enterprise bosses to suspend or withhold the salaries of "migrant workers". To get their salaries, "bleeding, sweating, and weeping" migrant workers may climb the tower crane, jump from a building, be assaulted for no reason, and even chased.

On October 24, 2003, Premier Wen Jiabao travelled to a remote small mountain in Yunyang County, Chongqing, and asked villagers: "Do you still have any difficulties? What can we do for you?"

Xiong Deming, a peasant woman sitting to the left of Premier said shyly: "Premier, I'd like to talk about the salary of my family." She directly raised the issue of wage arrears.

Listening to Xiong Deming, Wen Jiabao frowned and said after a thoughtful moment: "Wage arrears for farmers must be handled well." At 11 p.m. that night, Xiong Deming and her husband got the delinquent salary of RMB2,240.

They would never have expected that a wave of salary claims would start in China.

High-speed rail: Maximum speed up to 486.1 km per hour

During Spring Festival travel in 2007, China's own high-speed rail "motor train unit" first appeared in the Shanghai-Nanjing line and Shanghai-Hangzhou line.

On April 18, China's sixth great railway speeding was completed, with the running speeds of 200 kilometers per hour for main arteries, and 250 kilometers per hour in certain sections, which was the most prominent highlight.

From then on, China stepped into the high-speed era. Chinese people proudly referred to their trains as "bullet" trains.

On December 3, 2010, China's home-built "Harmony" CRH380 bullet train travelled at the highest speed yet of 486.1 km/h during a trial run on the

Motor train unit 157. Motor train units mark China's international advanced technology of railway passenger transportation equipment. As a result, China has become one of the few countries which can independently develop the motor train unit with the speed of 300 km/h.

Beijing-Shanghai express railway from Zaozhuang to Bengbu.

This was a world record set by China's railway and the beginning of an important chapter worth writing in global railway development.

In June 2011, the Beijing-Shangai high-speed railway opened, with "the world-class engineering quality... safety, comfort, and environmental protection" and generating new expectations for China. However, the "7-23" Wenzhou train crash led the deaths of 40 people and injuries among 200. Developing the safest high-speed railway system emerged as the desire of all Chinese people.

"Golden Week" lets people play

In September 1999, the State Council introduced the new statutory holiday system, a seven-day holiday that included the statutory holiday plus work day shifts for National Day, the Spring Festival, and May Day.

From then on, three "golden weeks" every year bring about the tourism consumption boom, which has influenced the national economy and changed people's lives. Controversy on advantages and disadvantages of Golden Weeks always exists and Golden Weeks need to be improved.

During Golden Weeks people enjoy themselves and businesses reap big benefits. During the May Day holiday in 2000, the holiday economy exploded. Cash registers ran continuously and the television news reported that various scenic spots were full of tourists. Shopping and tourism consumption showed both momentum and strength. Tourism revenue for the week reached RMB18.1 billion.

In late November 2005, the United Nations Educational, Scientific and Cultural Organization identified the Gangneung Danoje Festival in South Korea as an intangible heritage. The fierce Dragon Boat Festival battle applied for the status but victory went to South Korea. Some argued that the Gangneung Danoje Festival was different from our Dragon Boat Festival, but a tremendous response has been created in Chinese academic circles around the application.

Since January 1, 2008, the revised "Measures on Having a Holiday for National Annual Leaves and Memorial Days" took effect. According to the measures, there is one day off on Tomb-Sweeping Day, Dragon Boat Festival, and Mid-Autumn Festival since 2008, and the May Day Golden Week, which had been in place for seven years, was cancelled.

Feng Jicai, the famous writer, believes that to change the traditional festival into a legal holiday is an effective way to protect intangible cultural heritage, which is helps preserve the cultural connotation of theses traditional festivals and the roots of the Chinese nation.

Traditional festivals have received more attention and some foreign festivals are increasingly popular in China. Christmas, Valentine's Day, April fool's day,

Mother's Day, Father's Day, Thanksgiving Day and other festivals from western countries have slowly become part of the daily life of ordinary Chinese people. Christmas gifts, chocolates, roses and carnations, with freshness and romance, evoke the tender feelings hidden in the bottom of our hearts. Their popularity is give thanks to clever marketing by shrewd business people and speculation of the mainstream media. Among these foreign festivals, Christmas and Valentine's Day are the most fun.

Enhancement of individual income tax exemption

Promulgated in September 1980, China's first "Individual Income Tax Law" set the income of RMB800 per month as the income tax exemption, while the average monthly wage was no more than RMB60 at the time. At the time, the individual income tax was aimed at musicians and movie stars who made a lot of money and foreign executives in foreign companies, of course.

The wage-earning class began to pay the income tax in 1994. In October 1993, the "Modification of the 'Individual Income Tax Law of the People's Republic of China'" was passed, stipulating that regardless of nationality, all Chinese and non-residents with income from China should pay individual income tax in accordance with the law. On January 1, 1994, an enforcement regulation was enacted. Since then, many people found one more item on their salary sheet: Tax.

In August 2005, the National People's Congress revised the individual income tax law, raising the income tax exemption to RMB1,600. In December 2007, the law was modified again and the exemption was raised to RMB2,000 from 2008.

On February 7, 2007, a photograph of Yi Jianlian, a basketball player, appeared on the front pages of dozens of national newspapers. Without showing his skilled three-point shot, the 7-foot-tall, 23-year-old superstar was queuing up to declare his income at the Local Tax Bureau of Dongguan, Guangdong, along with his teammates and coach. He told reporters that "tax is the duty of high income people… I'm clear about my income last year."

The year 2007 was the first in which people with annual income more than RMB120,000 were asked to take the initiative to pay taxes in China. A total of 1.63 million declared their income like Yi Jianlian had done. However, the number was just a quarter of the previous estimate. Experts had expected six to seven million people would surface with an annual income of RMB120,000 throughout the country.

Many people believe that tax authorities should strengthen levies on the rich and famous, to limit tax evasion of this class.

Chinese citizens now frequently repeat the American saying that: Only death and taxes are inescapable.

On June 30, 2011, Standing Committee of the National People's Congress modified the individual income tax law. On the basis of giving full consideration to public opinion, the tax exemption of payable individual income tax for wages and salaries was raised to RMB3,500 from RMB2,000.

Credit cards have altered the tradition of "no pay, no goods"

The year 2003 was called "the first year of China's credit cards". The direct cause was that when SARS hit, people found the credit card was more convenient than cash, which led to the rapid growth of credit cards. The circulation of credit cards in 2003 surpassed the total in previous years. By the end of the year, there were 4.8 million credit cards, more than twice the number in 2002. Inter-bank trading exceeded RMB380 billion, double that of 2002.

After 2003, a variety of credit cards in young men's wallets – Great Wall Card, Peony Card, Dragon Card, Golden Spike Card, Sunflower Card – overwhelmed and dazzled people.

When Bank of China issued the first credit card in China in 1985, it was impossible to anticipate the fast spread of credit cards. As the credit card just entered China, it was received with doubts. In the beginning of the reform and opening up, there was little household savings. The long-standing goal of "making ends meet" had made people accustomed to "no pay, no goods". The low engagement ratio of bank cards and their uneven distribution made it difficult for credit cards to become popular.

Today, it's common to see several bank cards in the wallets of people living in cities.

Credit card has changed people's traditional way to trade.

Before 2004, the issuing bank would generally charge an annual fee. The annual fee could be avoided if the cards were used for transactions of a certain value. Later, in addition to no annual fee, card companies would sent gifts and allow customers to accumulate points. Other value-added services were added. At present, some cards allow customers to buy goods in instalments, without limitations on the range of goods or merchants.

Watching Wang Zhizhi, Yao Ming and the Chinese NBA

In February 2001, David Stern, the NBA President, said in the all-star game in Washington that Chinese players Yao Ming, Wang Zhizhi and Bartel were very talented. With the proper training the could join the starting line-up of NBA teams in just two or three years.

"I've been looking forward to their joining," he said.

On March 29, Wang Zhizhi flew to the United States launching Asians' dreams of joining the NBA. A few days later, the formal signing ceremony for Wang and the Dallas Mavericks was held in the Landry Sports Center. Wang singed a two year contract and became the first Asian player to join the NBA.

At 8:30 p.m. on Wednesday, October 23, 2002, the Houston Rockets started playing the San Antonio Spurs. Nine minutes and 40 seconds before the end of the second quarter of the game, Yao Ming, seven-foot-five and the number one draft pick of 2002, replaced Steve Goodrich to join the game on behalf of Rockets. That was Yao's debut in NBA.

Tim Duncan, from the Spurs, gave Yao a memorable welcome. A few seconds after Yao's stepped into the court at the SBS Center, the home court of the Spurs, Yao got the ball within the three-point line and moved towards the basket but Duncan, who had been named most valuable player (MVP) in the previous season, knocked Yao down just as the Chinese player was lifting his right arm to shot. The fans roared in support Yao.

With a bloat on, Yao stood up and walked quietly to the free-throw line and easily hit two penalty shots, getting his first two points in the NBA.

Before October 13, Yao was attending the 14th Asian Games on behalf of the Chinese national team. In the men's basketball final, host South Korea defeated the Chinese team, which won the silver medal. When Yao returned to China, he signed a guarantee for the Chinese Basketball Association, stating that he would come back to participate in international competitions whenever the Chinese team needed. He then got a visa for the US and went to play in Houston on October 22.

After Yao's participation in the full-court practice and training on October 22, the Rockets coach arranged for Yao to attend his first NBA game against the Spurs.

On July 20, 2011, in Kerry Hotel in Pudong, Shanghai, Yao announced during a news conference: "As a basketball player, today I want to say that I will end my sports career and retire."

He also said: "At last, I must give thanks to the great era, which has provided me chances to realize my dreams and value."

WTO helps China realize its auto dream

On November 10, 2001, the 4th Ministerial Meeting of World Trade Organization (WTO) was held in Doha, Qatar, on which China's accession to the WTO protocol was passed unanimously. On December 11, China formally became a member of WTO, which is of great significance in China's reform and opening up, being an iconic event for Chinese economic integration into the world and its participation in international competition.

Many people who doubt the WTO shouted that "the wolf is coming" and "we are going to dance with the wolf." Now, more and more people understand

China's social economy has been developing increasingly. China has gradually become the world's first automobile consumption power, with the car ownership rate shocking the whole world.

that the key to "dancing with the wolf" is to cooperate and achieve win-win conditions. By the end of 2006, when the five-year transition period after China's accession to WTO ended, people had felt the changes in their life, the tangible and actual changes.

The first benefit from entering the WTO for civilians was the provision of abundant products with excellent quality and reasonable price, and high quality service.

In the second half of 2001, the state formulated policies to cancel the initial installation charge for local calls, mobile access fee, initial installation charge for rural telephones, and other government fund projects attached to phones.

The monopoly in communication market was broken and the cost brought down steadily, which brought about gains for people. Before entering the WTO, the price of a Motorola V998 was RMB7,000. The price of the mobile phone fell to RMB1,800 a few months after the entry. People who had seen owning a mobile phone as the goal of struggle would want to laugh at themselves.

The competition among state-owned banks, between state-owned banks and joint stock banks and between domestic and foreign banks will eventually promote and perfect the bank business and lead to better services.

Accession to the WTO stimulated the automobile industry and made it possible for many to fulfill their dreams of automobile ownership.

On December 11, 2001, China officially joined the WTO. Three years later, the prices for the Tianjin Xiali, the small car for masses was slashed. In the same month, Jili, a privately-owned brand whose cars sold for RMB30,000 was given permission to produce cars after many hardships. That same year, Sail, the RMB100,000 "home car" produced by Shanghai General Motor came out.

Since then, demand for cars in China grew rapidly. Domestic car production and marketing saw double-digit growth for six years in a row, from 820,000 vehicles sold in 2001 to some 5.32 million were sold in 2007. The highest annual growth rate was more than 50%. Although the five-year buffer for Chinese cars was up and tariff were reduced as required, domestic cars still accounted for 95% of China's car market. For three consecutive years, China was the second largest car producing nation in the world, with production only second to that of the U.S., exceeding that of Germany and Japan.

In place of introduction and joint venture, China's car industry moved towards independent innovation. In recent years, relying on the development of cheap and quality cars, a number of independent brands such as Geely, Brilliance, Chery, SAIC, Great Wall, and BYD have stood firm in the domestic market. Shanghai Volkswagen, FAW Volkswagen, Guangzhou Honda and other joint ventures have successfully launched indigenous development models. China is actively encouraging and advocating R&D of energy conservation and environmental protection security for cars and high efficiency for small cars.

From 2007 to this day, the proportion of private cars in China's car market has reached 83.2%. Among the 16 million cars, privately purchased, dominate the market.

Strongest nail house: real estate rights shall not be infringed

Corresponding to the bull market in 2007, the expression "history supreme" (which sounds like 'bull' in Chinese) became popular.

In the center of a big hole, a dozen meters deep, stood a house, like an islet, with a five-starred red flag at the top. A compensation agreement was not reached between Wu Ping, the owner of the two-story house near the light rail in Yangjiaping, Jiulongpo District of Chongqing, and a real estate developer. The house of 219 square meters remained in the development site and it was called "the strongest nail household", and it became famous on the Internet.

On April 1, the two sides came to an agreement under court mediation and the "nail" was pulled out at 10 p.m. on April 2.

On March 16, 2007, the "Property Law" was passed by an absolute majority of votes during the Fifth Meeting of the Tenth National People's Congress – 2799 affirmative votes out of the 2889 delegates attending the closing meeting.

The "Property Law" stipulates: "The state, collective and private property, as well as the property of other obliges are protected by law, and shall not be infringed by any unit or individual."

After the implementation of the "Property Law", many respondents went to court with the "Property Law of the People's Republic of China" in hand.

The first property law case involved the owner charging the real estate service company and asking for the return of parking fees. The accuser Xiaowen alleged that in September 14, 2007, she signed the parking service agreement with Beijing Haoyuan Longji Property Management Co. Ltd. It stipulated that the company would provide a parking space for Xiaowen's car in the community where Xiaowen lived from September 14, 2007 to October 13, 2007, and Xiaowen should pay RMB150 every month and RMB20 for the car card. Soon afterwards, Xiaowen paid the service fee, but the company did not offer the parking space. Xiaowen had to park her car on the community road or the free field.

After the introduction of the "Property Law", Xiaowen used it to sue the company at the Fangshan District court, claiming the company should return the service charge she paid.

Abroad, there is a proverb: In a private hut, the wind can enter, rain can enter, but the king has no right to enter. The "Property Law" is the confirmation of a great number of existing systems since China's reform and opening up, and it is beneficial for people to enjoy the fruits of reform and development and further stimulate people's enthusiasm to create wealth.

Huawei incident and the new Labor Contract Law

Starting in the second half of 2007, the Huawei incident embodies the warm response of social parties before the implementation of the new Labor Contract Law.

Since the end of September, a total of more than 7,000 senior employees who have worked for eight years at Huawei have submitted their resignations to the company voluntarily. The company arranged the widespread resignations.

Soon, these resigned employees would fill jobs through competition at their original salaries and position but they had to resign from their original contracts and the lengths of their services would be changed. All resigned senior staff could obtain compensation from the company of up to RMB1 billion.

On January 1, 2008, the "Labor Contract Law" was implemented and led to intense debate.

The competition for position after a resignation at Huawei was seen as the evasion of relevant provisions under the Labor Contract Law.

Anyway, the protection of workers' rights and interests in the new "Labor Contract Law" surpassed that of any time previous time with obvious significance.

Under the low compensation system, labor surplus was replaced by labor shortage. It became difficult to recruit workers without paying higher wages. Labor shortages gained more and more attention. Some argued that China reached the Lewis turning point, the point when a nation's labor force shifts from surplus to shortage.

In theory, the industrialization process is accompanied by the gradual transfer of rural surplus labor to non-agricultural industries and the surplus labor is reduced until it disappears. Although there are diverse opinions, it is beyond all doubt that the "cheap" Chinese labor force no longer exists and China's demographic dividend is coming to an end.

Along with the labor shortages is employment pressure.

After 2004, the "sea turtles" and "seaweeds" emerged. They were the overseas returnees and students who have studied abroad are unable to find employment. In the beginning, returned talents who have studied abroad were referred to as "sea turtles", which alluded to their identity, status and competitive salary. Over time, as the number of sea turtles grew, they became known as seaweeds.

In 2009, the term "Antizen" emerged, referring to highly educated people with low incomes. Generally speaking, they usually live in marginal areas and suburban rural areas of big cities, with characteristics similar to ants: intellectual, weak and social. Based on research carried out in Beijing, Shanghai, Guangzhou, Wuhan and Xi'an, there is a large number of antizen in each city.

Unequivocally, some white-collars shout out the slogan of "escaping from Beijing, Shanghai and Guangzhou" and the idea spreads quickly among white-collars in first-tier cities. Because of the excessive cost of housing, the difficulties finding employment and the pressure of life in these cities, many white-collar workers choose to move to lower-tier cities or their hometowns.

SARS, let us live another way

In early 2003, SARS spread through 32 countries and regions in the world, including China, Singapore, the United States and Canada.

As of June 18, 2003, there were a total of 8,465 SARS patients (including suspected cases) globally, with 801 deaths. In Southeast Asia along, the economic losses reached $60 billion.

Through the joint efforts of the governments and the people, the global SARS outbreak was basically under control at the end of June.

In the first half of 2003, nearly all Chinese people wore face masks in public in case they coughed, because all eyes would be on him or her.

On May 1, 2003, the *Shanghai Youth Daily* published a commentary:

"Pace of life will not be cut off. If SARS had not come, you may once again take your bag and head for the fascinating place you have been waiting for resolutely during the May Day holiday, go hiking, go swimming, and enjoy the lovely spring. If SARS had not come, you may pull yourself out of the office and head into the bar or tea house, to enjoy the city night to your heart's content… If SARS, the sudden disaster hand not come, life would continue ticking like a clock."

During the SARS period in 2003, hospitals implemented the strict control for going in and out, to prevent infection.

Seen from the sights we captured, SARS has changed people's lives.

During the SARS period, some people with many dinner parties go home before dark, appreciating the connotation of "family". Friends meet with each begin the "atypical" greetings, realizing the truth of peace equals to happiness.

Some lovers still embrace and kiss. Just the slightly fashion masks force them to watch each other sometimes. In the face of the SARS virus, people have to experience concern and even fear. However, they have become brave, responsible and delighted to offer help. In particular, people pay more attention to the things that would be ignored in daily life. Temporarily transforming people's lives, SARS can't change people's reflections, dedication and love of life. In the human-virus competition, a life concept and logic will be implanted. Although we are now living a happy life, we should remember that we come from misery. Besides, we should be aware that in the future we may also encounter hardship and misfortune. Disasters will remind us to live humbly, cherish life, and live on bravely."

We are all Wenchuan People: May 12, 2008

2008 was destined to be an unusual year.

At 14:28 on May 12, an 8.8 magnitude earthquake occurred in Wenchuan County (31 degrees north latitude and 103.4 degrees east longitude), Sichuan Province, which was revised later to 8.0 magnitude.

Every scene was horrible.

There were too many heart-warming events in the disaster.

At 4 p.m. on May 16, the first 31 teammates of The Japan international emergency rescue team arrived at Qingchuan County and began the search-and-rescue on the dormitory building of the Traditional Chinese Medicine Institute.

Using life detection instruments and gas leak detectors, rescuers searched the ruins carefully. When the position of a body was determined, many Japanese teammates wore gloves and removed bricks one by one manually and cautiously. At 7 am, a mother and daughter were found. Song Xuemei was still holding her daughter in the arms tightly, near the bedroom and on the passage to the door. Rescuers believed that when the earthquake hit, the

(above) On the morning of May 14, 2008, the People's Liberation Army soldiers were carrying the wounded soldiers in Beichuan, the severely afflicted area.

(below) At 7 a.m. of May 14, 2008, a baby, who was buried for two days and two nights, was saved in Beichuan. His parents were killed in the earthquake.

mother and daughter were in the bedroom. After the mother came to herself, she picked up her daughter and rushed to the door. But the building collapsed and buried them. There were no bruises on the daughter but the mother was scarred. Song Xuemei was 28 years old, and her daughter had been born 75 days earlier.

At 7:30 a.m. on May 17, their bodies were put on a stretcher and covered by a piece of white cloth. The Japanese rescue team lined up on two sides, bowing their heads and mourning for the dead. Some wiped their tears and said: "The mother is too great. She was embracing her daughter to the last moment of life." ("Japanese Rescue Members Shed Tears in Silent Tribute for the Victim Mother and Daughter", May 18, 2008, *Youth Daily*)

At 23:50 on May 13, ambulance sirens resounded through the whole Hanwang Town. In succession, four students were rescued from the collapsed school buildings of Dongqi Secondary School in Deyang City by the rescuers of National Earthquake Response Support Service of China.

Tan Qianqiu, the hero teacher, protected his four students.

"When we found him, he was lying on the desk with his open arms, covering his four students rigidly. The four were all alive," one rescuer told reporters of the scene. (May 14, Xinhua News Agency)

At 3 a.m. of May 14, 2008, a victim who lost her relatives was weeping alone in Jiuzhou Gymnasium, Mianyang.

According to local customs, the students' parents set off a string of firecrackers for Tan on the playground.

One after another, touching stories about relief, self-reliance and camaraderie came out. Humanity shined through the ruins and demonstrated the unparalleled tenacity of the Chinese nation to the world.

The country would emerge stronger from adversity. Instead of being knocked down in front of the disaster, Chinese people helped one another with cohesion.

They shouted out that we were all Wenchuan people.

The world's attention focused on the disaster in China.

Six rescue teams from Hong Kong, Taiwan, Russia, South Korea and Singapore arrived at the disaster area one after another to help.

People of all nationalities' expressed their profound condolences to the victims of the Wenchuan earthquake. The State Council announced on May 18 that May 19 to 21, 2008 would be National Mourning Days. From east to west, from north to south, the vast Chinese land was totally immersed in sorrow.

Global opinion was that setting up the National Mourning Day "is a breakthrough by the Chinese government and also another embodiment of its 'people-oriented' policies, to help those overwhelmed with grief and wish all unfortunate a peaceful rest. All lives and the dead have been respected, and more care and humanitarianism by the regime and country have been shown."

The United Kingdom's *Daily Telegraph* published a photograph, recording a touching moment in China's earthquake relief effort. Making all his efforts to render a last dignity to his wife, a man tied his beloved dead wife on his back and rode a motorcycle to the morgue.

Author Rabindranath Tagore said: "The living should have immortal love, and the dead should be given the immortal reputation."

For tens of thousands of victims of the Wenchuan earthquake, we sincerely hope that they will be endowed with the immortal reputation by our immortal love.

"Bird's Nest" feast

At 8 pm on August 8, 2008, the national stadium shaped like a "bird's nest" was glorious. The opening ceremony of the prestigious 29th Olympic Games was held in Beijing. At 11:36 pm, President Hu Jintao announced the opening of the 29th Beijing Olympic Games.

Sounds of nature by the violin solo and the Olympic theme song *You and Me* was sung by Liu Huan, the famous Chinese singer and Sarah Brightman, "the Queen". The melody flowed in the venue: "You and me, from one world, we are family. Travel dream, a thousand miles, meeting in Beijing."

With the magnificent layout, novel imagination and high-tech innovation, the Beijing Olympic Games presented an audio-visual feast of "telling Chinese stories with the world language" to more than 4 billion TV viewers around the world.

The most touching scene came when the Chinese delegation entered the arena. In the forefront was Yao Ming, the flag bearer of the Chinese team and famous basketball player, holding hands with Lin Hao, a second-grade student from Yuzixi Elementary School, Yingxiu Town, Wenchuan County of Sichuan Province. When the Wenchuan earthquake happened, the 9-year-old Lin Hao was very brave and rushed into the ruins to rescue his classmates. He was named the "Hero-Youngster Struggling Against Disaster". Chinese and foreign audiences was so touched by Chinese people's perseverance and unyielding tenacity in the face of adversity. The auditorium rang with applause and cheers and the shouting of "Go China" resounded through the stadium.

On August 24, the Olympic flame, which had been burning for 16 days, extinguished slowly. The "Bird's Nest" for flying dreams lit the farewell night with so much warmth and put a successful end to the 29th Summer Olympic Games.

During the 16 days, more than 10,000 athletes from 204 countries and regions, and 4.5 billion viewers made the Beijing Olympic Games

Impressive Beijing Olympic cauldron in the Bird's Nest (National Stadium), setting fire to the national passion and pride.

Beijing Olympic mascots (Fuwa)— Huanhuan, Beibei, and Yingying.

Track and field competition scene in the Beijing Olympic Bird's Nest (National Stadium)

Young Volunteers in Laoshan Cycling Venue during the Beijing Olympic Games.

with most participating countries and regions in history.

An editorial in the *People's Daily* noted on August 25 that glory belonged to the great Olympics!

On August 8, 2009, China set August 8 as national fitness day to commemorate the 2008 Olympic Games.

Narrow dwelling

Some have very definite requirements from one to ten for mates since 2000: one degree, two languages (Chinese plus English), a three-room apartment, famous brands for four seasons, well-featured in five sense organs (attractive and well put together), deny all the six relatives, at least seven thousand yuan a month in wages, (of speech) eloquent covering eight sides beautifully, , no drinking or smoking, ("wine" sounds the same as nine in Chinese)and honest(ten points).

The harshest one is the wedding room. Some girls often use "confessions coerced" to torture their boyfriends. Questions such as "did you buy a house", "do you have a house loan" and "how much is your mortgage left" are often used.

In Shanghai, mothers always teach their daughters a pet phrase that you must date the boy with car and house or I will feel anxious.

After all, high housing prices scare young people. There was a saying for the generation after 80s. "It doesn't matter that one party can't afford a house. But, if neither one has the ability to buy a house, it is a big deal."

After the new millennium, with soaring house prices from 2005 to the first quarter of 2006 in particular, it became almost impossible to purchase real estate with a lower price in the market, causing a heavy repayment burden for a large number of buyers. In addition, the people's bank of China announced a push to raise interest rates in 2004 and 2006, which increased people's concern for heavier mortgage burden. Therefore, the word "mortgage slave" was created.

In 2009, *Narrow Dwelling*, a TV series with social concern aggrieved many people. There is a classic line, "Why are we fastening our lives and dreams on a house? All of our efforts and hopes come down to a house. What a miserable life!"

The Chinese livelihood issues and people's survival pressure are more serious.

China during the Financial Crisis

Spreading in 2008, the international financial crisis intensified in 2009. It moved from developed countries to emerging markets and developing countries, and from financial sectors to the rest of the economy, wide and deep, its impact defied expectations.

China could not stay out of the aggressive international financial crisis.

The rare severe test rendered by the international financial crisis was unable to hinder China to take Chinese road. The Party Central Committee decisively put forward the proactive fiscal policy and moderately loose monetary policy and quickly launched a series of policies and measures, especially ten actions for boosting domestic demands and ensuring growth. In the fourth quarter, RMB100 billion from the Central Government was added and RMB20 billion of the restoration and reconstruction fund after disasters was allocated in advance. By the end of 2010, a total of RMB4 trillion had been invested to "ensure growth, expanding domestic demand, adjusting structure, and attaching importance to people's livelihood".

In March 2009, *Unhappy China* was published and the authors also wrote *China Can Say No* in 1996, which influenced many Chinese people, especially those called "angry youth". It attracted widespread media attention and reports worldwide because the Chinese book caused a stir in America in 1996. One famous passage in the book is "The United States can only lead itself, but no other countries. Japan can't lead any countries, even itself sometimes. China just wants to lead itself, not other countries."

Some pointed out that China had no need to say no since China can choose to say nothing. Today, we still can say that there is no need for China to be unhappy. China participates in global cooperation and peaceful development and, at the same time, China insists on its own way and develops scientifically.

A consensus has been formed: As long as Chinese people don't sway back and forth, relax our efforts or get sidetracked, but adhere to the establishment of socialist road with Chinese characteristics, a better tomorrow is in sight.

"Better City, Better Life"

The World Exposition 2010 was held in Shanghai, China, from May 1 to Oct. 31. As another grand international event hosted by China after the Beijing Olympic Games, the Shanghai World Expo can be defined as the first registered exposition held in a developing country with a theme of "Better City, Better Life".

Participants from 246 countries and international organizations created a passionate movement for the harmonious coexistence of human civilization through exhibitions, forums and performances over 184 days. The Shanghai World Expo received 73.08 million people and its highest passenger traffic reached more than 1.03 million people in a single day, which set a new record in the history of the World Expo. It showed further improved demands of people for cultural life and a broader global vision.

Visitors were impressed by the hot weather and long queues. Thousands of visitors braved the intense heat of summer to queue up at the entrance of the World Expo and its pavilions, something pretty rare during the history of the World Expo. Visitors from around the world lined up patiently at the entrance of several hot pavilions. In the country with a population of over one billion, people are familiar with queuing, but this was different given the significance of the World Expo 2010.

If it was necessary for people to queue up to snap up goods in the past just to meet their needs for clothing and food and improve their living conditions, it was a bit elegant that they line up for the exotic culture of this World Expo.

From Weibo To WeChat

The year 2010 was known as "The First Year of Weibo".

More netizens are now using Weibo. Users only need to post messages of 140 words with text, pictures, video and links embedded and they can also make new friends, get information and air news through Weibo. With its short and fast features , it is also jokingly called "Scarf".

More and more netizens started to master and use this new instrument rapidly in 2010. From hot social issues to numerous grassroots stars, Weibo gave people an edgy tool to participate in social consensus.

Weibo is a result of social progress in China, rather than its reason. It is not only a new technology, but peoples' growing rights of participation and expression in the Internet era that made Weibo quite popular. Currently, government departments communicate with people through Weibo as well, which promotes government transformation.

After Weibo, WeChat emerged.

WeChat is a piece of phone chat software launched by Tencent in early 2011. Users can send voice, video, pictures and text quickly by cellphone and tablet. It provides a public platform, social media outlet, a push message service and more. Users can add friends and follow public platforms by "shaking", "searching numbers", "people nearby" and "scanning QR codes". They can also share content with friends. The slogan in its official website is "WeChat, A Way of Life".

Networking has so deeply ingrained itself in civilian life that unknowns quickly become popular for strange reasons. For example, in the cold February 2010, a ragged beggar with messy hair hit the Internet in just one week and was called "Sharp Brother" by millions of netizens for his gloomy look.

An article called Jiangsu Province, the Gelivable "Cultural Province" was published in the *People's Daily* on Nov. 10, 2010. Chinese and foreign media regarded this innovation, the use of the buzzword "Gelivable", as a sign that Chinese social vitality had burst out and that Chinese social language had entered the official discourse.

Networking has changed China and the Internet has become a large platform for Chinese social vitality due to its features of openness, interaction, speed, mass appeal and convenience. The boundless cultural creativity, the enthusiasm of participation in public affairs, the supervision and the appeal of social justice in our society now have a great release thanks to the Internet.

Outbound tourism for ordinary people

National tours focused on sightseeing were part of the early stage of development of tourism. The whirlwind tours can be described as "sleeping in the tourist bus, peeing off the bus, taking photos at sights and remembering nothing after coming back home".

Profound changes have taken place in national tours in the new millennium. From whirlwind tours to in-depth travel, package tours to DIY tours, various experiential vacation tours have become quite popular among people that are personalized to meet tourists' demands.

With the promotion of Chinese economic strength, some Chinese have become rich and began to travel around the world. Currently, 150 countries and regions are outbound tourism destinations for Chinese citizens. In 2003, the number of Chinese domestic tourists reached 3.26 billion, while the number of outbound tourists hit 98.19 million.

Not only signs in Chinese and Chinese-speaking guides, but also the services of Chinese interpreters and receptionists have been provided in many famous shopping places due to the consumption boom caused by Chinese outbound tourism, which had not yet appeared a decade ago.

Being much younger and more independent, Chinese outbound tourists now know more about local culture and they are more willing to blend with it and become more internationalized. Paying more attention to the image of civilization, China has begun to gain cultural recognition and win the world's respect by respecting its own culture and those of other countries. To attract Chinese tourists, governments have been in intense competition.

The uncivilized behavior of some Chinese tourists has also been exposed and has had a negative effect on the overall image of Chinese tourists, which some country labeled as "low quality".

In May 2013, a family from Nanjing made a public apology after their 15-year-old boy inscribed the words "Ding Junhao was here" on a wall at the Pyramids of Egypt, an ancient cultural relic. His parents said that they wanted to apologize to the Egyptian people and the Chinese people.

In addition, Chinese tourists have also shown other uncivilized behavior such as queue jumping, making rude noises in public, littering, wasting food, and more. Thus, measures must be taken to improve the quality of Chinese people from now on.

The era of leftover women

As one of the 171 new Chinese neologies published by the Ministry of Education in August 2007, the term "leftover woman" refers to women beyond the generally accepted marriageable age but still single.

There are four categories of leftover women. First are women of 25 to 28 that are called junior leftover women, who still struggle to look for their partners and that's where the term "leftover fighters" (Saint Seiya) comes from. Second are women of 28 to 32 called intermediate leftover women, who are so busy working that they have few opportunities and little time to look for their partners and are called "doomed single" (Pizza Hut). Third, those of 32 to 35 are called senior leftover women, who survive in the cruel struggle in the workplace but are still single and are thus known as "the last is the best". Fourth are women of 35 that are called the super leftover women and are regarded as "the Great Leftover Equaling Heaven" (the Great Sage Equaling Heaven).

Leftover women have aroused public concern.

You Are the One is a reality TV show about marriage and dating, launched in Jiangsu TV on Jan. 15, 2010. *Run for Love* in Zhejiang TV, *My Destiny with You* in Anhui TV and *When Love Knocks the Door* in Shangdong TV were not far behind. The public airwaves became a battlefield for dating shows. What we know of these similar battles of blind dating on screen is that guests' values about "standing out" have been indulged and even misled just to get public attention. And it has caused concern.

A female guest in *You are the One* said: "I would cry in a BMW rather than smile in a bicycle."

"I do not care about her appearance, but she must have an annual salary of RMB1 million to RMB3 million that can help me in my career," said another male guest who participated in the show to find a rich woman.

Gaofushuai (a tall, rich and handsome guy) and *baifumei* (a fair skinned, rich and beautiful girl) have become the most sought after mates.

All the men seem to be classified into *gaofushuai* and *aicuoqiong* (a dwarfish, poor and ugly guy) in a short time. Another term, cocksure (similar to *aicuoqiong*) became quite popular due to the self-mockery of people on Weibo in 2012. The German mini-series *Knuller Frauen* and its Chinese version pushed up the terms.

There are both cocksure and *tuhao* (a Chinese person who is rich but lacks taste). The meaning of words like *tuhao* has had derogatory connotations in the past, but has now become entertaining on account of the activity: "*Tuhao*, Let us be Friends" launched by Weibo. Unlike today's pursuit of *tuhao*, there has long been a dislike for tycoons and upstarts.

"It would be better to be a female with men's body among men than compete for wisdom among females." From leftover woman to the Holy virgin, winning women and to today's tough girls, the rise of women has become clearer and clearer.

PM2.5

Many areas of China were shrouded in smog in the winter of 2011, which caused much concern about particles suspended in the air. Professional items like PM2.5 became a focus for netizens.

A key factor in smog and air pollution, PM2.5 (small particulate matter) are liquid or solid particles with 2.5 micrometers diameter or smaller suspended in the air. With smaller diameter than other airborne particulates, PM2.5 are filled with toxic and harmful substances that can stay in the air for a long time and be transmitted over a long distance. So it has greater impacts on people's health and the quality of ambient air.

The measurement of PM2.5 was first regulated by *Determination of Atmospheric Articles PM10 and PM2.5 in Ambient Air by Gravimetric Method* published by the Ministry of Environment Protection, which brought PM2.5 a step closer to become the standard of air quality monitoring in China.

In early 2013, smog again became a problem in many areas, particularly seriously polluted regions such as the Yangtze River Delta, Pearl River Delta and Beijing-Tianjing-Hebei-Shangdong region. There were also 25 provinces and cities shrouded in smog from the northeast of China to Hainan Province in winter, such as Harbin, Hangzhou, Nanjing, Haikou, etc.

Facing smog, netizens described themselves as "having a broad mind to carry smog, but strive not to take in the smog" and "working hard for more smog in the smog weather".

On the morning of March 13, 2014, Premier Li Keqiang met with Chinese and foreign press in the Great Hall of the People.

Press (China National Radio): There have been growing public complaints about smog. In your government work report, you said the government will declare war against pollution. I wish to ask you what do you mean by that?

Li Keqiang: I said the government will declare war against smog and pollution as a whole, because this has become a serious issue on the top of the minds of our people. For many people, the first thing they do after getting up in the morning is to check the PM2.5 figure for the day. This has become a major issue that concerns our people's lives.

To declare war against smog and other pollution does not mean that we are declaring war against nature. Rather, what we mean is that we are going to declare war against our own inefficient and unsustainable model of growth and way of life. Last year, the State Council issued a ten-point plan of action on the prevention and control of air pollution. We now conduct PM2.5 monitoring in 161 cities across the country, which is the most extensive scope among all developing countries. This is not just a reminder for our people to take precautionary measures, but also placing additional responsibility on the shoulder of the government. This year we will take further measures. For example, we have set the target of cutting energy intensity by 3.9% on top of the 3.7% reduction we achieved last year. This is equivalent to cutting coal burning by 220 million tons.

There are complex causes for smog and it will take a long time to tackle this problem. But we cannot sit here and wait for wind or rain to drive smog away. We have to take action ourselves. I hope that the government, the businesses and each and every individual of the society will act together and make persistent efforts to win this tough battle against smog.

Mo Yan

Mo Yan was awarded the Nobel Prize in Literature in October 2012 and then became the first Chinese writer to win this prize.

Chinese people felt full of pride in Mo Yan. It should be mentioned that it was a dream of China's literary circle to win the Nobel Prize in Literature. As a great encouragement for Chinese writers, this news bolstered confidence in Chinese contemporary literature, for it is the world's highest recognition for writers.

Mo Yan's works show the scene of Chinese contemporary literature. His prize can be defined as an important symbol that Chinese literature has earned global recognition due to its artistic standards and cultural capacity, which has drawn the world's attention and provides opportunities for communication between Chinese literature and world literature.

The Nobel Prize Committee said that in Mo Yan's work "hallucinatory realism merges folk tales, history and the contemporary".

Mo Yan has restored the confidence of Chinese Literati.

Mo Yan was fond of reading in his boyhood. At that time, there was only one small kerosene lamp in his house. His elder brother and him read books under the bad lamp at night at the entrance of their house. Several years later, the entrance was hollowed by the weight of the two brothers. Mo Yan did everything to find books and he even helped other people grind and scythe wheat just to borrow their books.

Besides Mo Yan, there are many unique writers with considerable creativeness and potential in China as well, such as Jia Pingwa, Chen Zhongshi, Wang Anyi, Yu Hua, Su Tong, Liu ZhenYun, etc. Their works are also quite popular among overseas readers.

Two-Child

The term "Two-Child" refers to couples that can have a second child if either parent is an only child. The Third Plenary Session of the 18th Central Committee of the Communist Party of China proposed adhering "to the basic policy of family planning and couples will be allowed to have two children if one of the parents is an only-child."

"Two-Child" has become a hot topic in the society.

Some people thought the new policy made them both happy and ambivalent. Actually, how many families are willing to have a second child among the 20 million "single-child" families in China? Two children can take care of each other and share the pressure of caring for the aged in the future. However, nowadays, "it costs more to raise a child than to buy a house" and sometimes "child slaves" mooch off their parents. To have, or not to have, that is a question.

It is a common concern of how to raise children.

In 2013, *Dad, Where Are We Going*, a reality TV show about stars' parenting, was popular for a while. The word "father" became one of the most popular by the end of 2013. People believe that the most important standard for a man is to be a good father rather than to have a successful business.

A US survey in 2010 revealed that 71% of Americans thought the most important role of a man was to be a father. More than 90% of fathers living with their children could chat with children and listen to their daily experiences. However, in China, although most people know that fathers play an important role in the growth of their children, the ultimate symbol of a man's success is more or less his career.

Children have an opportunity to grow up in the special journey and so do their fathers but the show helped more parents rethink the way they raise their children. Therefore, the popularity of this show is not accidental, and it is time to improve family education in China.

Running towards the "Chinese Dream"

The figures of gross domestic product (GDP) in 2010 released by Japan on Feb. 14, 2010 showed that the nominal GDP of Japan that year was US$547.42 billion, US$404.4 billion less than China, Xinhua News Agency reported.

Japan slipped into the third place after the US and China. Since then, Japan has ended its decades of "economic miracle" after the US, and China became the world's second largest economy.

The 18th National Congress of Communist Party of China (CPC) was successfully convened in November 2012. On the morning of Nov. 15, the new Standing Community of Political Bureau elected by the first plenary meeting of the 18th CPC Central Community met with Chinese and foreign press. Xi Jinping, the new General Secretary of the CPC Central Community, said:

"It is our responsibility to rally and lead the whole party and Chinese people of all ethnic groups, take up the historic baton and continue working hard for the great rejuvenation, so that we will stand in family of nations and make fresh and great contributions to mankind.

Our people love life and yearn for better education, stable jobs, more satisfactory income, great social security, improved medical and health care, more comfortable living conditions, more beautiful environment. We want our children to grow up well, have better jobs and lead a more enjoyable life. The people's desire for a better life is what we shall for fight for."

In November 2013, the Third Plenary Session of the 18th CPC Central

Committee led to comprehensive deepening of reforms and the adoption of the *Decision of the CPC Central Committee on Some Major Issues Concerning Comprehensively Deepening the Reform*, which marked the new phase of China's reform and opening up from 1978. Efforts are to be made to accelerate the improvement of the modern market system and the transformation of government roles, deepen the reform of the fiscal and taxation systems, enhance the construction of political systems, strengthen the system of supervision of power, and more.

In December 2013, the Chang'e 3 detector successfully landed on the lunar surface and so did the "Jade Rabbit" rover, which marked China as the third country to achieve a soft landing of the celestial body after the Soviet Union and the US. Reuters noted that the success of Chang'e 3 lifted national pride and China's reputation and "the Chinese dream was lit again by the dream to explore on moon."

The propaganda poster of the Chinese Dream

 Decision of the CPC Central Committee on Some Major Issues Concerning Comprehensively Deepening the Reform

The statistics bulletin of the national economy and social development in 2013 released by the National Bureau of Statistics reveals:

The total population of the mainland was 1.36072 billion by the end of 2013. According to the preliminary accounting, the annual GDP was RMB56.8845 trillion. Total annual retail sales of consumer goods were RMB2.3781 trillion. The per capita net income of rural residents was RMB8,896, while the per capita disposable income of urban residents was RMB26,955.

The core of the Chinese dream is the great rejuvenation of the Chinese nation and its connotations include national prosperity and rejuvenation and people's happiness.

To realize the Chinese dream is to realize the people's dream, as they are the same after all.